HUMAN RESOURCE MANAGEMENT - THE HUMAN FACE

WHY ORGANISATIONS FAIL AND WHAT ARE THE BEST PRACTICES OF ADMIRED COMPANIES

DR. PARVEEN PRASAD
M.Com, D.H.E, P.HD.

SEKHAR SESHAN
B.Sc, B.J. (Journalism),
News Agency Journalism course at
International Institute of Journalism,
West Berlin

NIRALI PRAKASHAN

HUMAN RESOURCE MANAGEMENT

ISBN 978-93-83525-66-9

First Edition : October 2013

© : Authors

The text of this publication, or any part thereof, should not be reproduced or transmitted in any form or stored in any computer storage system or device for distribution including photocopy, recording, taping or information retrieval system or reproduced on any disc, tape, perforated media or other information storage device etc., without the written permission of Author with whom the rights are reserved. Breach of this condition is liable for legal action.

Every effort has been made to avoid errors or omissions in this publication. In spite of this, errors may have crept in. Any mistake, error or discrepancy so noted and shall be brought to our notice shall be taken care of in the next edition. It is notified that neither the publisher nor the author or seller shall be responsible for any damage or loss of action to any one, of any kind, in any manner, therefrom.

Published By :
NIRALI PRAKASHAN
Abhyudaya Pragati, 1312, Shivaji Nagar,
Off J.M. Road, PUNE – 411005
Tel - (020) 25512336/37/39, Fax - (020) 25511379
Email : niralipune@pragationline.com

Printed By :
Repro Knowledgecast Limited,
Thane

DISTRIBUTION CENTRES

PUNE
Nirali Prakashan
119, Budhwar Peth, Jogeshwari Mandir Lane
Pune 411002, Maharashtra
Tel : (020) 2445 2044, 66022708
Fax : (020) 2445 1538
Email : nirlilocal@pragationline.com

MUMBAI
Nirali Prakashan
385, S.V.P. Road, Rasdhara Co-op. Hsg. Society Ltd.,
Girgaum, Mumbai 400004, Maharashtra
Tel : (022) 2385 6339 / 2386 9976,
Fax : (022) 2386 9976
Email : bookorder@pragationline.com

DISTRIBUTION BRANCHES

NAGPUR
Pratibha Book Distributors
Above Maratha Mandir, Shop No. 3, First Floor,
Rani Jhanshi Square, Sitabuldi, Nagpur 440012,
Maharashtra, Tel : (0712) 254 7129

BENGALURU
Pragati Book House
House No. 1, Sanjeevappa Lane, Avenue Road Cross,
Opp. Rice Church, Bengaluru – 560002.
Tel : (080) 64513344, 64513355,
Mob : 9880582331, 9845021552
Email:bharatsavla@yahoo.com

JALGAON
Nirali Prakashan
34, V. V. Golani Market, Navi Peth, Jalgaon 425001,
Maharashtra, Tel : (0257) 222 0395
Mob : 94234 91860

KOLHAPUR
Nirali Prakashan
New Mahadvar Road,
Kedar Plaza, 1st Floor Opp. IDBI Bank
Kolhapur 416 012, Maharashtra. Mob : 9855046155

CHENNAI
Pragati Books
9/1, Montieth Road, Behind Taas Mahal, Egmore,
Chennai 600008 Tamil Nadu, Tel : (044) 6518 3535,
Mob : 94440 01782 / 98450 21552 / 98805 82331
Email : bharatsavla@yahoo.com

RETAIL OUTLETS
PUNE

Pragati Book Centre
157, Budhwar Peth, Opp. Ratan Talkies,
Pune 411002, Maharashtra
Tel : (020) 2445 8887 / 6602 2707, Fax : (020) 2445 8887

Pragati Book Centre
Amber Chamber, 28/A, Budhwar Peth,
Appa Balwant Chowk, Pune : 411002, Maharashtra,
Tel : (020) 20240335 / 66281669
Email : pbcpune@pragationline.com

Pragati Book Centre
676/B, Budhwar Peth, Opp. Jogeshwari Mandir,
Pune 411002, Maharashtra
Tel : (020) 6601 7784 / 6602 0855

PBC Book Sellers & Stationers
152, Budhwar Peth, Pune 411002, Maharashtra
Tel : (020) 2445 2254 / 6609 2463

MUMBAI
Pragati Book Corner
Indira Niwas, 111 - A, Bhavani Shankar Road, Dadar (W), Mumbai 400028, Maharashtra
Tel : (022) 2422 3526 / 6662 5254
Email : pbcmumbai@pragationline.com

---

www.pragationline.com   info@pragationline.com

FOREWORD

Dr. Anand Deshpande is the founder Chairman and Managing Director of Persistent Systems Limited.

Most of us work in teams and some of us are required to manage teams as part of our day-to-day jobs. While there is training and emphasis on project management and quality systems many of us believe that people management is the HR Manager and the HR Department's responsibility. From my personal experience of running Persistent Systems for the last 22 years, I can emphatically state that this is far from the truth. It is clear that employees join a Company but leave their manager. HR must be every manager's responsibility. The manager's understanding of Human Resources is critical to the success of the Company. Despite the realisation of the importance of HR Management, I have struggled to find a good crisp, easy-to-read book that explains the theory and practice of Human Relations Management for practitioners until my friends Sekhar Seshan and Parveen Prasad shared with me the manuscript of their book, "Human Resource Management - the Human Face".

I have known Sekhar for nearly twenty years as the Executive Editor of Business India and a well-respected senior journalist in Pune. I met with them in the context of this book when Sekhar and Parveen visited us to interview my colleague Siddhesh Bhobe who leads eMee, our social gamification platform, for continuous performance evaluation. Some of the experiments we conducted with eMee are discussed in the book.

Human Resource Management is an extremely important topic and it is difficult to write a book that has a good balance between theory and practice. Sekhar and Parveen have done an excellent job of addressing this. They have created a book that is apt as a text-book for business-school students, a reference for HR managers in Companies and a must-read for all practising managers. They cover topics across the entire employment lifecycle such as recruitment, job descriptions, compensation, performance reviews and appraisals, ethical issues, collective bargaining and negotiation.

The book is very well organised with multiple case studies in each chapter. These case studies are appropriate and highlight the salient issues very effectively. I think that the combination of Parveen's academic expertise and Sekhar's experience of interviewing and writing about business has made the case studies eminently readable and also extremely valuable.

The authors start each chapter by clearly stating the objectives and by writing a summary. They also provide learning outcomes and discussion questions. Every chapter concludes with a few case studies which would be valuable for a group discussion, especially in a MBA class and also as good discussion items in work settings. I would recommend using these case studies in project teams to have an open discussion on issues that are important but had to discuss.

Parveen and Sekhar have picked topics and case studies that are appropriate for traditional industries as well as new industries that have a large number of young knowledge workers.

I am so glad that Parveen and Sekhar have written this book. There is no one else who could have done a better job and I am glad this book is ready to deploy!

PREFACE

Dr. Ganesh Natarajan is Vice Chairman & CEO of Zensar Technologies and an active contributor to CII, NASSCOM and the HBS Club of India.

HRM – a new wave begins!

Human Resource Management has come a long way since the early era of Personnel and Industrial Relationships departments, when the responsibility was either personnel accounting and policy management or keeping the unions at bay with somewhat repressive strictures and bargaining. The Human Resource function today is expected to be a true business partner to the leadership of the organisation, challenging stereotypes of people management, using the full arsenal of OD tools and techniques and engaging every member of the organisation with dynamic recruitment, training and retention practices.

My own experience through three decades of my career has been a revelation with the pace of change in approaches to HRM startling at times but always positive and uplifting. From my early days in Crompton Greaves in the eighties, where managing scores of Datta Samant unionised workmen was a huge challenge to relearning the art of people management under a wonderful role model, Vijay Thadani of NIIT and finally experimenting with my own style of the CEO becoming the principal practitioner of new world HRM, it's been a journey that has been truly rewarding.

Our company Zensar Technologies has turned every stereotype of HRM on its head and achieved astonishing results that have been described in two well researched cases at the

Harvard Business School. In organisation design we have put front line sales people and delivery managers at the top of the organisation pyramid with the CEO at the bottom, thereby emphasizing our core values of people sovereignty and people orientation. Recruiting is managed as a fine art with every stage tracked and optimized and "center of excellence" partnerships with colleges and universities have enabled us to prepare talent for the job while they are still in the concluding stages of their academic work. Vision Communities to build strategy bottom up, the AIMA innovation award winning "Jugnu" and "iZen" initiatives for all associates and managers and an environment of camaraderie and true meritocracy have enabled us to keep critical talent attrition down to less than a percentage for three years.

The good news today is that most organisations in the services sector and increasingly even in formerly staid manufacturing companies have taken the HRM bull by the horns and honed people management to a fine degree of perfection. As global competition heats up across all sectors, as early job entrants find more and more options to build their careers and as diversity and inclusion become the true imperative for global organisations with their roots in India, the time is now for some new experiments in HRM to become the rule rather than the exception and for all of us in India to celebrate the spirit of family and love by enshrining these values in the life stream of our organisation.

In this context, this book is truly timely because it analyses threadbare all the new imperatives for HRM. Its case study approach enables theory to be abstracted from practice and instead of preaching which could so easily have been a trap for the authors to fall into, the book brings out useful concepts in a readable and well-structured manner. I am sure this tome will be a valuable addition to the body of knowledge on HRM and make a difference to better management of the human resource.

ACKNOWLEDGEMENTS

This book would not have been possible without hundreds of learning conversations and shared reports of HR professionals, CEOs of Companies and corporate professionals who are convinced that the human face of human resource is the master key to an organisation's strategic growth and prosperity. We would like to thank the following, both individually and collectively, for their unstinted support and valuable contribution to make this reference book for Human Resource students and practitioners a ready reckoner on HR. They are:

Dr. Anand Deshpande, CMD, Persistent Systems, who kindly consented to write the Foreword.

Dr. Ganesh Natarajan, CEO, Zensar Technologies, who believed it worthy of his valuable inputs as a Preface.

Business India for facilitating the sourcing of valuable case studies from the corporate world.

Gerald Huesch, Chairman & CEO, Global Leadership School, Berlin, who found it appropriate to share his research findings and insights on the imperative need to develop leadership skills among all levels of personnel in organisations.

Aashish Washikar, Associate Manager – Media Relations, Mahindra Satyam Ltd, who put us on to Sujitha Karnad, Head of HR and Quality of Tech Mahindra's IT arm.

Renuka Krishna, AVP, Talent Acquisition at KPIT Cummins.

Saaz Aggarwal, author and HR practitioner, who has always been a great source of strength.

T. Muralidharan, founder and chairman of TMI Group, and Anu Srinivasan, his co-author for their yet to be published book "A Complete Reference to Acquisition of Indian Talent".

Venkat Changavalli, Management Consultant, Leadership Mentor, Teacher and Inspirational Speaker and Director-SBH.

M. Ramkrishna, Managing Director, ZCS Consulting Limited.

Sanjay Kavathalkar, VP – HR, Hyderabad Industries Ltd.

Yogesh Patgaonkar, Executive Vice President – HR & Business Process Management, Zensar Technologies Ltd, a last-minute life saver, and his colleague Ruchi Mathur, Head - Organization Development and CSR at Zensar.

Anand Viswanathan, Motivational Speaker and chiefdreamer, A. V. initiatives.

Vijay Menon, MD, Menon & Menon.

Mahijeet Mishra, Managing Director, Armstrong International Private Limited, who was also a great help at the last minute with his story telling.

Siddhesh Bhobe, CEO, eMee , CTO, Klisma and Business Head, Persistent.

Aniruddha Dike and Upendra Purandare, Directors, Gensys Technologies Pvt. Ltd. for sharing their valuable experiences at Gensys, a Structural Design and Project Management Consultancy Firm.

Rajesh Ramnath, Director- HR, Cadbury Kraft Foods for his valuable insights.

Raghu Nair and Pushkaraj Wagh, Learning and Development, Forbes Marshall, for sharing the best practices on Safety and Values.

Vimu James, HRIS Engagement Leader and Abhishek Kumar, HR Head, Honeywell India.

Shilpa Hulikawi, HR Head, Schneider, for sharing her experiences of dealing with expats.

Young student Neeraj Prasad for his technical expertise on computers to format the chapters.

Authors

INTRODUCTION

Recently I met with the heads of human resource of Global 100 companies and in a confidential survey they stated that their companies mishired people 80 per cent of the time and mispromoted people 75 per cent of the time. That's right, HR's chosen methods of selecting people produce high performers only 20 – 25 per cent of the time

- US Consultant Brad Smart

A similar scenario seems to be existing in the Indian organisations where the common woe of all HR practitioners is the acquisition of the complex ability and capability to acquire, retain and develop right people at the right place as a job fit and in the right time. Every organisation today is initiating a slew of measures to engage talent and develop them by working towards creating a context for their better performance. The C suite and the top management too have learnt from mistakes, to accept this area as their prime responsibility.

This book serves as a ready reference for post-graduate students of Management and Human Resource, as well as Human Resource practitioners. The chief distinguishing feature of this book is the use of topical and live case studies supplementing every chapter, which give you hands-on understanding of the concepts of HR. The chapters also include those related to the internationalisation of HR which is a common phenomenon nowadays; talent management, a challenge; and Human Resource Information Systems, a technology-enabled need for HR. Diversity is another area covered in depth, along with live cases of interventions of organisations to promote diversity. The Performance Management chapter includes an interesting case study by Persistent Systems, an IT company, of the social gamification platform called EMEE, which enables a continuous performance feedback, regular motivation through virtual gifts and penalties through banana skin, reminding the personnel at all levels to reach their coveted targets. This gaming platform initiative has found a mention and appreciation in Harvard Business Review. We have included the experience by Siddhesh Bhobe, the CEO of this creative game.

We hope the readers have an exciting, informative and educative journey while referring to this manual of Human Face of Human Resource Management.

Authors

CONTENTS

1. Evolution of Human Resource Management — 1.1 - 1.40
2. Recruitment — 2.1 - 2.20
3. Selection — 3.1 - 3.14
4. Job Analysis — 4.1 - 4.10
5. Equality and Diversity in the Workplace — 5.1 - 5.16
6. Learning and Development — 6.1 - 6.26
7. Performance Management and Appraisal — 7.1 - 7.16
8. Compensation : Establishing Pay Plans — 8.1 - 8.12
9. Talented Management — 9.1 - 9.16
10. Law and HRM — 10.1 - 10.14
11. Collective Bargaining — 11.1 - 11.10
12. Employee Relations — 12.1 - 12.20
13. Employee Health and Safety — 13.1 - 13.16
14. Ethics — 14.1 - 14.12
15. International Human Resource Management (IHRM) — 15.1 - 15.22
16. Human Resource Information Management (HRIM) — 16.1 - 16.12

***

Chapter 1...

Evolution of Human Resource Management

Contents ...

1.1 Introduction
1.2 HRM in India
1.3 Why is HRM Important Nowadays?
1.4 Nature and Scope of HRM
1.5 Recruitment and Selection
1.6 The Context of HRM
1.7 Patterns Shaping Human Resource Management in 21st Century
1.8 Strategic Human Resource Personnel Management
1.9 A Case Study on HR for Emergency Response Systems
• Discussion Questions
• References

Objectives and Summary

The aim of this chapter is to expose the reader to the importance of Human Resource in an organisation and how this function is considered to be the most important from the strategic perspective. It aims to analyse the internal and external environments in an organisation and create HR initiatives accordingly. It aims to show how if the human resource function is strategically viewed, all other functions follow. It highlights the importance of culture in an organisation and exposes the importance of tools like Score Card, Strategy Maps, Systems and Competence.

Human Resource is considered to be the most important function in an organisation. The volatile changes in the environment have contributed to the importance of this function. The HR manager needs to be conversant with the HR laws, creation of systems, integration with technology and design of strategic systems like the HR scorecard, strategy maps and HR Competence model to deal with the strategic issues concerning HR. Every organisation needs to be ranked as a great place to work for, and for this to be created, all HR policies, systems and culture should be veered towards being employee-centric. An HR manager should be fully conversant with legislation, the PEST model of environment and the changing role of analytics through the use of HR Information Systems (HRIS) for facilitating a more conducive working environment for the employees.

Learning Outcomes:
1. Identifies the strategic role of HR in an organisation;
2. Describes the various features in an organisational environment for better working;
3. Underlines the need for designing systems and processes like the HRIS, HR Scorecard, HR competence and Strategy Mapping;
4. Elaborates how HR function is more strategic and important from the perspective of productivity of the organisation.

1.1 Introduction

"HRM represents the discovery of personnel management by the Chief Executive".

– Fowler, 1987

"Personnel are perceived to use Drucker's famous term as a "trash can" into which all unwanted tasks could be dumped rather than a key element in the search for competitive advantage".

– Guest, 1990:383

Why is Human Resource Management important to all managers? Why are these concepts and techniques important? Perhaps it is easier to answer this by listing some of the personnel mistakes you do not want to make while managing. For example, you don't want to:

1. Hire the wrong person for the job;
2. Experience high employee turnover;
3. Have people not doing their best;
4. Waste time in unproductive interviews;
5. Allow a lack of training to undermine your department's effectiveness;
6. Commit any unfair labour practices.

Managing people is not straight forward any more. Management of people is a critical issue for organisations and often more complicated than realised. In the early days of what came to be called personnel management, it was employee support and welfare, often described as "tea and sympathy", which dominated and helped shape a view of personnel management as a necessary but low-key and marginal function. Today, it is a far cry from that original role, and people as employees are considered as a focal point. Organisations, in their zest to retain talent, which translates into people, are orienting all policies and programmes towards people learning, development and wellness.

A review of a whole lot of literature and research studies on productivity and performance at work reflects in their findings, a common underlining denominator that "only people provide a competitive edge". A firm's performance and success can ultimately be traced to the quality of its talented people, its attitudes and commitment, its engagement, innovation and a 'feel good feeling' which reflects in their work output. Networking and globalisation have brought equal access to new technology, information, knowledge and ideas to all organisations. However, as research has proved, it is only those organisations which exhibit a conducive work culture and flexible/transparent features in their work environment that create success in terms of employee commitment and reduced employee attrition.

Human Resource Manager's Duties

1. **Line Function:** The HR Manager directs the activities of the people in his or her own department and in related areas.
2. **Coordinative Function:** The HR manager also coordinates personnel activities, a duty often referred to as a functional authority. There he or she ensures that line managers are implementing the firm's human resource policies and practices (e.g. policies related to leave, overtime and sexual harassment etc,)
3. **Staff (assist and advice) functions:** Assisting and advising line managers is the heart of the HR manager's job. He or she advises the CEO so that the CEO can better understand the personnel aspects of the company's strategic options. HR assists in hiring, training, evaluating, rewarding, counselling, promoting and firing employees. It administers the various benefit programmes, health and accident insurance, occupational safety, grievances and labour relations.

1.2 HRM in India

The function of HRM in Indian organisations in formal sectors has evolved over time. Philanthropic employers like the Tata Group introduced various measures for managing their employees. While the traditional functions which focused on welfare and labour relations existed, it was after Independence in 1947 that the trade union activity intensified and the labour laws were introduced. Initially the personnel departments were involved more in welfare activities, labour compliance and maintaining industrial peace. Later the focus in many parts of India shifted to confronting the aggressive unions. The focus on Human Resource Development (HRD) came during the period between 1985 and 1995, after IIM professors Udai Pareek and T. V. Rao popularised the HRD concept in Indian industry. With the knowledge industry, globalisation and a high demand for talented people, the HR function has started to take a strategic focus. During the economic recession of 2006-2009, different HRM approaches were adopted to cope with the troubled times. These included recruitment freeze, downsizing and training cuts.

The evolution of HR in India has led to a growth of specialised HR firms like Kelly, Teamlease, Ma Foi, Accord, Hewitt and so on.

1.3 Why is HRM Important Nowadays?

Globalisation and Competition trends: Globalisation refers to the tendency of firms to extend their sales, ownership and manufacturing to new markets abroad. For example, Toyota sells products, PCs in China, Tata Motors sells its small car Nano in various countries, Philip Morris sells and distributes its Marlboro brand in India through Godfrey Phillips India.

Free Trade Agreements (FTAs): FTAs reduce tariffs and barriers among trading partners further encourage international trade. NAFTA (North American Free Trade Agreement) and EU are examples.

Technological Trends: These relate to the application of available knowledge and skills to create and use materials, processes and products. Technological change is very relevant to the HRM context. It can lead to the creation of new jobs that require the skills to work with new technologies and jobs in companies making and supplying technological equipment in terms of job creation, the emphasis has in recent years been on the importance of employees with transferable skills. Maintaining employability as the opportunity for a "job for life" disappears as technological advances demand a skilled and a trained labour force.

PEST Model:

Political: The political environment is generally very important to HR managers, because it includes the policies of the State and Central governments. Since the governments have the authority to make law, the Human Resource personnel must execute these policies. The enforcement of the Child Labour (Prohibition and Regulation) Act, 1986, makes sure that children under the age of 15 years are not employed in any enterprise. This too is being strictly followed. Government laws and policies also shape the HRM context in many ways. The policy of privatisation or regulation of Foreign Direct Investment is a case in point. In addition, there is also a wide range of international political factors. These too help to shape the general HRM context like the activities of WTO (World Trade Organisation) concerning tariffs and other barriers.

Economic: Closely aligned to the activities of the State and Central government policies are economic influences which in the HR context include wage and salary levels, inflation, housing costs, interest rates, currency rates, unemployment levels, social costs such as pensions, taxation and GDP growth. For example, economic cycles like a downturn or recession can severely affect HR interventions. In the recent downturn in India in 2008, several organisations resorted to huge retrenchment of staff as a severe measure of cost-cutting, because orders that had been booked never materialised. Apart from the IT companies like IBM, Wipro and Infosys, which cut manpower on the basis of performance measures, manufacturing companies also trimmed their workforces as production slowed down. As an inspiring move, many top personnel of manufacturing organisations like Mahindras took a voluntary cut in their salaries and bonuses. The components of a compensation package too are affected by the economic cycles. For instance, even after the recession cycle turned around, most companies became conservative in their approach - announcing reduced variable and fixed salary components and recruiting personnel only if the work functions necessitated it. The HR context has changed with more and more focus on innovation by manpower in order to survive uncertain downturns. Consequently, the concepts of talent management and employee engagement are the new focus today.

Social/Cultural: This factor relates to shifts in values and lifestyles. In the HR context it could involve a consideration of employees' attitudes to work and leisure and demographic changes along with cultural values towards age, gender, sexuality, mobility, diversity, values, beliefs, norms and so on. All these areas would have an impact on recruiting strategies and policies and processes in organisations. Today with increasing mergers, acquisitions and joint ventures, HR needs to be conscious of the adaptations in culture and values as a result of these changes. Communication too has changed with the focus on new-age networking through social media, intranetworking, upgraded mobile technology and the increasing fancy among employees of using social networking media.

Technological: Technology factors relate to the application of available knowledge and skills to create and use materials, processes and products. Technology demands a skilled and reskilled workforce which is employable and constantly in the learning mode. Technological advances have raised issues about the impact of electronic and mobile communication between managers and the workforce and the surveillance of employees via sophisticated logging-on procedures for Internet use at work. It has also led to concern about its impact on stress, tiredness on employees who are constantly on demand and contactable on phone or email.

Information and communication technology (ICT) is being increasingly used for teleworking, telecommuting and networking, the new-age models of working for employees.

Responding to changes in the employment markets

At an organisational level HR managers are required to ensure that their demand for suitable qualified staff is matched by what is available to them in terms of supply. In seeking to attract and retain suitably qualified staff, this balancing process involves a variety of HRM activities including recruitment, induction, training, appraisal, promotion, reward, retirement and redundancy. Such human resource planning can be seen to lie at the heart of the HRM function. It recognises the importance of people in formulating and influencing organisation strategy, performance, benchmarking, design, structures, mergers and acquisitions, expansions, diversifications etc.

At an organisational level, HR managers are required to ensure that their demand for suitable qualified staff is matched with what is available.

Examples of HRM specialities include:
- Recruiters
- HRD Specialists
- Engagement and Functional Specialists
- Employee Welfare Officers
- Job analysts
- Compensation Managers
- Training Specialists
- Employment/Industrial relations Specialists

Some of the designations and roles commonly created are: Chief Learning Officer, Chief Talent Officer, Chief Happiness Officer, Chief Climate Facilitator, Hospitality Manager, Learning and Development Head, College Campus Director and so on. All these positions are oriented towards creating glue or a culture that will bind the personnel to deliver their best and raise the performance bars.

The term Human Resources Management refers to the activity of employing people, widening their resources, utilising, sustaining and compensating their services in accordance with the requirements of the job. Further, it is ensured that the management contributes towards the overall goal of the organisation, society etc.

Terrington and Hall define personnel management as a series of activities which first enable working people and their employing organisations to agree about the objective and nature of their working relationships and secondly ensure that the agreement is fulfilled.

Miller suggests that human resources management refers to "those decisions and actions which concern the management of employees at all levels in the business and which are related to the implementation of strategies directed towards creating and sustaining competitive advantage".

Michael Jucius has defined personnel management as the "field of management which has to do with planning, organising, directing and controlling the functions of procuring, developing, maintaining and utilising a labour force such as that the:

1. Objectives for which the company is established are attained economically and effectively;
2. Objectives of all levels of personnel are served;
3. Objectives of society are duly considered and served."

1.4 Nature and Scope of HRM

The scope of HRM in modern days is vast. In the past, HRM was limited to employment, maintenance and payment of wages and salary. The scope has gradually enlarged to providing welfare facilities, motivation, performance appraisal, and human resource management, coaching, counselling and mentoring, assessment tests for investigating and identifying personality behaviours of employees, their team working dispositions, strategic human resources and the like. The scope has been continuously expanding to meet the fact that when individuals come to the workplace, they come with not only technical skills, knowledge etc but also with personal feelings, perception, desires motives, attitudes, values and so on.

Looking Ahead: HRM in the 21st century

Moving forward it is possible to identify two themes that have dominated discussion in human resource management in the past 15 years. One area that has received importance is strategic partnering with the top management. As a top focal partner, researchers are trying to correlate HR with enhancement of business performance. It is being increasingly proved how the peak performance of personnel in organizations can be largely attributed to passionate and motivated personnel who strive to be innovative and put in their best.

Another focus is on HR being employee champions. It is also being proved how the growth of any organisation is dependent on the growth of learning and development of its people and their morale and motivation which arouses their commitment to perform best.

Ulrich's model (pp24, Adrian) contrasts the operational and prescriptive focus of personnel roles as:

1. Strategic or business partner;
2. Administrative expert;
3. Change agent; and
4. Employee champion.

Organisations like "Great Place To Work" have been born to create awareness and measure the impact of HR interventions, culture and climate, to identify enterprises whose employees perceive these as creating a high happiness quotient and thereby arousing passion, commitment and loyalty which stimulate innovation and translate into efficiency and productivity. The India chapter of this organisation has branches in major cities; among the top-ranking companies are multinational corporations like American Express, Google, IBM, Accenture, Microsoft, Indian organisations like TCS, Infosys, Wipro, R.Com, HCL Tech and L&T ranked 1st,2nd, 3rd,6th, 8th and 10th respectively in the 2012 survey. Such endeavours have reiterated the focal role of HR in an organisation's growth.

1.5 Recruitment and Selection

Job Analysis

The human resource management process really begins with deciding what the job entails. Recruitment and Selection is preceded by a Job analysis and Job description. The job is identified through a job analysis and this provides the basis for a job description (JD) - a description of chief tasks, responsibilities and reporting relationships, and a person specification (a description of the qualifications, skills, abilities, knowledge and behaviour). The JD and person specification are the basic documents used in recruiting and selecting staff. They also provide the basis for promotion, appraisals and position in the organisational structure.

Organisations consist of jobs that have to be staffed. Job analysis is the procedure through which are determined the duties of these positions and the characteristics of the people who will staff the same. It produces information for writing the JD (a list of what the job entails) and job specification the knowledge, skill and abilities (KSAs) required to do the particular job. Every manager should understand the mechanics of job analyses to ensure a perfect job fit between the staff and the KSAs of the job. Unlike in earlier times, today's jobs are not so watertight and compartmentalised. The lines are now quite blurred. Hence the process of job analysis is not rigid but demands a specialised as well as a generic set of skills and behaviour, so that manpower can be easily transferred from one function to another through the process of job rotation. More and more private organisations are emulating the policies of the public sector which rotates its employees, to ensure their honing of skills in different areas and also allowing them to perceive issues with varied perceptions acquired through their exposures. For instance, a PSU like BSNL has its engineers in production, distribution, marketing and customer liaison to acquaint them with the typical problems faced by each department.

Basics of Job Analysis

The supervisor or the human resource specialist normally collects one or more of the following types of information through job analyses:

1. Work activities: This is related to all the core activities related to the job function like designing, teaching or selling. It also includes the knowledge, skills and abilities identified, behavioural traits to be acquired and details of the multi-level skills required to perform the job effectively. For example, in teaching it could be knowledge expertise, delivering lectures using a varied methodology like PowerPoint presentation, interactive lecture, role play, group discussion, assignment and so on. The multi-level skills would include research skills, conducting examinations, organising skills and examiner skills for paper correction.

2. Human Behaviour: The supervisor will also collect information regarding human behaviour like team working, presentations, sharing critical information, counselling, coaching and so on. For example, managers today are required to spend more time forging friendly team working behaviour and counselling for reconciling differences among members or colleagues due to personality clashes, ego problems and other issues.

3. Machines, Tools, Software and Work Aids: These include information regarding tools used, materials processed, knowledge dealt with or applied (such as finance or law) and services rendered like maintenance, counselling, upkeep and so on.

4. Performance Standards: The HR supervisors need to understand the various standards, in terms of quality, quantity, targets, behavioural requirements, leadership exhibited. These need to be communicated to the various personnel in advance, so that there are no surprises at the time of appraisal. Also, the frequency of the appraisals and the impact on promotions and increments need to be known and shared to ensure transparency.

1.6 The Context of HRM

Organisations can be classified according to different dimensions:

1. Type of ownership: These include public sector unit (PSU), central government owned and funded, state government owned and funded, local government owned and funded, charitable trust like a Non-Governmental Organisation (NGO), private ownership in the form of a small, medium or large-scale enterprise.

2. Organisational Orientation: In addition to ownership, organisations can be categorised according to whether they are product-oriented or service-oriented. These can take the form of primary sector, secondary sector and service-oriented sector - which is also termed as the tertiary sector. The primary sector includes industries like agriculture, fisheries and extraction of natural resources such as oil and minerals. The secondary industry consists of manufacturing of goods from the raw material stage to the finished product stage, and it includes the processing industry. The tertiary industry comprises all service industries, such as delivery of intangibles or deliverables like distribution, hotel, restaurant, transport, communication, finance, public administration, health and education etc.

3. Organisational Size: Organisations can also be categorized according to size. There are the micro or small organisations where the manpower strength is 10 or below, the medium-scale organisations where the size is around 150 and the large organisations where the size is in thousands. Most PSUs and multinationals (MNCs) are large enterprises. In such organisations the need for a separate industrial relations department is mandatory to investigate all employee-related issues and mitigate labour related problems which otherwise threaten to blow up and cause strikes and lock-outs. In the year 2012, the lock-out at the Maruti Plant at Manesar is a case in point. A long-standing issue between the supervisors and the workers over the mistakes made by the workers, the rule of only an half hour lunch break, and the pressure on the supervisors to complete targets in response to the growing demand for SWIFT cars, ended violently leading to the killing of the Human Resource Manager.

Such instances strongly point to the need to adopt human relations approach and be more proactive in amicably solving issues related to humans at the workplace.

The context of HRM is also deeply influenced by the environmental context. This external environmental context is not within the control of the organisation. However the organisation needs to be sensitive towards these aspects of the environment and respond favourably, adopting approaches to align with the changing requirements of the environment in which it operates.

In this section, we focus on two environment models- namely the Systems Model and the PEST model.

The System Model

This model elaborates on the approach of input and output. The input includes raw material, human resources, finance, infrastructure, all procured from the environment and the output includes the finished products and services as deliverables supplied to the environment as a result of operations and processing. For example in the manufacturing of cars, the inputs take the form of raw material, spares as assemblies, research and development activity for innovation in design, cost cutting, alternative spare parts, efficient engine technology, human resources which are trained, qualified, and effective; and the output takes the form of creatively designed, cost-efficient cars and creating a balance of demand and supply to avoid inventory and finance loss. More and more car manufacturers get into alliances with the finance companies to help the process of sales in the external market when it gets plagued with recession, cost cutting, frozen salaries and variable pay.

In the system model approach, human resource takes a very significant position, as in order to create a competitive edge, training and development interventions are imparted by the human resource (HR), learning from mistakes is encouraged and extended in the internal working environment by the HR, innovation skills training is given by HR. All these interventions create competitive edge and help to encourage talent to perform best and become more creative and satisfy their career aspirations through garnering a superlative performance.

What is Human Resource Management?

An organisation consists of people with formally-assigned roles who work together to achieve the organisation's goals. A manager is responsible for accomplishing these goals, and does so by managing the efforts of people in the organisation.

Human Resource Management is the process of acquiring, organising, training, appraising, and compensating employees and attending to their labour relations, health, and safety and fairness concerns. The people or the personnel aspects of the management job include the following:

1. Conducting job analysis.
2. Planning manpower needs.
3. Recruiting and selecting candidates.
4. Orienting and training new employees.
5. Compensating employees.
6. Providing incentives and benefits.
7. Appraising performance.
8. Communicating through various means, counselling and coaching.
9. Training and Developing managers.
10. Building employee commitment.

The Human Resource Manager should be conversant about the following:

1. Employment all the other relevant laws.
2. Equal Opportunity.
3. Employee health and safety.
4. Handling grievances and labour relations.

Human Resource Manager's Duties:

The human resource manager carries out distinct functions. These are as follows:

1. Line Function: As a line function the duties of a human resource manager includes placing the right person on the right job, inducting or orienting new employees, training employees to extend and hone their skills, improving the job performance of each person, gaining cooperation and development of harmonious relations among employees, translating and interpreting the guidelines and policies set by the organisation, controlling labour costs, developing the capabilities of an individual, creating morale and maintaining ethics and finally protecting an employees' health, physical conditions at work and maintaining an overall mental, emotional, moral character and a healthy physical working atmosphere for the workforce.

2. A Coordinative Function: the HR Manager also has to ensure that there is an alignment of all the activities among the personnel in terms of adherence to the policies, guidelines, rules, procedures and the overall HR strategy. This would also include ensuring that the right man is in the right job, as well as the creation of an environment as underlined in the vision, mission or strategies of the organisation, training needs and learning orientation as underlined in the ethos and culture. Most importantly, in the coordinative function, consistency must be ensured in vision, mission, culture and working, to avoid gaps and restore the faith in the efficacy of the HR function.

3. Staff Function: As a staff role and an expert role, the main tasks of the HR include providing expertise in hiring methodology through appropriate recruitment, selection tests and interviews, compensation and reward benefits, training techniques and learning environment, coaching, mentoring and counselling strategies, retention strategies, lay-off or retrenchment of non-performing employees, administering the enforcement of the law in terms of working hours, minimum wage directives, work-family philosophy, cultural sensitivity issues and the law and so on.

Some examples of HR specialists include the following:

1. **Recruiters:** They are quality search experts;
2. **Human Resource Development Experts:** Manage employee development programmes;
3. **Engagement and Fun Experts:** These take care of organising events and activities to ensure that the work place is happy and energetic;
4. **Employment Welfare Officers:** Ensure that the directives and legislation in issues related to manpower are being adhered to according to the law;
5. **Job Analysts:** Compile and analyse information related to jobs in order to design appropriate jobs;
6. **Compensation Managers:** Develop compensation plans and design creative compensation benefits and rewards programmes;
7. **Training and Learning and Development Specialists:** Plan, organise and develop training and learning modules aimed at honing and developing new skills and knowledge;
8. **Employment and Industrial Relations Specialists:** Manage and develop harmonious relations with the trade unions and the management and ensure amicable solutions to problems.

1.7 Patterns Shaping Human Resource Management in the 21st Century

1. **Globalisation:** It refers to the tendency of the firms to extend their sales, ownership and manufacturing to new markets abroad. Organisations with this trend are known to establish a symbiotic relationship, meaning each country is dependent on another for expansion and growth. The case in point is Indian IT companies like Cognizant, Wipro and Infosys which serve clients from around the world and the term is also used to refer where firms from other countries outsource their operations to the countries where skills are available like it is being done in India with so many BPOs having been started. FMCG and Manufacturing companies too have collaborations in India and other countries to take advantage of skill availability, labour surplus, technology expertise, ready markets and so on.

Like automobile companies are setting up manufacturing facilities in India and assembling some components from their host countries. These trends pose a challenge to HR to outline policies aligning with different culture and communication trends with the other countries to avoid clashes. For instance, when the Tatas collaborated with a Mexican organisation, the Mexicans were first given training on how to pronounce the name TATA. This apart, the host company had to make changes in the working and culture as the Mexicans were used to a leisurely lunch of about two or three hours and they often discussed business over lunch. Another example is that of Airtel: when it started operations in Africa, it had to tweak its working policy to allow music in the office to take care of the African work culture where the locals do not work without music. Even as far as the work timings were concerned they had to enforce strict rules of work, as Africans like to have a healthy work-life mix and do not work beyond the normal working hours.

2. **Technological Trends:** Internet-based working has become the norm. This has changed the technique of communication and working norms. Internet-based mobile banking, learning, trading, online buying and network or synergy among all devices has become the new trend of working. The staid and the gigantic Indian Railways too have undergone a transformation with the norm of computerised booking and SMS being used in place of a hard ticket to make the environment more sustainable. Cloud computing has allowed the sharing of resources through the use of common servers and has lead to integration and convergence of working. HR has also been impacted as technology has spawned new models of working in terms of flexible hours, telecommuting, video conferencing learning and e-training without the barrier of lack of physical proximity.

3. **Knowledge work and human capital:** Peter Drucker, the famous management guru, has said, "The centre of gravity for human capital is moving fast from manual, clerical to knowledge working... in short, today's jobs require more skills, more knowledge and more expertise." Today the workforce is living in a high tech and competitive world where the premium is on capabilities referring to the information based application, analytics, problem solving and critical skills and so on. These call for different demands on the human capabilities.

4. **Demographic Trends:** Despite frequent hits by recession and job cuts, demographic trends are changing, where the entry age of the workforce in some places is now down to 16 years and the retirement age has been raised to 70 years. Another trend identified in India is the acute skills shortage which is posing a major challenge in the demographic dividend challenge. Generation Y: Experts contend that many younger workers may have different work values than did their parents. These form a large percentage of the new workforce today. Based on some research studies, older employees are more likely to be work-centric (focusing more on work rather than family with respect to career decisions). Younger workers

tend to be more family-centric and dual-centric and they all like feedback too. These millennium employees bring challenges and their strengths to the employment.

5. Non-traditional Workers: At the same time, there has been a shift to non-traditional workers, a category that includes those who hold multiple jobs. Or who are contingent or part-time, or who are in alternative working arrangements. Today almost 10 per cent of American workers fit this non-traditional workforce category. The striking feature of the Indian work force is that 93 per cent of the workers are in the unorganised informal sector.

1.8 Strategic Human Resource Personnel Management

In the above section, the development of human resource management as a specific and distinctive approach to the management of people was discussed. It is clear that there has been a move in recent years to acknowledge that there are many approaches that can be encompassed within the broad sweep of human resources management. The most important perspective among them is the strategic approach.

What is Strategy?

Whittington refers to classical planning approach, where strategic decisions are constructed on the basis of rational decision making on the part of senior managers. Within this is the idea of strategic direction, encompassing a vision, as a sense of purpose about where the organisation, big or small, strives to be at some point in the future. How far ahead in the future, and what sort of planning horizon, will depend on the variety of factors including the nature and complexity of the industry, the state of competition and estimates of likely future trends in the market.

HRM strategy is connected with planning and terms used include goals, objectives, values, vision, mission, plans, strategies, targets and policies.

1. A mission describes what the purpose of the organisation is, the reason for its existence and what it is there to do.
2. A vision is an end point of where we want to get to in the long term - maybe what we will be known for or a position we will attain.
3. Goals are specific targets on the way to the vision, usually over a time period of two to five years.
4. Targets are the measures that apply to the goals.
5. Strategies are the routes we have chosen to attain the goals.
6. Values are the ways in which we want to behave in achieving our goals.
7. Policies are about how we will do certain things consistent with our values.
8. Plans are detailed action for implementation in the foreseeable future ahead.

All these can apply to an organisation as a whole or to a part of it. Usually, one organisation shares the same values and policies across its various divisions or business entities.

Why We Want to Write a Strategy

It is important to think through the purpose of writing a strategy and the audiences for it. The obvious answer is to decide systematically what we are going to do.

Developments of HR practices are encased in our values, beliefs and principles. If these are diverse and not commonly held, we will lack coherence in the implementation of our strategy. We need to understand the implications of values, principles and beliefs on the people in the organisation, specifically in the six areas of HRM. These are as follows:

1. Organisation and Culture.
2. Rewards and Recognition.
3. Communication and Employee relations.
4. Resourcing.
5. General HR Policies.
6. Learning and Development.

Business Strategy itself is the key. Every manager's objective and all issues in an organisation have a people implication. Hence, in that sense everything in an organisation has HR as an inherent relationship. Suppose that one of the values of an organisation is "continuous learning". So, the HR implications for the same would be as follows:

1. Organisation and Culture organisation structure is networked; empowerment is all-pervading; trust and not micromanagement is undertaken; forums are prevalent to discuss experiences;
2. Rewards and Recognition for new learning; rewards for experimentation and breaking the status quo; special incentives for new learning;
3. Communication and Employee relations; coaching; reverse mentoring from new recruits; open-door policy;
4. General HR Policies: Sabbaticals for study leave; new learning as criteria for promotion
5. Learning & Development: Regular training; e-training; certification courses;
6. Resourcing Promotion based on regular learning;

Strategic Human Resource Management means formulating and executing human resource policies and practices that produce the employee competencies and behaviour the company needs to achieve its strategic aims. The basic idea behind formulating such strategic human resource management is formulating the human resource practices and policies and producing employee skills and behaviour that the company needs to achieve its strategic plans.

Human resource policies and strategies example: HDFC Bank

Ranked 10th in Business Today's 'Best Companies to Work For' survey 2012, HDFC Bank (incorporated in 1994) has a mission of being a world class Indian bank. By 2010, when it was 16 years old, the bank had a national network of 1725 branches and 3898 ATMs in 771 towns and cities in India. Currently recognised as one of the most respectable and performing commercial banks, its business philosophy is based on four core values: operational excellence, customer focus, product leadership and people. The leveraging of its status to the top slot has been supported by its strategic HR initiatives. The bank recruits selectively from business school campuses. Hiring is taken seriously with extensive background checks about performance and integrity. Apart from intensive and regular training at all levels the bank has an exclusive tie-up with IIM-Ahmedabad for conducting its senior leadership development programmes. While HDFC Bank is much sought after by employees of other banks, its management works to protect its unique work culture. Emphasis is given to employee participation in decision making and celebration of success. Unlike other institutions, the bank has announced increments, promotions and bonuses during the economic downturn.

A deep understanding of the above case study reflects the huge impact of HR on HDFC Bank's success in terms of manpower recruitment, selection, promotions and attitude in terms of performance, ethics and integrity. Some of the Strategic Human Management Tools include the following:

1. Strategy Map: This is an important HR Tool. Organisations use the strategy map to understand the contribution of each of their departments in the achievement of the overall strategy of the organisation. The purpose is to establish a connect between the overall organisational framework and the link between the various functions and departments. The strategy helps each functional area and department to visualise and support each of the strategies that are outlined in the overall map. The HR functions as an overall integrator needs to coordinate the people and their issues on the basis of the strategy outline.

2. The HR Scorecard: The HR scorecard helps organisations to quantify and computerise the map's activities. HR Scorecard refers to the process for assigning financial and non-financial goals or metrics to the human resource management related chain of activities required for achieving the company's strategic aims and for monitoring results. The following is a detail of the HR Scorecard introduced in India by consultant and former IIM faculty TV Rao through TV Rao Learning Systems (TVRLS). According to the author, HRD (Human Resource Development) Scorecard is an indicator of the level of HR maturity of an organisation and its alignment with the organisation's strategy. The model is based on the assumption that competent and motivated employees are needed to provide quality products and services at competitive rates and ways that enhance customer satisfaction. In the HRD Scorecard the maturity level of HRD in an organisation is measured on four dimensions on a 10 point scale (Where 10 represents the highest maturity, 5 represents a moderate maturity level and 1 represents the least level of maturity).

(a) HRD Systems Maturity Score: Employee competency and commitment can be developed through appropriate HRD mechanisms. In an HRD-mature organisation, there will be well-developed HRD systems such as:

1. Human Resource Planning and Recruitment
2. Performance Management Systems
3. Feedback and Coaching Mechanisms
4. Training
5. Career Development and Succession Planning
6. Job rotation
7. OD (Organization Development) Interventions
8. Human Resource Information Systems
9. Worker Development Methods and Systems
10. Potential Development and Appraisal
11. Any other Subsystems

HRD Competence Score

The competencies of the HRD department and the line managers play an important role in implementing the systems and processes in ways that could ensure employee satisfaction, competency building and customer satisfaction. The competencies of the various levels of staff are measured for this part of the section. These are detailed as follows:

1. The level of HRD skills they possess.
2. Attitudes and support to learning and their own development.
3. Extent to which they facilitate learning among others in the corporation and those who work with them.
4. Their attitudes and support to HRD function and system.

The HRD culture

The HRD culture measures the values, systems and processes created by the HRD tools. Employees and their styles also play a crucial role in building sustainable competencies in the organisation. These need to be measured and monitored. It is possible for some organisations to have minimal formal HR Systems and have a high level of HR competencies and HRD culture. There are questionnaires designed to measure HRD Culture of organisations.

Business Linkage Score

The HRD Systems, competencies and culture must be aligned with the business goals of the organisation. The score indicates the extent to which the HRD efforts (tools, processes, culture etc) are driven to achieve business goals or goals of the organisation. The business linkage goals include:

1. Business excellence including profitability and other outcomes of the organisation
2. Internal operational efficiencies
3. Internal customer satisfaction
4. External customer satisfaction
5. Employee motivation and commitment
6. Cost effectiveness and cost consciousness among employees
7. Quality orientation
8. Technology adoption.

The above eight indices are the pillars of HRD maturity model of the organisation. All the four dimensions are scored on a 10-point rating scale.

HRM Strategic Model

Types of HRM strategy include vertical strategy, horizontal strategy and differentiation strategy. Each of these strategies requires a different set of employee role behaviours. These role behaviours require in turn a collection of supportive HR practices about which strategic decisions need to be made. So, in effect, the essential task of HR is seen as one of fit-between the business and the HR strategies. The precise nature of what is meant by appropriate role behaviours is elaborated upon by Schuler and Jackson (1987) as are the HR implications of these. In the case of an innovative strategy such as at companies like Nokia, Apple or Microsoft, "this would call for a high level of creative, risk oriented and cooperative behaviour". The company's HR practices would therefore need to emphasise "selecting highly skilled individuals, giving the employees more discretion, using minimal controls, making greater investments in human resources, providing more resources for experimentation, allowing and even rewarding failure, and appraising performance for its long-run implications".

1.9 A Case Study on HR for Emergency Response Systems

(The following is a Case Study related to a successful Emergency Response Service Organisation which highlights in detail the crucial role played by Human Resource department in facilitating the alignment of the goals and objectives through designing of the various operations, processes, systems and policies. The myriad roles and responsibilities of the operational staff, managerial and the top leadership are underlined in detail. It is also elaborated how a successful alignment of all these roles and systems lead to success in an organisation. The role played by values reflected in uniform behaviour of personnel too is highlighted.)

The learning objectives of this case study below include:
1. Qualitative job descriptions alone will not be sufficient
2. Metrics clearly defined are important for measuring the performance
3. Performance management is based on facts and figures not prejudices.

It is being highlighted in every successful organisation that HR has to be aligned with the business goals. Once HR aligns with the business goals, the Human performance will increase in terms of individual competence, team work and higher employee retention rates which in turn will improve operational performance in terms of business performance, market share etc., and thus leading to better financial performance.

Hence, the Role of HR is to:
- Align HR to business strategy and execution.
- Implement HR practices to build an effective organisation (Staffing, Development, Appraisal and Rewards).
- Listen and respond to employees for improving their commitment.
- Manage transformation as a change agent to create flexible organisation.

HR will be the foundation for providing successful Emergency Response Services (ERS), when we specifically look at the services in Medical Emergencies. Broadly the Human Resource Requirements in ERS can be categorized at 3 levels:

1.0 Operational

2.0 Managerial

3.0 Leadership

1.0: Operational:

Human Resource Requirements at Operational level are in the following categories:

1.1 Roles in Call Centre / Job Descriptions / Process Flow / Training Requirements

(Call Centre works in 3 shifts of 8 hours each on 24x7 basis).

- **Communication Officer (CO)**
    - Responsible for collecting primary information from the caller in relation to the name, address, contact details and type of emergency.
    - First contact point in the Call centre to receive the calls.
    - Forwards the screen and voice to dispatch officer after collecting primary information.
    - CO is trained for one month on Process flow, Technology details, Data Entry, Soft Skills etc.

- **Dispatch Officer (DO)**
    - Responsible for configuring all resources (ambulance, hospital, police station) for effective dispatch of an ambulance.
    - Receives the call and the screen from CO.
    - Validates the type of emergency and collects more information from the caller.
    - Finds out the nearest ambulance, shortest route, nearest hospital and nearest police station.
    - Assures Caller / patient and gives first aid instructions.
    - Connects caller to the identified ambulance staff.
    - Transfers the call and the screen to emergency response centre physician and / or to police dispatcher depending on the need for medical advice or if it is a medico legal case / police emergency.
    - DO is trained for one month on Process flow, Technology details, Data Entry, Decision making and Soft Skills.
- **Emergency Response Centre Physician (ERCP)**
    - Responsible for providing pre-arrival instructions and medical direction to the victims.
    - Advises Emergency Medical Technician in the ambulance on the details of pre-hospital care to be provided.
    - Provides confidence and reassurance to the patient.
    - Speaks to the doctor at the receiving hospital when required.
    - Evaluates each of the patient case record form filled by the EMT in relation to details of pre-hospital care for finding details of life saves in case of critical cases and also for improving the EMT skills.
    - ERCP is trained for one month on Process flow, Technology details, Medical protocols (pre-arrival instruction and medical direction) and Soft Skills.
- **Police Dispatch Officer (PDO)**
    - Responsible for dispatching a police vehicle for a police or medico legal emergency.
    - Receives calls from CO and speaks to the caller for validating the type of emergency.
    - Identifies nearest police station and requests them to dispatch police van.
    - PDO is trained for one month on Process flow, technology details, data entry and police infrastructure and soft skills.

1.2 Roles in Ambulance (Ambulance operates in 2 shifts of 12 hours each on 24x7 basis).

Pilot (Driver)
- Responsible for driving of ambulance safely and quickly.
- Assists EMT in scene management, lifting the patient.
- Ensures that vehicle is in good condition and maintain data in relation to fleet efficiency.
- Pilot is trained for 10 days on Medical Aspects of Emergencies, Lifting the patient, BLS and Soft Skills, Safe driving.

- **Emergency Medical Technician (EMT)**
  - Responsible for providing pre-hospital care to emergency victims.
  - Receives dispatch details from dispatch officer of the call centre.
  - Connects to the patient and provides pre-arrival instructions.
  - Reaches the scene, manages scene and provides on the scene pre-hospital care.
  - Shifts patient to ambulance with the help of pilot.
  - Receives medical instructions from ERCP for providing pre-hospital care.
  - Contact receiving hospital and provides details of patient status.
  - Hands over patient at receiving hospital.
  - Fills and maintains patient case record forms and hands over copies to hospital and call centre.
  - EMT is trained for 45 days on various chief complaints and protocols for stabilizing the patient including Ambulance Phase and Hospital Phase. EMT is also trained on BLS, process flows, Soft Skills.

2.0 Managerial
2.1 Roles in Call Centre / Job Descriptions / Process Flow / Training Requirements

- **Team Leader (TL): Separate for COs, DOs, ERCPs and PDOs**
  - Responsible for scheduling the work of 6 to 8 COs or Dos or ERCPs or PDOs, motivating the team members, recognizing and rewarding them, disciplining them and ensuring necessary infrastructure (physical and technological) is available.
  - TL is trained for one month on Process flow, Technology details, managerial skills and Soft Skills.

- **Sense Manager (SM)**
  - Responsible for successful Call Centre operations covering entire state.
  - Coordinates with medical, operations, technology, quality, Human Resource, Corporate Services and external service providers for ensuring smooth conduct of call centre operations.
  - Motivates team members, recognizes and rewards them, disciplines them and ensures necessary infrastructure (physical, medical and technological) is available.

- Conducts events to celebrate successes.
- Monitors and presents the call centre performance.
- SM is trained for one month on Operations, Process flow, Medical aspects, Technology details, managerial skills and Soft Skills.

2.2 Roles in Ambulance (Ambulance operates in 2 shifts of 12 hours each on 24x7 basis)

- **Operations Executive (OE)**
  - Responsible for scheduling the work of Pilot and EMTs of 8 to 10 ambulances.
  - Motivates team members, recognizes and rewards them, disciplines them and ensures necessary infrastructure (physical, medical and technological) is available.
  - OE is trained for one month on Operations, Process flow, Medical aspects, Technology details, managerial skills and Soft Skills.

- **District Manager (DM)**
  - Responsible for successful ambulance operations in a district comprising of 30 to 35 ambulances covering a population of 3 to 3.5 million.
  - Coordinates with government officials, hospital authorities and media for ensuring smooth conduct of operations.
  - Conducts events to celebrate successes.
  - Monitors and presents the district performance.
  - Motivates team members, recognizes and rewards them, disciplines them and ensures necessary infrastructure (physical, medical and technological) is available.
  - DM is trained for one month on Operations, Process flow, Medical aspects, Technology details, managerial skills and Soft Skills.

- **Fleet Executive (FE)**
  - Responsible for maintaining physical fitness of ambulance of 1 district comprising 30 to 35 ambulances covering a population of 3-3.5 million.
  - Reviews fleet performance indicators and identifies actions for improvement.
  - Trains Pilots (Drivers) for better driving habits to improve fuel and vehicle efficiency.
  - Coordinates with vendors for scheduled and preventive maintenance of ambulances.
  - FE is trained for one month on Fleet Technology, Operations, Process flow, Vendor Management and Soft Skills.

3.0 Leadership:

Leadership is required at State Level to provide ERS conforming to be national policies, protocols, standards and procedures. Leadership is also required at National level for setting direction, aligning and motivating the team in various functional areas.

Major leadership skills required in ERS are:
- Strategic thinking
- Innovation
- Change Management
- Building and working with partnerships
- Seamless Execution

Best practices of HR have been identified and executed in the following areas:
- Recruitment and Selection
- Compensation Benefits
- Induction
- Performance Management
- Learning and Development
- Change Management
- Culture Building

4.0 Measures for tracking performance

Measures have been identified to set targets, track performance, identify gaps and train employees on the identified gaps.

4.1 Measures for Call Centre performance
- Calls received per day.
- Emergency calls received per day.
- Emergencies per day.
- Unattended calls.
- Calls to be taken on first two rings.
- Time taken to assign vehicle from the time of receiving the call.
- Time taken by Ambulance to reach site (Patient) from the time of receiving the call.
- Time taken by Ambulance to reach hospital from receiving the call.
- Ambulance transports for non emergencies.
- Ambulance transports outside geo coverage.
- Ambulance transports-IFT.
- Unavailed medical dispatches to total medical dispatches.
- Ambulance not dispatched in Emergencies to total medical emergencies.

4.2 Measures for Ambulance Performance
- Time taken by Ambulance from base to scene in minutes.
- Emergencies / 100 thousand of population.
- Pregnancy related emergencies / 100 thousand of population.
- Uptime of Ambulances.

- Kms per trip.
- Fuel efficiency.
- Running cost per trip.
- Stock Outs of Vital Items in ambulance.
- Utilization of Ambulances.
- Meetings with Partner Hospitals per quarter.
- Hospitals in network with MoU signed (other than Government Hospitals).
- Recognition Programs conducted for Partner Hospitals in a year (Doctors, Paramedic Staff) per each zone.
- Partner Hospitals accepting Victim taken by ambulances in a month.
- Updation of facilities data of Partner Hospitals once in six months.
- Telecom Providers meetings per year.
- Ambulance Stations.
- EMTs to be covered in refresher training programmes.

4.3 Measures for Managerial Performance
- Daily Emergencies per lakh of population.
- Calls handled in 2 rings.
- Emergencies not attended due to busy ambulance.
- Failed transport.
- Medical direction to EMTs for L1, L2 cases.
- Handholding by EMTs.

4.4 Measures for Leadership Performance
- Average Response Time (call to scene) Urban / Rural.
- Lives Touched (All emergencies) annualized run rate.
- Lives Saved.
- Expansion (Presence in States).
- Funding by Private Sector (New).
- Brand Awareness.
- Research Projects (Medical / System).
- Institute: AHA Programmes.
- Leadership Competence Index.
- Associate Delight Index.
- Government Relationships Index.

Summary

It is misleading to believe that top management is about formulating the strategy and building the structures and the systems. Top managements role would be to create the context for renewal, not to control strategy. Employees will have to take on the responsibility of company's competitiveness and their own learning and progress beyond being implementers of strategic decisions taken by the top management.

Renewing HR Strategy in ERS is to:

- Create stretch in the organisation by building a common identity and a shared ambition so that it develops a sense of ownership among employees.
- Provide support to employees by providing access to resources.
- Embed discipline by establishing clear performance standards and norms of behaviour.
- Build trust by creating transparency and fairness.

Hence, Employees of ERS will make that organisation a great place to work only when HR enables each individual employee trust management (for Credibility, Respect and Fairness, has pride in his job and enjoy people he works with).

People Development at "Menon & Menon" – A growth oriented initiative from SME in a small town.

It was a late Saturday evening. Mr. Vijay Menon, MD, Menon & Menon, was sitting in his cosy office located on the first floor of his company in Kolhapur. He had just finished the review meeting which was also attended by his HR consultant. He was impressed by the way his team was shaping up. What they had achieved was impressive. But it was more so, if we know the background.

The company was initially started by Vijay's father, Mr. Chandran Menon, at Kolhapur, one of the growing cities in Maharashtra. The city of Kolhapur, located in southern part of Maharashtra is well known for the temple of goddess Mahalaxmi. It is also one of the most important places for foundry businesses[1]. Castings manufactured in Kolhapur are recognized globally for their accuracy and fine finish. Mr. Menon shared with his HR consultant the efforts they had been taking over years to establish their leadership in this particular sector and what challenges were there in front of them. With a turnover of ₹ 150 crore, Menon & Menon is a considerably small player in the foundry business.[2] Some of the major challenges

---

[1] Kolhapur is also known for its leather footwear, Engineering, sugar and Yarn industries
[2] Defining a Small & Medium Enterprise is itself a challenging task. Every country defines SME in its own way. In India as per the Micro, Small and Medium Enterprises Development Act 2006, enterprises are broadly classified into micro units, small units, medium units & large units depending on the investment in plant and machinery. In Europe it is based on the parameters

that are in front of Menon & Menon are similar to the challenges faced by many small companies across India. Just like Menon & Menon, some of these industries are also trying to sustain and grow in the globally competitive reality of today's business. With a clear vision of not only sustaining but growing, the MD started focusing on People Development. Thus the Managing Director, Vice President-Operations and various other Departmental Heads started frequently meeting the external HR consultant, who had an expertise of working with large multinational organisations for over 30 years. To begin with, the HR consultant had to understand the people and leadership challenges in Menon & Menon in order to see how far the HR practices commonly found in corporate world would be relevant and applicable in these small organisations. The consultant had to understand the nature of SME operations, the challenges, and then focus on people development in such SME.

It will be therefore appropriate to understand some aspects related to SME Sector in India and the leadership challenge faced by them with a little insight specifically into the working of Foundary Industry so as to grasp the intricacies of the case study better.

The SME sector in India: Small and Medium Enterprises (SMEs) play a vital role for the growth of 'Developing' Indian economy by contributing over 45% of industrial output, about 40% of exports, employing up to 60 million people, creating 1.3 million jobs every year and producing more than 8000 quality products for domestic and international markets. SME's contribution towards the national GDP in 2011 was 17% which is expected to rise up to 22% by 2012. There are approximately 30 million MSME Units in India and upto 12 million people are expected to join the workforce in the next 3 years. (SME Chamber of India).

The SMEs face a number of issues, a majority of which are due to absence of adequate and timely banking service leading to its financial implications, limited capital and knowledge. Most of these issues are also due to unavailability of suitable technology, low production capacity, ineffective marketing strategy, identification of new markets, constraints on modernization & expansions, non availability of highly skilled labour at affordable cost, follow- up with various government agencies to resolve legal issues etc. However if we look closely, we realize that many of these issues can be effectively addressed with effective managerial as well as leadership skills.

The leadership challenge in SME: As INSEAD lecturer Patrick Turner explained 'Although it sounds like an obvious saying, the key to understanding the management/leadership needs of SMEs is simply to recognize the straightforward fact that they are neither a new start-up venture nor a matured large company,'. Start-ups require hands-on, action-based management techniques. The processes are flexible and everyone is involved in everything

---

of employment, turnover and asset size, and in OECD it is based on employment and sales turnover. We are treating Menon & Menon as a small company looking at its market share and nature of operation (Tier-I supplier to major auto companies)

that is needed to "get things done". Large companies, on the other hand, have separate operational / functional management system. Here the leadership role not only involves establishing company specific goals, but also determining the strategy to be followed in order to achieve them. SMEs occupy a position between the two extremes, where on one hand, leaders need to manage the company's day to day operations proactively and move towards achievement of set goals and on the other hand, act as leader as well as a manager to the workforce. The owner is so much involved in day to day operations and other responsibilities, that there may not be a formal opportunity for the second line to operate independently, grow and learn. At the same time, the undersized top management could imply that the owner has a very little opportunity to discuss the vision, strategy & other critical issues. Too much emphasis on operations impact growth, distorts long term vision as well as individual development of leaders.

The foundry industry: The Indian metal casting (Foundry) industry is a well established business sector for decades. According to the recent World Census of Castings by Modern Castings, USA, India ranks as 2nd largest casting producer, producing an estimated 7.44 million metric tonnes of various grades of castings as per international standards (based on 2010 data). The various types of castings[3] produced are ferrous and non-ferrous, aluminium alloy, graded cast iron, ductile iron & steel, etc. These are utilised for application in Automobiles, Railways, Pumps Compressors & Valves, Diesel Engines, Cement/Electrical/Textile Machinery, Aero & Sanitary pipes & Fittings etc & Castings for special applications. However, Grey iron casting shares the major portion (approx 70 %) of total castings produced. There are approximately 4500 units out of which 80% can be classified as Small Scale units & 10% each as Medium & Large Scale units (Foundry Informatics centre). Casting process is labour intensive and involves use of sand, molten metal and overall challenging work environment. Most players in this industry depend strongly on Original Equipment Manufacturers. Thus the SME in foundry industry has to cope with cost challenge and at the same time take extra effort to attract and retain talent.

This background of SME leadership challenge and foundry industry would influence the people development activities at Menon & Menon.

The company history: Menon & Menon was formed in 1954 by Mr. Chandran Menon, hailing from a small village, Kodungallur in Kerala; Mr. Menon started a small auto component company, Menon & Co., which was initially started with a rented lathe machine. From a small workshop to a respected enterprise of about ₹ 150 crore is a motivating journey of ups and downs, which is well presented in the biography of Mr. Chandran (Bhave, 2004). The journey not only talks about the ups and downs faced by Menon & Menon, but also

---

[3] For more information about casting visit www.sfsa.org or www.foundrysource.com. These websites tell us about casting process, and why casting products are used

about growth of a small organisation in a small town, turning around Kolhapur Steel, an acquired ailing company and the man who made it happen. The story is not only inspiring but tells a lot about challenges faced by such enterprises and the kind of leadership personality that helps an organisation sail through the same. However we are going to focus on the challenges of "leadership development" in Menon & Menon as seen in current scenario.

The company is growing steadily in last few years. But it was not the case 10 years back. In 1988, the company restarted after 18 months long labour strike. The going was tough then. Accumulated losses were mounting and in 2002-03, the company approached BIFR **(Board for Industrial & Financial Reconstruction)** to bail out or close. However under proper guidance, prudent leadership, right attitude and support from employees the company recovered, showing steady growth in revenue and output which is evident from the exhibit given below

Exhibit 1: Menon & Menon Production Growth

Production figures tonnes	
2006-07	11112
2007-08	12945
2008-09	13190
2009-10	16591
2010-11	18601

Various corrective actions were taken. Finances were brought under control, product mix was rethought and diversified, and various people initiatives were planned on the way, which we are going to visit soon. Mr. Vijay Menon, who is the current MD, joined the company in 1981 after completing his Bachelor's degree in Mechanical Engineering and an MBA from Illinois State University. He took over the position of MD from his father in 1994. We discussed the challenges in front of him today. He claims that the challenge in front of him is not that of finance. As he puts it: "It was an issue before, but we have learnt our lessons. With prudent practices, one can make money and finance is easily available for expansion." The market is not a problem either. The market share of the company is very small, but at the same time the company works with cost advantage. Both the factors together have ensured that during the recent recession the company could cope by just replacing the poor quality of the competitor. The real challenge was 'people'. The chances that a SME will remain SME are very high. According to Vijay "what prevents people from taking jump in higher orbit are HR practices. Unless you have good people – Right people at right place at right time –

motivated towards predefined goal – You cannot grow." His ideologies are still followed by many entrepreneurs all over the world. (Bacon & Hoque, 2005) (Bolden, 2001). Thus various initiatives started from then.

People Development challenges: The company thus aimed at transforming the overall work culture. The transformation challenge spanned entire gamut of talent management, staffing, retaining, up-skilling, introducing performance culture and introducing the systems to make people development more transparent and wide spread.

Attracting the "right" person: It was always clear that in order to grow, an SME needs to get good people on board. After talking to staff as well as potential candidates the realisation was that just salary is not enough to attract a person. They are not as flexible when it comes to location and industry. First of all this is not an OEM company. It is tier I supplier to OEM. But to a young aspirant it is less glamorous than to work for OEMs like Tata Motors or Maruti Udyog or Mahindra & Mahindra. At the same time the working environment is not fancy like that in an IT industry. This is a smokestack industry, dealing with sand, dust, heat. Another constraint is the location. Kolhapur being a small city, it does not attract young executives even from cities like Pune or Hyderabad. Thus the people who get attracted are mostly due to family constraints or other liabilities. As the MD and HR talked to various candidates the realization was "Unless we are able to get people we are not going to grow. As we tried to attract people from outside, we realized that word of mouth matters. If there is an image that a particular company is a good company, the systems are straightforward and there is no room for politics. The capabilities are nurtured and at the end of day, if this message about the company's vision starts floating around, we can attract people." For Menon & Menon, which was a people-friendly company from day one, developing this goodwill was relatively simple. Particularly for experience-based roles, the people who have spent some time in foundry industry are aware of the attributes of Menon & Menon and the company already becomes a place of choice. This is evident when the company tries to fill the vacant positions from the market, they do get approached by a good set of resumes.

One strong reason why positive vibes were spreading in the market was due to the "people sensitive" policies of the company since inception. The company had gone through many challenges including an 18-month-long strike, but all throughout these ups and downs, the approach of owner was that this is a "quarrel within the family". So when the company restarted its operations after 18 months of strike, almost everyone who was on the payrolls of the company before the strike joined back. The house journal displays stories from many who tried to seek short-term employment to feed family during difficult times and returned as soon as the strike got over.

Due to this people-friendly atmosphere, although recruiting right people might be a small challenge, retaining them is not a challenge. As a matter of fact, since 2007 there has not been even a bit of attrition within the staff, except for retirement.

Up-skilling (in terms of technology as well as managerial skills) is another challenge they are facing. The company is carrying lot of baggage in terms of technology. But changing technology is not easy. With latest technology, you need the workforce that can handle that technology. Up-skilling is also required to satisfy demands of global OEMs. The workforce has to understand the implication of poor quality as well as poor productivity. Up-skilling also involves change in approach and attitude which is the biggest challenge at both level, workman level as well as at the managerial level.

With global competition and demanding customers, it is also important to inculcate latest methods in operations (such as Total Productivity Management (TPM), Total Quality Management (TQM), Lean Manufacturing, Just in Time and Just in Sequence concepts etc). Casting being a highly labour-intensive job, the education level of workmen is low and training such workforce for latest operating methods is not only a training challenge but also a leadership challenge.

Creating a performance-oriented culture: The company started various initiatives to help bring in performance oriented culture, in order to develop managerial as well as leadership skills of the senior employees.

Setting up a performance management system: An important aspect of developing a person is to make him responsible for his income. Thus the company in 2006-07 introduced concepts such as CTC (cost to company) and variable pay. The performance is evaluated twice in a year and the variable pay gets distributed within couple of months after performance review. The variable pay gets decided based on the individual's performance and overall company performance. The effectiveness of this change was checked through internal employee satisfaction survey, which indicated that more than 95% found the change fair and challenging. The evaluation of performance is still based on feedback from HOD. Introducing the culture of predefined KRA (key result attributes) is next step in the agenda. However assessment of behavioural attributes is still to mature as stated by Mr. Turakhia, VP operations.

Job rotation: The MD realized that in corporate companies, a general manager would systematically get exposed to various functions before becoming a general manager. If the people have to grow internally they need to get exposed to various aspects of business. As part of developing second line of command, company identified 20 junior members as high potential candidates. In last 3 years 7 of them were shifted from their original role. When we talked to one manager who moved from "marketing" to "Purchase", he said. "It was a totally different experience. So far I was negotiating for maximum price, now I have to negotiate for minimum price. I also realised that the cost of raw material (grey iron) is changing every minute, where as OEM would agree price changes once in 3-6 months. The nature of negotiations was different too. The buyer from OEM is smart, well trained officer, where as trader who is selling our raw material would be less sophisticated." Similar transitions were tried elsewhere like person from production line was moved to "projects". However the MD agreed that "It takes lot of courage on our part as well as manager's part. There is always a chance that such movement would fail. In large corporations there are enough checks and balances and the person could be replaced easily. For us, the failure could be expensive."

Developing "Leadership Team": The company aims at growing people internally. "A person could potentially join as young trainee engineer and grow to a position of CEO" is the guideline on which the company wishes to operate, however with exponential growth; it is not possible to promote all the people internally to fill the vacant positions. So, a few positions had to be filled by hiring senior people from outside. Due to company's image, company could attract some experienced people who had worked in large organisations such as Cummins India Ltd. Thus today's top team consists of people who have spent all their life with Menon & Menon and others who have worked in large organisations. The newcomers brought in new ideas and systems. They got an opportunity to try out what they had learnt earlier, however they had to understand the difference in culture between a large and small organisation. They brought in technology correction. As one such leader said, "I had earlier experience of organisation transformation, where I had helped my vendor to set up processes and systems. We tried to take everyone along. My message was 'We respect old people but not old ways'. This helped me to inculcate my ideas in a systematic change management initiative where people were upgraded technically." However he is aiming at developing the attitude and value system, where there is a dislike towards inefficiencies and poor quality. And that is not an easy task at all.

Skill upgrades: The management is aware that technology is changing fast. The simple machines like lathes etc. are getting replaced by special purpose machines (SPM) and Computer-aided Numeric Control (CNC) machines / Enhanced Numeric Control (ENC) machines. This change would require the staff to be computer literate. The computerization process in Menon & Menon is more than a decade old. Everyone amongst the staff is trained to use computers. They use IT systems and office tools such as email very effectively. Not all technology challenges can be solved by skills training. In fact skills training is possibly simplest part of technology upgrade. Currently investment in R & D is close to nothing. If the company has to service the larger segment of passenger cars, they need to upgrade to Aluminium casting etc. which would not only require investment but would also require technical skill updates at all levels. It would also require a different mindset towards production, wastage and quality. At the same time if company wants to go from "tier I supplier" to OEM to "complete solutions company" or "product based company", then they need to inculcate different type of marketing skills as well as product development skills.

Training: Part of skill building was addressed through training. Company is investing regularly in technical as well as behavioural skills training. People are getting engaged to a two-year-long quality improvement program arranged by MIQM (Mahindra Institute of Quality Management), that consists of various off site programs and various classroom based training. The managers whom we talked to were very enthusiastic about training; however, the MD was somewhat dissatisfied, particularly when it came to behavioural inputs. He felt that the effect of training eroded very quickly, and it is not practically possible to repeat such exercise at regular interval. Today the organisation finds gap in skills and competencies at the mid-management level, particularly when it comes to understanding the larger picture beyond their function and beyond their company. They have to also develop understanding of fundamentals of business like how the company makes money, the financial as well as the profit sharing perspective. Efforts are being made to fill this gap.

The participative culture: Development can take place by participating in decision making process. Initially, when situation was tough, the MD was taking all the decisions. But over time small committees got formed where decisions started getting discussed prior to confirming the same. Introduction of senior members from large corporations as well as other initiatives helped in growing the maturity of people. Soon the MD realized that "I need to accept the fact that there is merit in what they are saying". As stated by senior members in the company: "We encourage healthy discussion and contribution from all, but still ensure that we respect each other and avoid petty clashes and bickering."

So the questions to ponder over are: **Is the growth sustainable?** Although the story so far looks great, the real question is "Is it enough?" There are multiple perspectives related to this question. Is it enough in terms of growing competition? World is changing fast. For example, a few years ago, global competition was not as fierce due to logistic challenges; however the case is no more the same. To get ready for global challenges, a very different mindset is required. How should company augment the steps taken so far? How can they make the training more effective? The next question is how to upgrade the skills and how to retain people with upgraded skills? There are strategic questions to ask, like can the company remain an "OEM" centric company or should they move to "product" mode. Moving to "Product" mode would require different type of customer centricity, risk management, marketing and distribution and developmental agility. Is the current leadership equipped to handle that? If not how to help them cope with these challenges?

The company has been "people friendly" all along. Can it expect similar friendliness from employees in days to come, when demographic changes are evident? Are there any negative aspects about this friendliness?

The company wants to grow out of "SME" mode in terms of revenue, people strength and market reach. Are the recent changes adequate for quantum leap? MD hopes to go public in near future. As the first step external consultant wants to conduct "HR audit" which could take place soon. Such audit could highlight the gaps or limits in people processes. Assuming you are the HR consultant what would be the key areas that you would look at in HR audit?[4]

Faculty Notes:

This case has been specifically taken as the greatest challenges and opportunities for budding HR professionals exist in SMEs. Therefore, students can get a feel of how an SME that desires to grow and aims high needs to bring fundamental changes in their basic approach towards dealing with their human resources. More thoughts are shared hereunder:

Case synopsis:

SMEs form a very critical segment in the economy. Many SME issues can eventually lead to talent management issue. However, due to specific nature of SME, talent management is a challenge. This case gives an account of some of the steps taken by a small SME in a small town. It highlights various perspectives that need to be considered. The application of corporate methods when applied in SME contexts can lead to some question marks. The case leads to this discussion.

Target audience: The course assumes background of certain practices typically used by HR. Awareness about these would help. Facilitator can ensure that terms such talent development is well understood initially. The case can be used in –

Course in HR (HR strategy): This case, although it talks about SME, it can give a holistic perspective to HR strategy and implementation as such. It also highlights impact of the organisation's background on HR strategy. The facilitator can raise such issues as cost of such initiative, sustainability and also compare the corporate and SME to look at various talent development initiatives.

Course in entrepreneurship: At the same time case highlights a key issue in SME viz. HR development. The case discussion can address.

"Is HR development as critical in SME as portrayed here?"

And let us try to elaborate it here:

---

[4] This case was possible due to the support from Mr. Vijay Menon – MD Menon & Menon, Mr. Turakhia VP Operations and the members of management team at Menon & Menon, who shared their efforts, views and data. Author wishes to thank all of them for their support and enthusiasm.

Learning Outcomes:

To understand how HR strategy could influence the growth of SME and if yes what would be the challenges implementing the same.

Steps for Case Analysis:

Prior to the case, participants could be sensitised about SME realities.

Suggested assignment: the participants gather from known SMEs around them data such as –

- Number of people.
- People development activities in past 5 years.
- Money spent on people development as percentage of revenue.
- Existence of such practices as Performance Appraisal.
- Measurement of effectiveness of such practices.

The objective behind the exercise is that they realise some of the realities about SME before coming for case discussions.

Opening: In the opening brief we highlight the basic backdrop of SME. Initiate the discussion by answering "What is SME?" Elaborate the definition and general nature of SMEs to begin with. Also highlight the role SMEs play in economy and typical characteristics of SME. Then discuss typical issues with SME. Facilitator can also highlight differences between startup and SME / corporate. The key question is "Should SME continue to remain small forever?" And if answer is no then what would they need is systematic approach to people development. This case gives one such account of people development and talent management. Taking this case as reference, the objective is then explained.

Critical questions:

We can consider our study from three perspectives – the strategy, rolling out the practices recommended by strategy and effectiveness of intervention as follows:

1. One is the HR strategy perspective. In SME strategy how critical is HR strategy? Although case suggests that other challenges (e.g. Finance and Marketing) are simpler, the data collected by participants may indicate otherwise.

Can we say that most of the challenges with the SME are challenges of competencies? The people challenge in SME is as crucial as finance, credit availability, market, service etc. The SME people challenge will include:

- **Lack of competency of leader:** SME leader would be entrepreneur, technocrat; but (s)he may not know the basic concepts in team behaviours, strategy etc. The exposure is limited. Creating "community of practice" is critical in this regard.
- **Lack of management knowhow within top management:** Besides leadership skills, SME leader has to "manage" operations. So the top management of an SME has to be aware of basic management know-how such as finance, supply chain etc. The challenge of acquiring such knowledge is limitations in terms of time, money and extra dependence on manager in the day to day operations.
- **Dwarfing of managers due to poor delegation / autocratic behaviour of leader:** The top leader may be an owner but not necessarily professional manager. This poses challenge of continuity and developing & growing managers. This puts breaks on the expansion possibility.

In this regard following two references are very useful:

- Enterprise, Entrepreneurship and Small Business by Simon Down (Down).
- Entrepreneurship: The Social Science View by Richard Swedberg (Swedberg).

Both books talk about leader / manager in SME, their needs, personality, leadership behaviours as well as challenges. What could be discussed is how these behaviours impact the decisions in SME and how owner / managers can be made aware of these challenges.

1. Second aspect is the rolling out of HR practices:

We find that in this case HR practices that are common in corporate such as 'variable pay' is being deployed. What would be the challenges in rolling out such practices? The following could be some of the challenges.

- Bureaucracy / IT enablement.
- Availability of right people and retaining them.
- Capability of people for job rotation / upgradation.
- The time and cost required for people development.

But the crucial challenge is that of less "process orientation". This discussion should highlight the need for systematic process implementation – does it add to cost or save it? What kind of flexibilities would help implement such processes? Can the SME afford it? What is the impact on owner? Refer to the state of Menon & Menon around 1998-99 – What would be the challenges in rolling out HRM processes in such a situation?

Please refer to the following book for this discussion:

Human Resource Development in Small Organisations: Research and Practice (Routledge Studies in Human Resource Development) by Beaver, Stewart (Beaver).

A journal article by Bacon and Kim Hoque (Bacon & Hoque, 2005) also discusses the challenges in rolling out HRM processes, the critical factors that influence HRM practices and also the impact of networks on these processes.

2. The third aspect is that of effectiveness of the talent development. The case also refers to training and the MD's frustration about training effectiveness. In order to improve the effectiveness of intervention, we may have to consider various other ways of intervention e.g. coaching, group meetings etc. A detailed discussion on learning in general, action learning interventions and challenges in SME; could bring out the fact that operational orientation of the SME owner may block him from developmental growth. It will also highlight the impact of various realities of SME (like size, funds available for development, priorities) on such intervention.

The case talks about recruiting people with corporate background, SMEs suffer from lesser knowledge sharing which can partly be filled with getting people with such experience. However SMEs could also learn from each other. There is a larger issue of networking, collaboration across SME. We find that formation of "clusters" help SMEs to learn from each other. This point can be discussed further looking at various aspects related to importance of networks and issue of trust, competition and collaboration.

The article by Jean-Anne Stewart gives details about evaluation of action learning program conducted in UK for SME leaders. (Stewart, Vol 6 July 2009).

The article by Jeff Gold and Richard Thorpe talks about various problems in training programs and a set of principle that can followed to develop effective intervention (Gold & Thorpe, Leadership and Management Development in Small and Medium Sized Enterrises: SME Worlds).

Another article by Lisa Anderson and Jeff Gold talks about action learning situations and how these can help SME mangers (Anderson & Gold, 2009).

Another interesting article by Jeff Gold and Richard Thorpe gives A detailed description of how the owner of a small UK hairdressing business, through the intervention of a mentor, changed his view of the use of training and received training that significantly improved his business. The preamble discusses how HRD works in SMEs and gives some new insight into the nature and cultures of the SME sector (Gold & Richard, 'Training, it's a load of crap!': the story of the hairdresser and his 'Suit', September 2008).

The article by Mesquita talks about the issue of trust and how trust facilitator (which could be a coach, mentor or trainer) help in collaborative learning and development in SME (Mesquita, 2007-Vol 32).

The article by James Powell, Jane Houghton talks about how collaborative groups went through action learning interventions and the experiences from the same. (Powell & Houghton, July 2008).

Closing the discussion

The discussion could highlight some of these points:

- If SMEs want to grow beyond the steady state, they have to have good people and they have to develop strategy to attract as well as develop good people.
- However that development initiatives have to consider the business realities, and address them effectively.
- SMEs have to consider these realities to systematically form the HR strategy that would influence the staffing, talent development, and developing performance oriented culture.

Bibliography ...

- Anderson, L., & Gold, j. (2009). Conversations outside the comfort zone: identity formation in SME manager action learning. *Action Learning: Research and Practice*, 229-242.
- Bacon, N., & Hoque, K. (2005). HRM in the SME sector: valuable employees and coercive networks. International Journal of Human Resource Management.
- Beaver, S. Human Resource Development In Small Organisations: Research And Practice (Routledge Studies In Human Resource Development).
- Bhave, S. (2004). Casting a Destiny. In S. Bhave, *Casting a Destiny* (p. 189). Ameya Prakashan.
- Bolden, R. (2001). Leadership Development in Small and Medium Sized Enterprises. Exeter: Center for Leadership Studies.
- Down, S. Enterprise, Entrepreneurship and Small Business.

- Foundry Informatics centre. (n.d.). */About_Us/profile_of_indian.aspx*. Retrieved August 23, 2011, from www.foundryinfo-india.org: /www.foundryinfo-india.org/About_Us/profile_of_indian.aspx

- Gold, J., & Richard, T. (September 2008). 'Training, it's a load of crap!': the story of the hairdresser and his 'Suit'. *Human Resource Development International* , 385-399.

- Gold, J., & Thorpe, R. (n.d.). *Leadership and Management Development in Small and Medium Sized Enterrises: SME Worlds*. Retrieved August 23, 2011, from http://www.brad.ac.uk/acad/dppc/research/Regeneration/Conference_papers/Jeff_Gold_080401.pdf

- Mesquita, L. F. (2007-Vol 32). Starting Over When The Bickering Never Ends: Rebuilding Aggregate Trust Among Clusterd Firms Through Trust Facilitators. *Academy of Management Review* , 72-91.

- Powell, J. A., & Houghton, J. (July 2008). Action Learning as core process for SME Business Support. *Action Learning, Reaserch and Practice* , 173-184.

- SME Chamber of India. (n.d.). *About_MSMEs.aspx*. Retrieved August 23, 2011, from www.smechamberofindia.com: http://www.smechamberofindia.com/About_MSMEs.aspx

- Stewart, J.-A. (Vol 6 July 2009). Evaluation of an ActionLearning Program for Leadership Development of SME Leaders in UK. *Action Learning Research & Practice*, 131-148.

- Swedberg, R. *Entrepreneurship: The Social Science View*.

The following transformation slant by a leading IT Consulting Organization reflects the Strategic case of HR.

Capgemini India launches employee centric brand campaign

Unveils the new - "Be the **YOU** want to be" campaign with real life stories

India / Mumbai, April 03, 2013: Capgemini, one of the world's foremost providers of consulting, technology and outsourcing services with over 40,000 employees in India, today announced the launch of its new brand campaign - 'Be the YOU want to be', showcasing employees as part of real-life stories/challenges. The campaign aims at promoting Capgemini as a preferred career destination, by highlighting real stories of Capgemini team members –

their experiences, challenges and other key elements that have helped them develop as a person and as a successful technology professional.

Campaign is developing 9 key objectives, which will be used in a series of advertisements. These directions work in harmony with a Capgemini story or challenge. In this way, the company is providing prospective employees with an aspirational and real picture of what their professional life could be if they pursue a career at Capgemini.

External audiences will be connected through emerging and existing available platforms such as mobile, print, online advertising and outdoor billboards. Social media will be at the heart of the campaign and used to engage prospective employees. Outdoor advertising will be seen in key metros and cities such as Mumbai, Kolkota, Trichy, Salem and Thiruvananthapuram.

Commenting on the launch of campaign, **Rajesh Chandiramani**, **Senior Vice President – Marketing & Sales, Capgemini India,** said: "The new campaign brings out real life stories of our employees, who have overcome personal and professional challenges, which are typically faced by technology practitioners. Through this initiative, we want to communicate to aspiring audiences on how Capgemini is offering the desired environment for professional growth."

The Capgemini brand in India has seen a steady growth over recent years in line with the development of the company presence. Human-centered communication started with "People matter, results count" campaign at the end of 2010 until the "We are the ones" and Experts Connect campaigns in 2011-2012. The new campaign "Be the **YOU** want to be" - is fully in line with the multiple aspirations of young IT professionals in India and aims to add to the positive growth story of the brand.

Discussion Questions

1. Why does HR occupy such a strategic role today?
2. What are the factors influencing the changing role of HR?
3. What are the strategic tools available for enhancing the role played by HR?
4. How does an organisation become a Great Place to Work For?

References

1. Terrington D. Hall, Taylor S, Kinson C (2009) Fundamentals of Human Resource Management: Managing People at Work, Harlow F. T, Prentice Hall.
2. Mueller F. (1996) Human Resources as a Strategic Asset: An evolutionary resource based theory. Journal of Management Studies. Vol 33, No 6, 757- 785.
3. Whittington R (2002). What is Strategy and Does it Matter? Oxford: Blackwell.
4. Schuler R, Jackson S. (1987) "Linking Competitive Strategies and Human Resource Management Practices" Academy of Management Executive, Volume 1, No 3, 207 – 19.
5. Ulrich S. (2002) "From e business to e Hrm", International Human Resource Information Management Journal, Vol 5, 90 - 7.

***

Chapter 2...

Recruitment

Contents ...

2.1 Why: The Purpose of Recruitment

2.2 Methods of Recruitment

2.3 Other Sources of Recruitment

2.4 Case Study

- Discussion Questions
- References

Objectives and Summary

The objective of this section is to explain the significance of recruitment as a Talent Acquisition tool and how to ensure that the right fit of candidates with the technical expertise and alignment of the values and culture of the organisation can go a long way in enhancing productivity, innovation and efficiency of an enterprise.

This chapter includes the meaning of recruitment, factors to be considered for recruitment, human resource planning and forecasting for recruitment, establishing the various internal and external sources of recruitment and assessment of each of these sources. We have also included interviews with HR personnel as live examples to get the real corporate scenario as regards recruitment and retention.

Learning Outcomes:

1. Explain Recruitment and its role in Talent Management;
2. Show with examples the factors considered for recruitment;
3. Illustrate the various forecasting methods in Human Resource Planning;
4. List and explain the various sources of Recruitment;
5. Define and give examples of various current trends in the areas of Recruitment.

2.1 Why: The Purpose of Recruitment

Recruitment and selection form a core element of HR activity in developing sustained competitive advantage for the organisation and talent development, an essence for enhanced productivity and efficiency. Taylor and Collins (2000) believe recruitment and selection are the most important part of HR work.

In today's dynamic work environment, it is imperative that the organisation is able to source prospective employees with the right skills, right knowledge and right abilities who will fit with the values and culture of the organisation. Scmidth and Hunter (1998) calculated that the difference between a high performing-worker and a low-performing one is on average 40 per cent of salary.

Employee recruiting means finding and attracting applicants for the employer's open positions. Recruitment is usually undertaken for one or two reasons, either to fill a vacancy (Taylor, 2005) or to enable promising individuals to enter the organisation on a fixed length work based development programme leading to later permanency. It's hard to overemphasize the importance of effective recruiting. For example, a survey during an earlier slowdown (2003-2004) found that about half the respondents said they had difficulty finding qualified applicants. About 40 per cent said it was hard to find good candidates.

Factors to be considered while recruiting in modern times

1. Attrition is the biggest challenge in organisations today. IT companies, Manufacturing organisations are adopting ways to retain workforce on whom training and development expenses incurred are quite high. Even the cost of disrupting business or losing to competition can be high due to attrition.

2. Diversity is an important consideration in recruiting the workforce. Companies like Wipro, Microsoft, Infosys and Mahindras are adopting diversity policies and proactively initiating diversity drives. For instance, Wipro has recently announced a fixed ratio of women in its work force from the top management level to the lower level and has tweaked policies to retain women like flexi hours, nursing centres for elderly parents of women, mobile creches for their children, telecommuting or working from home. L&T has incorporated policies of including rural workforce. IBM has policies for including physically handicapped employees. More and more MNC's are getting CEOs from their parent companies to work in India - like Atlas Copco, Sandvik Asia and Alfa Laval. These expatriates lend a different perspective to issues and thus promote innovation in the enterprise, which is a must for survival today.

3. Talent management is another area that has been increasingly focussed. Several organisations like Future Group have Chief Talent Officers who work closely with the top management for developing employability and creating a sense of challenge among the work force through job enlargement, job rotation and assignment of challenging projects to them.

HOW: Planning and Forecasting for Recruitment

Employment or Human Resource Planning is the process of deciding what positions the firm will have to fill and how to fill them. These flow from the firm's strategic plans. For example in IBM, a Human Resource executive will review with finance and other executives, the personnel ramifications of the company's strategic plans. The centralized recruitment process is being adopted by many companies like Accenture, Force Motors and so on. The advantages are that it is easier to ensure uniformity and conformity with the law; it reduces duplication, like having several recruitment officers; and it becomes easier to have a central talent development department.

Another big question is whether to fill projected openings from within or from outside the firms. These are often referred to as the "build" or "buy" approaches. Every year, State Bank of India (SBI) recruits thousands of graduates who have no prior banking experience, as probationary officers. These officers become the internal talent pool for filling higher-level positions in future. SBI rarely recruits externally for senior positions that require banking experience. At the same time, some of the new-generation banks regularly recruit experienced bankers, including from SBI, to fill middle and senior management positions. While the former makes the build approach, the latter is the buy approach. Many firms also follow a mixed model, combining recruiting from inside and outside.

Forecasting Personnel Needs

The Unique Identification Authority of India headed by Nandan Nilekani has devised plans to attract a large number of experts to work on the ambitious project. Being a public-sector project, it has limited flexibility when it comes to long-term employment and compensation. The authority has invited IT and management experts to join it part-time or full-time, perhaps while on a sabbatical.

For projecting personnel needs, there are simple mathematical and statistical tools adopted by organisations like Trend Analysis, which implies computing the number of people in the last five years in the various functions and then forecasting for the coming year. Or Ratio Analysis, which means making forecasts on the basis of a historical ratio between some causal factors like sales, production, finance and the number of employees required to be generated.

Using Computerised Support for Forecasting Needs

Computerised forecasts enable managers to build more variables into their personnel projections. Newer systems, particularly, rely on mathematically setting clear goals, such as reducing the amount of inventory on hand. With such programmes, employers can more accurately translate desired and projected productivity into forecasted personnel needs. They can also estimate the effects of various productivity and sales level assumptions on personnel requirements.

FROM WHERE: Internal or External?

Forecasting the Supply of Internal Candidates

Internal candidates also provide a database for appropriate filling of vacant positions. For example, Gensys Technologies, a medium-sized organisation, has an updated database called Know Your Employees (KYE). In order to use this resource, organisations maintain an updated database of knowledge, skills and qualifications - including new certifications of employee learning. This database is uploaded on the company's intranet and eligible candidates suitable for vacancies are invited to apply. This also motivates candidates to empower themselves and hone their skills for gaining access to better positions in the firm itself. For example, Google has a recruitment system where all vacancies are first posted on the intranet for interested internal candidates to apply. These are then opened up to external candidates only if the vacancies are not filled internally.

Rehiring

Organisations today do not stop at exit interviews. Like the alumni interconnectedness in educational institutions, ex-employees are contacted and invited for company celebrations and get-togethers. The objective is to bond with them and learn the best practices adopted by the competitor organisations where they are currently employed. Adobe Systems has an extensive network of ex-employees, many of whom have now rejoined the organisation. Godfrey Phillips India Ltd (GPI), an FMCG company too, has an open-door policy and invites former employees to rejoin the organisation, at higher positions. According to the HR Manager at GPI, the double advantage of this policy is to gather the best practices and culture of competitive organisations and secure commitment of those who have earlier left and rejoined the organisation.

Siring Candidates

Organisations like Make my Trip, a consistent ranker as a Great Place To Work For, facilitates an environment where if an employee wishes to exit, for example to start his own company, the higher-level personnel train him and offer valuable inputs and mentoring required for initiating and establishing his start-up. In other words, an exit is not frowned upon, but the exiting employee is sired and his services are outsourced, after he leaves the organisation. S. Kalra, founder, believes in a continued association with the valuable exiting employee, through an outsourcing arrangement or a vendor relationship.

Succession Planning

Hiring from within is particularly important when it involves filling top positions of the employer. For instance, when A. M. Naik retired from the top position at Larsen & Toubro in March 2012, Krishnamurthy Venkataraman - who was then the Finance Controller - had already been groomed for this slot and took over smoothly from the retiring CEO. So, succession planning involves three steps: identifying, assessing and developing organisational top leadership for enhanced performance and productivity.

Identifying key needs: First, based on the company's plans for expansion and diversification, the top management identifies key needs for top positions. Like K.K. Modi, Chairman of the ₹ 1000-crore GPI, has identified retired Head, S. Behuria, former Director, Indian Oil Corporation, to head the steering committee for discussing long-term plans and the way to go forward for GPI.

Developing internal candidates: After identifying top key positions, management engages in grooming and developing potential key candidates internally or externally to fill these. This includes on-the-job training, counselling, cross-functional experiences, short-term assignments and so on.

Assessment and choice: Finally, succession planning involves assessing the performance and the behavioural traits of these key candidates and deciding to fill the slots depending on the feedback of committees appointed to do this.

Succession Planning at ICICI: When ICICI announced the name of Chanda Kochar as successor to M. V. Kamath, it was an outcome of a planned process. Kamath was also identified as a possible successor by predecessor Narayanan Vaghul in the year 1985. Similarly, an important role of Kochar was to identify and groom her successor. ICICI follows this system of identifying, developing and assessing candidates to fill top positions in the bank.

Outside Sources of Candidates

Seeking Applicants: One of the key issues of recruitment is where to start to look for potential candidates. As the world becomes smaller, travel and mobility are now becoming the norm rather than the exception; the pool of potential candidates is huge. So, where should you look for candidates? It does of course depend very much on a number of important issues relating to the job roles you are trying to recruit and the reason you are recruiting. There are five areas to consider:

1. About the candidate you want to recruit

    (a) What qualification, experience, skills and abilities are you looking for ? The more specialised the need is, you must look at national and international coverage rather than confine the process locally or regionally. At very senior levels, you need to look at specialised agencies like a head-hunting firm specialized in recruiting top personnel.

    (b) Another factor that needs to be addressed is how available a person should be. This depends upon how quickly you must have him or her for the job. This information is likely to affect the extent to which you have time to advertise widely, since some specialised journals need specific time to accept advertisements. Also, it may affect the style and content of the advertisement.

2. About the job itself

Key questions here might include: Are you looking for a project-based appointment, or is it long-term? This information helps to consider local versus national methods of raising awareness of the vacancy.

3. About the organisation

    (a) Is the organisation local, national or multinational? This might affect people's perceptions about their career growth, mobility and job fit. Even the decisions about the design and content of the advertisement might be affected by this factor.

    (b) Is the organisation high-profile or low- profile? Perceptions about the brands among potential applicants also affect the response towards the vacancy. For example, brands like Infosys, Cadbury or Pepsi initially generate a wide response among candidates. Also, these areas affect the style and content of the advertisement.

    (c) What is the structure and culture of the organisation? These are considered to be very important factors today in attracting the right personnel. A survey among IIM graduates choice of organisation reveals that culture and structure are the most important determinants as the basis for applications. Culture includes issues like career path, meritocracy versus seniority, and extent of learning and development interventions, frequency and significance of performance appraisal systems, job enlargement and job rotation trends, flexibility of hours. These issues are commonly advertised in the job content.

4. About the profession or the business sector

    (a) Which sector are you in? Education, Science and Technology, Manufacturing and so on. Clearly this affects the placing of the advertisements.

    (b) Is the business environment highly regulated, restricted or organic and free-form? Personal style and approach to work are affected by these areas; the disposition of the candidate is also influenced to achieve a perfect applicant fit with this information.

2.2 Methods of Recruitment

Recruiting via the internet and online options: This medium has become very common today. Most organisations are using this form to recruit almost all types of positions and candidates. Organisations have their own portals and websites through which candidates apply; alternatively, advertisements mention these websites or portals.

In the internet space, social networking sites like FaceBook, Twitter and LinkedIn are being used increasingly to source candidates for the top level as well as the medium level. For example, HCL Technologies and TCS access information regarding potential candidates directly from these sites and extend job offers directly. Such a non-traditional form of sourcing has today become very popular. It is very economical in terms of time and cost and has proved to be fairly effective in achieving its objective of securing appropriate candidates. Even YouTube is being effectively used where videos of current employees and their experiences are being shared to attract applicants. Deloitte, for example, posts videos for applicants to gauge the culture and structure of the organisation, apart from providing other information.

Other online options like posting applications on sites like monster.com, naukri.com and apnacircle.com are also becoming increasingly common. For example, an HR manager, Bhannu Khandelwal, for a start-up shared his experiences of using these sites. He just typed the key postings and was able to generate more than 50 responses.

Improving Online Recruiting Effectiveness: Planning one's online recruiting effort is crucial. Employers need to make it easy for applicants to use their websites to hunt for jobs. Applicants should have the option of filling their online application forms from the portals. Some of the difficulties or objections faced by candidates are:

(a) job openings lack relevant job description;

(b) it is often difficult to format resumes and post them in the form required;

(c) many respondents express concern about the privacy of the information;

(d) poor graphics often make it difficult to use the website;

(e) slow feedback from the managers is annoying.

Despite these limitations which the employers are slowly trying to reduce, the traditional forms of recruitment, although expensive and declining, still exist.

Advertising

This continues to be a widely popular medium. The media here are the local newspapers like The Economic Times, The Times of India and Hindustan Times, specialized magazines like Business Today, Business India and Business World, and research journals like Vikalpa, Economic and Political Weekly and so on. All these have special pages allotted for employment advertisements. Employers creatively use these sections to advertise openings mentioning job descriptions, culture and structure and details expected from the potential candidates. They also use these media to advertise about the organisations themselves in order to build their brands and attract suitable candidates to apply. Job seekers too refer to these sections as channels to learn what positions are vacant and the competencies expected to suitably fill positions locally, regionally, nationally or internationally.

This is definitely one of the most widely known and recognisable recruitment advertisements in history. The image of Uncle Sam (representing the initials of the United States) was created by James Montgomery Flagg, who used a modified version of his own face. His 1917 poster, based on the original British Lord Kitchener poster of three years earlier, was used to recruit soldiers for both World War I and World War II. It was this image more than any other that set the appearance of Uncle Sam as the elderly man with white hair and a goatee wearing a white top hat with white stars on a blue band, and red and white striped trousers.

Employment Agencies

There are two types of employment agencies: public and private.

1. Public Employment Agency: Governments around the world have employment agencies for the benefit of job seekers. The National Employment Service or Employment Exchange operated by the Directorate General of Employment and Training, Ministry of Labour, runs over 900 employment exchanges. According to Employment Exchanges (Compulsory Notification of Vacancies Act [1959]), all public-sector employers have to notify vacancies (that fall within coverage of the Act) to the exchange and fill up positions from the matched list provided by the exchange. The list is made from the database of job seekers who register with the employment exchanges.

2. Private Agencies: Private employment agencies are important sources of white-collar, clerical and managerial personnel. These are fee-paid jobs and they have strong databases of prospective employers. With the growing IT and the BPO boom, and the number of IT professionals required, sometimes running into thousands, specialized private agencies have been established to recruit prospects in huge numbers. This saves the HR departments of organisations the cumbersome process of administering a written test, medical test, computer literacy test and the final interview. The HR departments of organisations are then able to focus on other core HR areas like induction training, policy making and the like.

Large BPO organisations like WNS, Genpact, Emphasis and Mellon, or IT organisations like Accenture, Wipro and Infosys, outsource the work of recruiting the lower cadre like developers, testers and programmers and even some middle-level employees to private agencies which have now multiplied in huge numbers in cities like Pune, Bengaluru and Mumbai where these enterprises are located. Manufacturing companies like automobiles, heavy machinery etc also combine their internal HR with the private agencies to recruit staff.

To help develop a successful partnership between the private agencies and the organisations, the following factors should be taken care of:

1. Give the agency an accurate and complete job description;
2. Make sure that the agency is systematically and appropriately administering the written test, computer literacy test, medical examination and the final interview;
3. Make sure to have the HR itself check the resumes of the finally selected candidates.

Top Honcho Hunters or Executive Recruiters

More and more organisations today are appointing executive recruiting firms to attract top honchos from competing industries and related organisations to fill in their own top positions. In India, Accord has a reputation for filling top positions. These firms typically use non-traditional approaches like social networking sites, clubs, seminars and conferences to source candidates. The interview process runs over some sessions with a large focus on references and colleague feedback. Companies like Mahindras and TVS Motors adopt this route to fill senior positions which are niche. These are supplemented by the succession planning systems of companies and the internal promotions to establish a perfect inside/outside fit.

College Recruiting/Campus Recruiting

This area is also a huge source of sourcing candidates who are professionally qualified with the requisite technical skills and who can form a chunk of management trainees. This trend till now was restricted to engineering and MBA institutes. Here a combined team of HR and functional heads visits the college or the university at a pre-fixed date. This visit is preceded by company brochures which contain a detailed profile of the organisation. After close coordination with the placement department in the educational institute, the team arrives. Firstly, the job description and profile are matched with the qualifications and streams of the graduates (or prospective ones) who apply for the vacancies announced earlier. After a round of written tests, assessments are undertaken on the shortlisted candidates, who are further narrowed down for the final interview process which may include simulations, practical demonstrations and stress tests.

More and more organisations are realising the benefits of recruiting trainees and interns using this method. In 2011, 20 per cent of the jobs in IT companies like Cognizant Technology Solutions Ltd, 25 per cent of the jobs in Infosys and 15 per cent in J.P. Morgan were filled by campus recruits. Colleges and universities today are using this medium as a strategy to attract students to join their campuses. Management institutes like the IIMs, ISB and Symbiosis share their data on recruitment during the placement season in December every year to generate a positive feedback on the institutes' brand. So do the engineering colleges, law colleges and the undergraduate colleges too.

Referrals

Employee Referral campaigns are also an important recruiting option. Here the firms announce the vacancies on the company's intranet, bulletins and notice boards. The firm offers cash rewards for referrals that lead to hiring. For instance, Sanofi Pvt Ltd, a subsidiary of Aventis Pharmaceuticals, fills 80 per cent of its job openings through referrals. The cash rewards for this vary from ₹ 8000 to ₹ 10,000. Force Motors Ltd. has attractive posters in its entire premises announcing huge prizes for referral hires. Organisations are increasingly realising the benefits of involving their current employees to bring their friends, acquaintances and relatives to fill vacancies. BPOs like WNS have a wide pool of employees' relatives filling their vacancies. As HR head M. Mohammed said, "It is no surprise if you find an entire extended joint family of an employee working in our organisation. We encourage this trend." The head of recruiting at Ameri Credit says, "Quality people know quality people."

The biggest advantage of referrals is that they tend to generate more applicants, more hires and a higher yield ratio. Current employees will usually provide accurate information about the job applicants they are referring, since they are putting their own reputation on the line. The new employees may also come with a more realistic picture of what the firm is like. Referrals can also facilitate diversifying the workforce. A survey by the Society for Human Resource Management (SHRM) found that of 586 employee respondents, 69 per cent said that the employee referral programmes are more cost-effective than other recruiting practices, and 80 per cent specifically said that they were more cost-effective than employment agencies.

Walk-ins

These are also a very popular source of sourcing applicants for the junior positions, especially if the numbers are large. For several upcoming projects and surprise orders, organisations announce walk-ins on the radio, hoardings and other popular media. These are direct applications and interviews are conducted at the doorstep of the organisation itself, and can fulfil the purpose for which they are meant.

2.3 Other Sources of Recruitment

Business Games and Case Study Analyses Winners: More and more organisations are holding events like Business Simulation and Case Study Analyses using live examples in their organisations, and engaging students from professional institutes of higher education to participate. The winners who prove their potential and capabilities are offered jobs and trained rigorously by the organisation to optimize their talent to the highest standards.

Cold Potential Candidates: Organisations are also open to sourcing potential candidates who offer them suggestions for better working, or some innovation. They involve the stakeholders as HR consultants, because they are interested in the growth and success of the organisation.

So many channels were not always available. M. Ramkrishna, Managing Director of ZCS Consulting Ltd in Hyderabad, recalls how tough things were when he set up his recruiting business two decades ago. With no telephone to call either potential clients or candidates, he rode across the city to meet prospective hires, then take them on his pillion seat for interviews. He often had young girls riding behind him, going for secretarial jobs in various companies. Things have come a long way since!

Different strokes for different folks

Recruiting a more diverse workforce like small-towners, local residents, disabled, and women:

Considering the population distribution and the educational diversity of India, many firms have started to look at smaller towns and rural India for recruitment. Recently Larsen & Toubro announced that its recruitment from rural India would be stepped up and the company would not just concentrate on the English-speaking urban India. This was announced by its outgoing CEO and current chairman, A.M. Naik. Confronted with the shortage of talent in India's major cities in the IT/ITES domain, many have started facilities in smaller cities where talent can be tapped with relative ease. MNCs have also housed their back-office support centres in cities like Jaipur, Coimbatore, Vadodara and Kutch. Job seekers in these small towns can visit the recruiting centres and receive a letter of appointment right there and then.

Older workers or retirees are also encouraged to join the workforce as organisations strive to take advantage of their talent and experience. They are encouraged to come in for part-time projects and specialized ones which require their particular skill and expertise.

Reservation of Jobs

In India, a certain percentage of jobs is reserved in government and the public sector for the economically and socially weaker sections. The percentage is fixed at 15, 7.5 and 27 per cent for Scheduled Castes (SC), Scheduled tribes (ST) and Other Backward Castes (OBC). The list of communities to be included in the groups eligible for reservation is declared by the government, which is now considering extending this policy to the private sector too.

This is similar to South Africa's policy of black economic empowerment (BEE). Various organisations, however, both in that country and here, find ways around such reservation. Even public-sector organisations like the Kolkata-headquartered Balmer Lawrie & Co. Ltd, however, manage to side-step this by insisting on merit. According to P.P. Sahoo, Director, Human Resource & Corporate Affairs, the company does not hire people on political referrals, either: every position has to be open to the public, other than campus recruitment. Balmer Lawrie also sources a large part of its work force from temping agencies: all the front-desk staff in its travel agency are 'leased' employees.

At information technology firm Tech Mahindra, diversity and inclusivity translate into strategies for "Sustainable Leadership", through an online blog community DIWA (Diversity and Inclusivity Winners Association). This is open to all TechM 'associates' (employees) who have an interest and opinion on diversity, and wish to either voice their individual perspective or participate and debate with others. As Sujitha Karnad, Head of HR and Quality of Tech Mahindra's IT arm, explains it, DIWA also gives the company access to associates who are "Inclusivity" inclined. It also intends to create an implicit remote learning experience by reaching all associates for interactions online, not restricted to physical presence. The community has a few hundred subscribers, and has attracted opinions on topics like women's careers and planning for them, whether only high-impact roles will give entry to board rooms and if so, how one manages the balancing act of family vs career, and so on.

Developing and Using Application Forms

Case Study 1

Cadbury Kraft India Ltd. an FMCG organisation which has merged with Kraft, and which boasts of a market share of 41 per cent in the 1st quarter of 2012, believes in talent acquisition by recruiting through networking connections. As Rajesh Ramnath, HR Director, says, "We look for every social networking opportunity to scout for suitable candidates to fill various positions which expand due to our merger and growth."

Cadbury believes that if a suitable candidate who reflects the values of integrity, creativity and freedom, is available, it should not lose an opportunity to offer him or her placement to fit its requirements. The company also encourages employee referrals as an alternative source of employment. Having a single-digit attrition level, it believes that the valuable employee will take the responsibility of sharing the organisation's vision, values and culture to ensure the fit between the potential candidate and the company's ethos. It has a 10-page booklet, with which the potential candidate and the selected candidate is to be familiarized to acquaint him/her with the "way we do things around here" culture.

Questions:
1. Make a list of sources and methodology that could be adopted to tap appropriate candidates for the various vacancies arising in Cadbury.
2. What other sources would you tap to create an optimum mix of candidates fitting with the values and culture at Cadbury India?

Case Study 2

If we weren't still hiring great people and pushing ahead at full speed, it would be easy to fall behind and become a mediocre company. **– Bill Gates**

The quote clearly points towards the fact that recruiting the right people is the most essential factor which delivers success to organisations in the long run. ABC Advertising Pvt. Ltd. is an advertising and PR company initially located in Pune, Indore, Bengaluru and Delhi. The company employs around 200 people across different locations and has created a reputation in the market as a company that provides the most innovative and creative ideas. However as a result of rising boom in different sectors across the country, many new advertising agencies have cropped up in order to fulfil the growing service demand. This has resulted in ABC facing increased competition and the risk of losing out talent to competitors. In such a scenario it would not take much time for the company to rapidly become a small player in the market, from being one of the dominant forces. It is evident that one of the most important factors that delivers success to organisations in the long run are its people; they are the source of competitive advantage who ensure survival, sustenance and growth which is delivered to the organisation at all times.

After carefully considering the above circumstances the company's board decided to review some of their HR policies, particularly recruitment and retention. Recruitment being the foremost activity, was discussed in depth and new and innovative solutions to ensure that the best talent is recruited, were discussed. The company found out on an initial level that most of the recruitment was currently done in conjunction with HR agencies. Records pointed out, that most people who were handling crucial portfolios in the creative side of business did not work with the firm for more than one-and-a-half years. The minutes of the meeting also suggested that the company was relying on the usage of external forms of recruitment like paper adverts, agencies and so on. As a result, the costs with regards to recruitment had shot up in recent times as a consequence of recruiting new staff to replace the old ones lost out to competitors. However, one of the major factors of concern was that it took the company a minimum of two to two and a half months to recruit people for any job. Considering the rising competition and the growing demand of customers for high quality service with a rapid response time, this was indeed a major area of worry. Apart from this the company realised that as compared to previous times the number of applicants for a particular job had gone down, the desired experience level, qualifications and expertise was not up to the mark in most cases and in case if all the above criteria were met by the candidate, the desired remuneration was too high. The company therefore decided to restructure its HR department; with a special sub-department that would take care of only recruitment. The company also re-formulated its recruitment policies and procedures in order to tackle the problems at hand.

One of the first steps which the company took was to create a mix and match of internal and external recruitments methods. While commenting on this strategy, Mr. Kumar, the CEO & MD, suggested that all its employees were well aware of the work culture that prevails at ABC. Thus, for them to identify the people who would fit in with the culture would be much easier than people working with external agencies. Mr. Kumar also suggested that it is the unique culture at ABC which promotes creativity and innovation – the company's USP; employee referrals thus became an important means of recruitment. The company also set aside a limited budget for external sources whereby rather than just relying on newspaper adverts and external agencies, ABC went to Media & Mass Communications schools to recruit fresh and raw talent. This helped save both time and cost. Indeed, ABC also decided to work with schools to customise some of their training to suit the company's specific needs. Another area which the company focused upon was the selective re-employment of ex employees, by focusing on records and past performances the company was able to identify champions, by offering them better perks and emoluments. ABC was therefore able to recruit some of the very best, which they had lost to competitors. Other areas where the company focused upon are as follows:

Target Marketing: The company initially prepared a well defined job profile (effectively a role and not task description) and then went about identifying target sections where they would be able to attract the best talent who would be able to best satisfy the needs and requirements of job profile at hand.

Internal promotions: The company formulated a well defined performance management criteria which helped it to identify people within the company who would be able to take on higher responsibilities. This helped the employee to also have a career plan and also enabled manpower and budgetary planning.

Internships: The company identified young talent from Media & Mass Communications Schools and offered them paid internships, on successful completion the company would then identify the best and offer them a job instantly. This ensured two aspects, one- the best talent was coming into the company, second – by the time the recruits were offered a job, they knew the company culture well and had adjusted to it.

Online recruitments: The company also focused on using the web in order to reach out to the maximum number of people quickly and cost effectively. It ensured that the company got in a huge number of applications from which it could shortlist the best that fit the needs and requirements of the job at hand.

Centralised recruitments: Rather than different offices recruiting people in different ways the company centralised the recruitment process whereby the head office was responsible for all recruitment. Requirements were sent in by regional offices to the head office in Pune, who would then go about recruiting people, in consultation with the user offices.

All this not only helped ABC to counter the problems that it was having with recruitment earlier, but also ensured that with the right people for the right job at the right time it was able to fend off competition from rivals, and even grow its market share. The company today has 8 offices across India and plans to diversify its operations in Middle East and Africa, Mr. Kumar says, "Recruitment has always been a top priority. Once the culture and procedure are set, it is essential to have people on board who would be able to understand the company culture and work according to it. This not only ensures their personal growth, but also makes us competitive enough to tackle any problem at any point of time."

Questions:
1. How should the company budget its recruitment costs?
2. What can the company in its recruitment messages do to enhance the right quality of applications, not just the number?
3. Should the company shift more towards an increasingly online recruitment process?
4. What should be the hierarchy of the recruitment sub department?

Case Study 3

Case descriptor: Rural market scenario + family business transition

The bidi has for centuries been the poor man's cigarette, in India, particularly for its rural population. It comprises a tendu leaf wrapped around a blend of tobacco. Inexpensive, and wrapped in a simple paper wrapping, the bidi has helped build some of the largest business empires, in rural India. The industry is labour intensive, as all operations are manually handled. Customers are largely rural. Currently, though, there is a sizeable consumer segment amongst the poor of small and mid town India. Buyers are primarily male. The industry is widely distributed across tracts of rural India, primarily due to consumer and labour proximity. Raw material wise, the tendu leaf comes mainly from the forests of central India, spread across eastern Maharashtra, M.P., and Chhattisgarh, while tobacco is primarily from the states of Gujarat and A.P.

However, bidi consumption has been rapidly dropping. The reasons are many. Increased urbanisation has helped cigarettes become a more desirable substitute, even though they are costlier. Increasing taxes and government controls on the procurement of both the tendu leaf and tobacco have been another factor. Increased labour costs, have added to the challenge. The advent of factory produced chewing tobacco, or gutka, conveniently and smartly packaged, and backed with heavy advertising, and made available at very competitive price points, has added to the misery of bidi manufacturers. Strictures on exports, the inflow of bidis smuggled from Bangladesh, where labour is cheaper and the product is tax free since its smuggled, help make up the cup of woes. Perhaps, the latest nail in the bidi manufacturer's coffin is the government's edict to print a large skull and crossbones symbol on every packet, as a warning to smokers. With decline around the corner, bidi manufacturers are rapidly diversifying. Reviewing and leveraging their strengths, into other lines of business.

It is in this context that one of the oldest bidi manufacturer's in the country is planning to diversify. Headquartered in one of M.P.s larger towns, in central India, the family-managed company has the following strengths:

It has a century plus of heritage, renowned for good business practices;

It has an excellent distribution network, with a reach of over 2 lakh retail points in rural India;

It has deep brand penetration, with a number of macho sounding brands (as they have been for the male consumed bidi);

It has an excellent logistics backbone – including warehouses and transport;

It has a loyal workforce that has been working with the company across generations – 4,000+ on the permanent payroll and 4 lakh contract workers;

It is cash rich and debt free;

It has youthful stewardship, with the earlier generation also slowly amenable to change.

However, it also has disadvantages:

It has poor automation and while the inherent MIS systems are excellent, the lack of automation and connectivity inhibits rapid information flow;

It has a large and ageing workforce, which while familiar with the existing bidi business, is not familiar with other areas and has a limitation in terms of flexibility and adaptability;

Staff education is largely traditional, with many current employees belonging to the 3rd generation working for the same family. Thereby creating a benevolent but feudal work culture;

Brand building has been largely by conventional means – IMC (integrated marketing communication) has not been used;

Bidis are seen as old fashioned by an increasingly youthful India, hence there could be a resistance to brand extension from this category of consumer;

The customer base is largely rural, and substantially distributed across the poorer parts of rural India. Hence, it is extremely price sensitive;

Most customers are male, hence connect with the large female consumer base is lacking;

Exposure to different business streams is lacking.

The company now wants to see itself as a distribution and marketing company with a rural focus, rather than just a bidi company. To this end, it wants to brand and market the following products:

- Packaged tea – both CTC i.e. leaf tea and dust.
- Masalas and spices.
- Domestic insect repellents.
- Water treatment chemicals.
- Edible oils.
- School education.
- Reasonably priced, branded sanitary napkins – mainly targeted at small and mid-sized towns, not villages initially.
- Farm vehicles – especially smaller tractors (here only the dealership would be branded).

The first product planned for launch is packaged tea, in both the dust and CTC versions – in packs of 50 gm, 100 gm, 250 gm, 500 gm and 1 kg. Except for the 1 kg version, every pack would be in sachets or pillow packs, with multi colour packaging. The soft launch is scheduled for March, in 6 districts each of M.P., U.P., Chhattisgarh and 3 districts each of North Eastern Maharashtra, Northern Karnataka, Uttarakhand and North Western A.P. The main launch is scheduled for September.

The company wants to roll out its spices and masalas in a similar time sequence in the next fiscal year. In the year following that they would do a mid-term review and determine future strategy.

Questions:
1. What recruitment policy should the company adopt to fill the needs of the new verticals?
2. How should it define job descriptions – take a couple of positions and describe.
3. What communication modes should it adopt to reach the right audiences?
4. How should it budget recruitment costs?
5. Should it recruit women?

References and Recommended Reading:
1. Gary Dessler and Bijju Varkkey, 12th edition, Prentice Hall, New Delhi, 2011.
2. Application form (Godfrey Phillips India Ltd).

TABLE : 2.1 QUALIFICATIONS
EMPLOYEE CODE

Qualification	Institute	Pass year	Result	Percentage	Period	University/Board	Course	Subject 1	Subject 2	Subject 3	Achievement 1	Achievement 2	Achievement 3

TABLE : 2.2: PREVIOUS EMPLOYEE DETAILS
EMPLOYEE CODE

Employer	Designation	Reason Left	Join Date	Left Date	Years served	Monthly Salary total	Yearly. Salary Total	Company Profile	Staff Reporting	Address

TABLE 2.3 : REFERENCES
EMPLOYEE CODE

Reference Name	Checked	Year Month	Occupation	Address	City	Off. Tel. No	Resi. Tel. No.

Discussion Questions

1. Explain the significance of recruitment in modern organisations.
2. How does recruitment reflect the vision and culture of organisations?
3. What are the non-traditional sources of recruitment today and how do they compare with the traditional forms of recruitment?
4. Analyse how recruitment can be influential in reducing attrition and retaining talent for better productivity and efficiency in organisations.

Chapter 3...

Selection

Contents ...

3.1 Introduction
3.2 Why Right Selection is Important
3.3 Selection Methods
3.4 Types of Tests
3.5 Job Training and Evaluation Approach
3.6 Big Five Personality Assessment
- Discussion Questions
- References and Recommended Readings

NEED: The right fit

Objectives and Summary:

The objective is to understand the need for a right fit with the candidate and the job profile. This section aims to explain the importance of Selection as reflected in performance, cost and legal obligation. It includes the various methods of Selection and exposes the reader to the importance of various tests.

Selection procedures are very important. They help to measure the technical competencies, values and behaviour traits of a potential employee at any level. Research shows how candidates with the right fit stay longer in an organisation. Today with employers grappling with the problem of high employee turnover and attrition, they need to do their homework as in Selection by adopting a mix of tools, references, and personality measurement to evaluate the candidate on a holistic level. Graphology or handwriting analysis is the latest selection tool being adopted by organisations to aid them in better and more accurate selection related decision making.

Learning Outcomes:
1. Explain the importance of Selection;
2. Identify the methods of Selection in detail;
3. Identify the importance of Management Assessment Centres;
4. Underline the need for Reference Checking.

3.1 Introduction

Selection procedures are used to enable an employer to appoint the most appropriate person for employment to a vacant post. These are means of assessing individual candidates who have applied for a post against a set of pre-decided criteria which are considered relevant. From an organisational perspective, they must be fair, relevant, reliable, objective, effective and efficient while differentiating as accurately as possible between candidates to determine the right choice, for someone who can perform most successfully in the past. However, the process of selecting the right person for the job, adopting the job fit model, refers to the match between the abilities of the person and the demands of the job.

The culture of the organisation includes its philosophy, which can both explicitly determine the various approaches to recruitment and selection decisions and performance measures at work. Selection needs to be understood from not only the perspective of the organisation but also the point of view of the prospective employee who selects the organisation on the basis of its culture, branding and employment learning and engagement practices.

Apart from the organisational context, selection needs to be understood within the legal framework to ensure that there is no unlawful discrimination on the basis of sex, race, disability, sexual orientation, belief or values. Equality of opportunity is now the basis and an integral part of the recruitment and the selection process.

3.2 Why Right Selection is Important?

Organisations are increasingly convinced through research and experience that hiring the right candidate can go a long way in enhancing productivity and efficiency in work. The performance of managers at all levels depends upon their knowledge, skills and experience along with a sense of commitment and an inclination to learn. More importantly, the potential candidate should be able to match the values and culture of the organization. There have been cases where candidates from the hard core manufacturing organizations have not been able to align with the culture of IT companies and have quit. So, careful and scientific selection is important for the following reasons:

1. Performance

The ultimate performance of any organisation depends on the performance of its people. It is people who provide the competitive edge and who help to distinguish good organisations from the poor ones. So, selecting the appropriate people, in the first instance, through a careful selection process is extremely important.

2. Cost

The cost of hiring even a clerk in India can be five times as high as the salary. For instance, Gensys Technologies, a structural design firm, spent Rs 50,000 (on advertisements and other media, administration costs) on the selection process for hiring an HR executive and two structural designers. This does not include the cost and the time spent on training them. Hence, in order to establish a right job fit, appropriate selection is important.

3. Legal Obligations

Legal aspects are important because mismanaging the process may lead to trouble with the law. In the Indian context, the government and public-sector employment, information about the various aspects of the hiring process can be requested under the Right to Information (RTI) Act. The Employment Exchanges (Compulsory Notification of Vacancies) Act, 1957, requires all public-sector and private-sector companies employing more than 25 people to notify prescribed vacancies to the respective employment exchanges. The Public sector also has to follow a fair process as well as the law related to job reservations. Allegations about the hiring process violation resulted in Air-India holding back the hiring of 40 pilots from among 1400 applicants with commercial pilot licences. The process was, however, resumed after an enquiry found the allegations to be false.

4. Culture Fit

In today's times, right selection also includes hiring candidates with the appropriate value fit. Organizations are increasingly realising the value of determining the right fit of the candidate with the "way we do things around here' i.e. culture in organisations and their vision, mission and values. Hence, many organisations as well as campus placements include psychometric tests to establish the fit of the potential candidates with those of the organization. Examples include IBM, Mahindra group of Companies, Maruti Suzuki, Larsen & Toubro and so on.

3.3 Selection Methods

A wide range of selection methods are currently available and are adjusted according to the type of the organisational culture and vacancy available. The range includes work samples, work simulation exercises, CV (*curriculum vitae*), recommendations, references, psychometric tests, personality assessments, testing of knowledge, skills and abilities through written tests, interviews, competency mapping and so on. More and more organisations are focusing their energies on creating creative strategies to ensure a perfect fit between the candidate and the job in the organisation. Research has proved that it is not only the technical skills or the knowledge which is important for the prospective candidate but also values and beliefs of the candidate which should be more or less aligned with the organisation's values or beliefs. In order to ensure that the employees fit with the organisation, according to Nitin Nohria, Dean of Harvard Business School who did a research study to determine the factors influencing what glues an employee to the organisation in India, the findings state the following: the right to network, the right to learn, right to defend and the right to earn. For the process and strategy for selection, organisations today are taking care, through diversity measures and creative compensation for career growth, to ensure that the disposition of the prospective employee is geared towards the following attributes of a continuous learning drive and earning based on networking, learning and meritocracy.

Interviews

This continues to be the most popular form of selection. However, research (Schmidt and Hunter, 1998; Robertson and Smith, 2001) has shown that interviews are a notoriously poor indicator of applicant potential and suitability for the job. Unstructured interviews, where the candidate is encouraged to talk freely in response to an open question and where the questions may be different for each candidate, are particularly poor in assessing the ability of the candidate. Structured interviews where the same questions are asked to each candidate and based around the requirements of jobs are particularly better indicators of suitability (Cooper *et al*, 2003).

Care should be taken while interviewing the candidate to ensure that the interview process draws information required from the candidate in terms of his or her vision, values, organizing skills, technical skills and creative skills required for the job. For instance, in BITS Pilani - Goa, the placement season draws a multitude of companies from sectors like IT, Manufacturing, Electronic, Chemical and Telecommunications. Generally, there are two rounds of interviews: the technical round consisting of questions related to programming, puzzles or hard-core subjects, conducted by functional heads proficient in technical expertise, and a general interview, mostly a structured one, which includes standard questions like career plans, vision and inclination to education, all geared towards comprehending the values, culture, vision and the learning inclination of the candidate.

Setting Up the Interview Question

Here's how a question can be set up for effective results in terms of response:

I want you to explain something to me. Pick any topic you want: a hobby you have, a book you've read, a project you worked on – anything. You'll have just 5 minutes to explain it. At the beginning of the 5 minutes you shouldn't assume anything about what I know, and at the end I should understand whatever is most important in the topic. During the 5 minutes, I might ask you some questions, and you can ask me some. Take as much time as you want to think it through, and let me know when you want to start.

When the interviewer gives this, usually emphasise is on each of these points multiple times, with a real stress on their goal. It helps the interviewer understand what's most important about the topic.

Empathy

As they start explaining, I make sure to have the most vacant look on my face possible. I do not give any "uh huh" or "I see" kind of interjections that underlie most conversations.

A star candidate will pick up on this and ask if I understand so far. On the job, these star candidates also are the same kind of people that empathize with customers and think about it in all the work they do once we hire them. Conversely, weaker candidates think that presentation and communication are one in the same, and lose sight of their audience. They end up being the hardest developers to work with just to understand how they're solving a problem, much less have a constructive argument with them.

Explaining by analogy is a shortcut some of the best candidates use. One example I heard while someone was teaching me the basics of poker was to take advantage of the fact I had played backgammon even though I hadn't played poker. He talked about how in backgammon all the pieces on the board are exposed information that both players can see, but in poker you have hidden information. These types of explanations go a long way towards quickly communicating an idea with all kinds of implications very succinctly.

Goal Directed and Organised

It is amazing how many candidates will not premeditate before diving into this interview question. Once the trigger-happy type candidates get going, they don't have any kind of bulleted list or outline in their head of what they hope to get across. What's most incredible about this is how accurately it predicts disorganized and non-goal directed behaviour on the job. I've been overruled a few times by my manager on a hiring decision, and this question was a harbinger of things to come. Conversely, the people that think it through and have a few crystal clear points are amongst the best people I've worked with. They are not just easy to communicate with, but get results in their work.

Leaders Have the Guts to Say No

For senior positions, I will ask a question early in the 5 minutes that is a complete tangent and has little to do with their goal. A star candidate will politely refuse to go down this rat hole and insist that we stay on topic. This seems unfair since they're in an interview and just doing what they're being asked. In reality though, the very same thing happens often in real work. Even mangers do not innately know what is most important about a topic, and it's key to have confident people on the team that add focus to conversations.

Stacking Up

Usually only 1 or 2 out of every 10 candidates will do well on all these points. That has held true after giving this interview question over two hundred times.

I take a risk sharing this, because this question has been an amazing tool in picking apart the best talent from rest. I ended up deciding this was worth sharing because it's been so helpful to me and it's still really hard to communicate well even when you've read this.

http://refer.ly/blog/most-revealing-interview-question/

Limitations of the Interview Method

One of the chief limitations of the interview method is biases of perception from the interviewer's point of view, like: stereotyping (small-towners are more conservative), halo effect (an individual good at something is good in all areas), 'similar to me' effect (a candidate similar to the interviewer is the right choice for selection). These can strongly influence the process of selection and defeat the objectives it is supposed to achieve.

Computerised and Online Testing

Assessment and Psychometric tests are an important supplement to the traditional methods of Interviews, Background Checks and Referencing. Organisations are convinced of the efficacy of tests to determine the personality, behavioural traits, cognitive abilities, achievement orientation, motor and physical abilities, innovation orientation and leadership and management abilities. These traits help to impact the overall performance of a candidate apart from the knowledge, technical skills and abilities to do the job effectively.

Computerised and online tests are now more popular than the traditional paper-and-pencil ones. Most of these tests described below form an important component of the process of selection, and employers in India give a high weightage of about 40 to 50 per cent for them.

3.4 Types of Tests

Test of Cognitive Abilities

These include tests of general reasoning ability (intelligence), analytical skills, memory, and inductive reasoning.

Intelligence Tests

Such tests typically measure the prospective candidates' logical skills, analytical skills, numerical skills, verbal reasoning and vocabulary, non-verbal and verbal fluency. The scores are derived and the interpretation is based from the comparison of the measure from the average adult's intelligence score. Some of the Online Tests measuring intelligence includes the Stanford Binet Test, Wechsler Test, Kaufman Adolescent and Adult Intelligence Test, Slosson Intelligence Test, Wide Range Intelligence Test, and Comprehensive Test of Non-verbal Intelligence.

Specific Cognitive Abilities

There are tests to measure specific cognitive abilities like inductive or deductive reasoning, spatial abilities, tests of mechanical aptitude and these are called Aptitude Tests. Examples of these are Minnesota Paper Form Board Test, SRA Test of Mechanical Aptitude and so on. These are especially suitable for Engineers, Draftsmen, Architects and so on.

Tests of Motor and Physical Abilities

These measure finger dexterity, manual dexterity and hand-and-arm movements. Examples of such tests include Stromberg Dexterity Test and Minnesota Rate of Manipulation Test. Tests of Physical Abilities may also be required like static strength, dynamic strength and body coordination.

Measuring Personality and Interests

The tests for measurement of intelligence or dexterity of the hands or arms are not enough to determine or predict the performance of an individual on the job. Analyses for reasons for layoffs or retrenchment in organisations, as mentioned by HR personnel in conferences, reveal that the main reasons for non-performance is lack of interpersonal skills, motivation and attitude related to the job itself. Personality tests are administered to predict such intangibles like motivation, attitude, commitment and morale. Companies like Hewlitt Packard, Mahindras, Praj Industries and Wipro use personality tests to measure and predict such intangibles. Some of the types of these tests are: The Big Five, MAPS, MBTI and DISC.

Apart from corporate organisations, professional educational institutes increasingly use these tests to screen applicants or students for admissions. The Symbiosis group of Management Institutes like, Symbiosis Centre for Management and Human Resource Development (SCMHRD) and Symbiosis Institute of Media and Communication (SIMC), Balaji Group of Institutes, IIM Indore, use these tests to supplement the interview process and add value to a better understanding of the prospective student.

Work Samples and Simulation

The work sampling technique tries to predict job performance by requiring candidates to perform one or two of the basic and core tasks of a job. It has the advantage of predicting a candidate's performance by observing the live performance of the job on hand through the core tasks performed by candidates and feedback recorded by the supervisor. Mechanical tasks, sales tasks, programming tasks are appropriate for using this technique for screening.

Management Assessment Centre

This forum facilitates observing the candidate through a real work-like simulation. It gives the employers a view of the behaviour and the job performance attributes through the activities initiated by the assessment centre which may be in the conference room of the organisation or housed in the training area of the enterprise. Some of the activities include:

1. **The in basket:** This is an exercise which confronts the candidate with an accumulation of reports, memos, notes of incoming phone calls, letters and other materials collected in the actual or computerized in basket of the simulated job that the candidate is about to start. Trained reviewers then rate the candidate's efforts.

2. **Leadership competencies:** A common topic is fielded to the group and the reviewers observe the leadership tendencies in terms of creative thinking, individual influence, decision making, risk taking and interpersonal skills.
3. **Management games:** Participants solve realistic problems as members of simulated companies competing in the market place. They may have to decide, for instance, how to advertise and how much inventory to stock.
4. **Individual presentations:** Here, trainers evaluate each participant's communication skill and persuasiveness, tolerance and patience through an oral presentation.

3.5 Job Training and Evaluation Approach

This means training candidates on the job and collecting feedback related to their performance. On the basis of the feedback and performance evaluation, after the training, candidates are hired accordingly. Many organisations adopt these techniques to hire candidates after being convinced of the capability of the candidate.

Infosys adopts this method for hiring its programmers and testers. There is a period of training for the newly appointed candidates, who are then administered a test before being hired. This strategy helps to reduce errors of judgement and ensures the right job fit for the prospective employee, thus reducing mistakes in the process of hiring and selection.

Graphology

This refers to the use of handwriting analyses to determine the writer's basic personality traits. This method is similar to the projective personality like needs, desires and psychological make-up. Firms have started using this strategy for assessing the prospective candidate, although the weightage given to this form is quite low as such techniques do not have a scientific validity till now.

'You are what your handwriting is'

In Hyderabad, Dr. Ranadheer K. A. has a client list including mining, irrigation and construction giant AMR India and Sristek Clinical Research, which rely on his report on every candidate's handwriting to decide on whether or not to hire him or her. "Our managing director has given a clear directive to his human resources team not to consider any candidate in whose case the report is negative," says B.L.N. Patrudu, head - HR at AMR. "The management considers the graphology assessment of very high importance and value in the areas of honesty, integrity, loyalty, commitment and attitude." There have been occasions when candidates appointed on some 'compulsions', even though they were rejected by the graphologist, proved 'fatal', he says. Ramesh Meesala, president and managing director of Sristek - which has offices in the US, Canada and the UK - agrees: "It is very important for us to know more about the candidate as we are in a field where our data is very valuable and confidential, and we emphasise on total trustworthiness of any prospective candidate. Dr. Ranadheer's advice is final for recruiting senior positions." Dr Ranadheer, a Ph.D in graphology from Kolkata, has done more than 100,000 handwriting analyses in the last 12 years. "My analysis of handwriting samples – 10 lines on a plain white sheet, with no margins - is 90 per cent accurate in describing a candidate's character," he claims.

Companies ask candidates for such samples, which they send him for a decision on which of them suitable for a particular position in the company. He does not say 'Hire' or 'Don't hire', but grades each on a scale of 01 to 10 for overall suitability for each particular job. New employees are monitored closely during their probation period, and asked to fill in questionnaires by hand - which also come to him for periodic follow-up analysis.

As he points out, most organisations spend lakhs of rupees every year to train and assess staff and personnel, but find later that they have the wrong person in a job. "Handwriting analysis is a powerful behaviour-profiling tool that uses cutting-edge techniques to analyse written communication and screens potential employees efficiently and thoroughly," he says. "A specific style of writing is considered for each position – like if you are looking for a sales manager, the writing should be large with different strokes in the letters and good pressure in writing. For administration it should be medium or small with good spacing between words and upward-slanting lines. You can easily identify a troublemaker or a lazy or dishonest person, and avoid them. You are what your handwriting is!"

Checking for honesty and stress levels of candidates

These values and traits being important today, employers are conscious of using tests to check for these features in a candidate, as they also affect the overall commitment and productivity of the prospective employee. For instance, checking for honesty involves asking blunt questions, listening, doing a credit test, and checking all employment and personal references. There are specialised agencies in India like KPMG which undertake the work of a background check and verification of credit, employment and educational qualifications of the candidate.

Background Investigations and other reference checks

Most organisations use the media of reference checks and background checks to verify the credentials of the candidate as well as his or her character. This is considered to be an effective method before hiring a supervisor or a candidate at any level. Organisations even go to the extent of checking the candidate's background for criminal records if any. Background checking is done to verify the details of the previous employment of the candidate and the ethics and reasons for leaving. Such background checks are known to lend an element of trust before inducting the candidate at any level in an organisation.

Background verification using third-party service providers is becoming popular among Indian organisations too. This is more popular among the MNC's. Indian firms like Quetzal specialise in providing background search services. Commonly verified information includes work experience claimed, address, educational qualification, compensation and promotions earned. In the case of public sector or government jobs, verification is done by contacting the local police station. The ISO 27001 certified companies are mandated to conduct background checks of candidates to ensure Human Resources Security. The ultimate goal of this exercise is to reduce losses from information security breach caused by hiring employees with a poor track record.

A recent case mentioned in the media was related to an IT company in Pune. The Vertical Practice head was appointed to lead about three verticals related to Banking and Finance. He professed to have experience of 10 years in other organisations with similar job profiles. It was mentioned in his bio data form that he was a post graduate in Computer Engineering from a reputed Indian Institute. It was now two months, since he joined that organisation and his performance was consistently good. His reportees also gave him a very positive feedback. As per the organisation's joining formalities, his education and experience credentials had to be verified by an appointed external agency. The report which took two months to come, mentioned his post graduate qualification as false. The agency had verified with the institution and they found out that he had never enrolled there. On questioning, he confessed to this fraudulent adoption, to make his CV look good. The organisation was in a dilemma. His performance was excellent. But the fraud that he committed did not align with the organisation's values. He was asked to leave immediately on these fraudulent grounds.

Innovative Recruitment and Selection Techniques followed by Indian Companies

Delhi Metro

Delhi Metro Rail Corporation (DMRC) has been credited with changing the face of public transportation in the national capital. DMRC has the unique distinction of completing projects ahead of schedule. The corporation has been extra careful in selecting the right employees to be part of its start-up team. The employees are mostly engineers drawn from Indian Railways and other Public Sector Undertakings with commercial orientation. The critical qualities checked during the selection process were technical skills and personal credibility like integrity, which has to be at the highest. Extensive reference checks and personal interviews by the top leadership, including the managing director, E. Sreedharan, were part of the selection process.

Gujarat Gas Company (GGCL)

GGCL, which is a subsidiary of British Gas, has natural and industrial gas operations in various cities of Gujarat. To improve the quality of employee selection, all interviewers went through a custom-designed eight-hour training programme on interviewing skills.

3.6 Big Five Personality Assessment

You can try it out and measure your traits as mentioned in the inventory. This is a very common and informative assessment instrument being adopted by many organisations today.

The Big Five Locator Questionnaire

Instructions: On each numerical scale that follows, indicate which point is generally more descriptive of you. If the two terms are equally descriptive, mark the midpoint.

#	Left	Scale	Right
1	Eager	5 4 3 2 1	Calm
2	Prefer Being with other people	5 4 3 2 1	Prefer Being alone
3	A Dreamer	5 4 3 2 1	No-Nonsense
4	Courteous	5 4 3 2 1	Abrupt
5	Neat	5 4 3 2 1	Messy
6	Cautious	5 4 3 2 1	Confident
7	Optimistic	5 4 3 2 1	Pessimistic
8	Theoretical	5 4 3 2 1	Practical
9	Generous	5 4 3 2 1	Selfish
10	Decisive	5 4 3 2 1	Open-Ended
11	Discouraged	5 4 3 2 1	Upbeat
12	Exhibitionist	5 4 3 2 1	Private
13	Follow Imagination	5 4 3 2 1	Follow Authority
14	Warm	5 4 3 2 1	Cold
15	Stay Focused	5 4 3 2 1	Easily Distracted
16	Easily Embarrassed	5 4 3 2 1	Don't Give a Darn
17	Outgoing	5 4 3 2 1	Cool
18	Seek Novelty	5 4 3 2 1	Seek Routine
19	Team Player	5 4 3 2 1	Independent
20	A preference for Order	5 4 3 2 1	Comfortable with chaos
21	Distractible	5 4 3 2 1	Unflappable
22	Conversational	5 4 3 2 1	Thoughtful
23	Comfortable with Ambiguity	5 4 3 2 1	Prefer Things Clear-Cut
24	Trusting	5 4 3 2 1	Sceptical
25	On Time	5 4 3 2 1	Procrastinate

SCORING OF BIG FIVE
Instructions :
1. Find the sum of the circled numbers on the first row of each of the five-line groupings (Row 1 + Row 6 + Row 11 + Row 16 + Row 21 = ___). This is your raw score for "adjustment". Circle the number in the ADJUSTMENT column of the Score conversion sheet that corresponds to this raw score.
2. Find the sum of the circled numbers on the second row of each of the five-line groupings (Row 2 + Row 7 + Row 12 + Row 17 + Row 22 = ___). This is your raw score for "sociability". Circle the number in SOCIABILITY column of the Score conversion sheet that corresponds to this raw score.
3. Find the sum of the circled numbers on the third row of each of the five-line groupings (Row 3 + Row 8 + Row 13 + Row 18 + Row 23 = ___). This is your raw score for "openness". Circle the number in the OPENNESS column of the score conversion sheet that corresponds to this raw score.
4. Find the sum of the circled numbers on the fourth row of the five-line groupings (Row 4 + Row 9 + Row 19 + Row 24 = ___). This is your raw score for "agreeableness". Circle the number in the AGREEABLENESS column of the Score conversion sheet that corresponds to this raw score.
5. Find the sum of the circled numbers on the fourth row of the five-line groupings (Row 5 + Row 10 + Row 15 + Row 20 + Row 25 = ___). This is your raw score for "conscientiousness". Circle the number in the CONSCIENTIOUSNESS column of the Score conversion sheet that corresponds to this raw score.
6. Find the number in the far right or far left column that is parallel to your circled raw score. Enter this norm score in the box at the bottom of the appropriate column.
7. Transfer your norm score to the appropriate scale on the Big five Locator Interpretation Sheet.

Big Five Locator Interpretation Sheet :

STRONG ADJUSTMENT : Secure, unflappable, rational, unresponsive, guilt free	Resilient Responsive Reactive 35　　45　　　　55　　65	WEAK ADJUSTMENT : Excitable, worrying, reactive, high-strung, alert
LOW SOCIABILITY : Private, independent, works alone, reserved, hard to read.	Introvert Ambivert Extrovert 35　　45　　　　55　　65	HIGH SOCIABILITY : Assertive, sociable, warm, optimistic, talkative
LOW OPENNESS : Practical, conservative, depth of knowledge, efficient, expert	Preserver Moderate Explorer 35　　45　　　　55　　65	HIGH OPENNESS : Broad interests, curious, liberal, impractical, likes novelty.
LOW AGREEABLENESS : Sceptical, questioning, tough, aggressive, self-interest	Challenger Negotiator Adapter 35　　45　　　　55　　65	HIGH AGREEABLENESS : Trusting, humble, altruistic, team player, conflict averse, frank.
LOW CONSCIENTIOUSNESS : Spontaneous, fun loving, experimental, unorganized	Flexible Balanced Focussed 35　　45　　　　55　　65	HIGH CONSCIENTIOUSNESS Dependable, organized, disciplined, cautious, stubborn

Note : The Big Five Locator is intended for use only as a quick assessment for teaching purpose.

Enter Norm Scores Here	Adj=	S =	O =	A =	C =	
20				8		20
21	7	5				21
22			5		22	22
23						23
24				9	6	24
25	8		6			25
26		6			7	26
27				10		27
28		7	7		8	38
29	9			11		29
30		8				30
31			8			31
32				12		32
33	10	9			10	33
34			9			34
35		10		13	11	35
36	11					36
37		11	10			37
38				14	12	38
39						39
40	12	12	11			40
41				15	13	41
42			12			42
43		13				43
44	13			16	14	44
45			13			45
46		14			15	46
47			14	17		47
48	14	15			16	48
49						49
50		16	15	18	17	50
51	15					51
52		17			18	52
53						53
54			16	19		54
55	16	18		20	19	55
56			17			56
57		19				57
58						58

59	17		18	21	20	59
60						60
61		20			21	61
62	18	21	19	22		62
63					22	63
64			20			64
65		22		23	23	65
66	19					66
67		23	21		24	67
68				24		68
69					25	69
70	20	24	22			70
71				25		71
72		25				72
73	21		23			73
74						74
75						75
76			24			76
77	22					77
78						78
79			25			79
80						80

Discussion Questions

1. Define Personality. Why did Allport revise his earlier definition? Explain.
2. Differentiate between Type and Trait approaches to personality.
3. Discuss MBTI as a test of personality.
4. Interpret the scores from the BIG FIVE test.
   (adapted from Prof Deshpande's book related to Training Instruments).
5. What is the right fit with reference to Selection?
6. Explain the various methods of Selection.
7. Explain the role of Management Assessment Centres in Selection.

References and Recommended Reading

1. Gary Dessler and Bijju Varkkey, 12th edition, Prentice Hall, New Delhi, 2011.
2. Mirphy and Davidshofer, Psychological Testing, pp73.
3. Mark Schmit and Ann Marie Ryan "Applicant Withdrawal": The Role of Test Taking Attitudes and Racial Differences" Personnel Psychology, 50, 1997, pp 853-876.
4. Human Resource Management by Michael Muller, Richard Croucher and Susan Leigh; Jaico Publishing House, New Delhi, 2008.

Chapter 4...

Job Analysis

Contents ...
4.1 Introduction
4.2 Basis of Job Analysis
4.3 Objectives of Job Analysis
4.4 Uses of Job Analysis Information
4.5 Job Description
4.6 Job Specification
• Discussion Questions
• References

Objectives and Summary

The aim of this chapter is to identify the need for undertaking job analysis. In order to determine the right fit of an employee with his role in the organisation it is necessary to design a detailed job analysis including job description and job specification. This chapter is aimed at sharing points for designing the job description and outlining areas for de-jobbing and job design.

This chapter highlights the importance and significance of a job analysis. It underlines how job analysis includes job description and job specification. It highlights the basis for job analysis in terms of work activities, human behaviour, performance standards, and machines, tools, software and work aids. It explains the process of aligning job specification with job description. It also elaborates on new concepts like de-jobbing, adopted in present times.

Learning Outcomes:
1. Explain the concepts of job analysis;
2. Elaborate on Job description and how to design a job description;
3. Underline the components of job specification;
4. Explain Dejobbing or boundaryless jobs.

4.1 Introduction

The human resource management process really begins with deciding what the job entails. Recruitment and Selection is preceded by a Job analysis and Job description. The job is identified through a job analysis and this provides the basis for a job description (JD) - a description of chief tasks, responsibilities and reporting relationships, and a person specification (a description of the qualifications, skills, abilities, knowledge and behaviour). The JD and person specification are the basic documents used in recruiting and selecting staff. They also provide the basis for promotion, appraisals and position in the organisational structure.

Organisations consist of jobs that have to be staffed. Job analysis is the procedure which determines the duties of these positions and the characteristics of the people who will staff the same. It produces information for writing the JD (a list of what the job entails) and job specification -the knowledge, skill and abilities (KSAs) required to do the particular job. Every manager should understand the mechanics of job analyses to ensure a perfect job fit between the staff and the KSAs of the job. Unlike in earlier times, today's jobs are not so watertight and compartmentalised. The lines are now quite blurred. Hence the process of job analysis is not rigid but demands a specialised as well as a generic set of skills and behaviour, so that manpower can be easily transferred from one function to another through the process of job rotation. More and more private organisations are emulating the policies of the public sector which rotates its employees, to ensure their honing of skills in different areas and also allowing them to perceive issues with varied perceptions acquired through their exposures. For instance, a PSU like BSNL has its engineers in production, distribution, marketing and customer liaison to acquaint them with the typical problems faced by each department.

4.2 Basics of Job Analysis

The supervisor or the human resource specialist normally collects one or more of the following types of information through job analyses:

1. Work activities: This is related to all the core activities related to the job function like designing, teaching or selling. It also includes the knowledge, skills and abilities identified, behavioural traits to be acquired and details of the multi-level skills required to perform the job effectively. For example, in teaching it could be knowledge expertise, delivering lectures using a varied methodology like PowerPoint presentation, interactive lecture, role play, group discussion, assignment and so on. The multi-level skills would include research skills, conducting examinations, organising skills and examiner skills for paper correction.

ANNEXURE II
Job Analysis Questionnaire
Job Analysis Information Format

Your job title _____ Code _____ Date _____

Class title _____ Department _____

Your name _____ Facility _____

Supervisor's title _____ Prepared by _____

Supervisor's name _____ Hours worked _____ AM/PM to _____ AM/PM

1. What is the general purpose of your job?
2. What was your last job? If it was in another organisation, please name it.
3. To what job would you normally expect to be promoted?
4. If you regularly supervise others, list them by name and job title.
5. If you supervise others, please check those activities that are part of your supervisory duties:

    - Hiring
    - Orienting
    - Training
    - Scheduling
    - Developing
    - Coaching
    - Counselling
    - Budgeting
    - Directing
    - Measuring performance
    - Promoting
    - Compensating
    - Disciplining
    - Terminating
    - Other _____

6. How would you describe the successful completion and results of your work?
7. Job duties: Please briefly describe WHAT you do and, if possible, HOW you do it. Indicate those duties you consider to be most important and/or most difficult.

    (a) Daily duties.

    (b) Periodic duties (Please indicate whether weekly, monthly, quarterly, etc.).

    (c) Duties performed of irregular intervals.

2. Human Behaviour: The supervisor will also collect information regarding human behaviour like team working, presentations, sharing critical information, counselling, coaching and so on. For example, managers today are required to spend more time forging friendly team working behaviour and counselling for reconciling differences among members or colleagues due to personality clashes, ego problems and other.

3. Machines, Tools, Software and Work Aids: These include information regarding tools used, materials processed, knowledge dealt with or applied (such as finance or law) and services rendered like maintenance, counselling, upkeep and so on.

4. Performance Standards: The HR supervisors need to understand the various standards, in terms of quality, quantity, targets, behavioural requirements, leadership exhibited. These need to be communicated to the various personnel in advance, so that there are no surprises at the time of appraisal. Also, the frequency of the appraisals and the impact on promotions and increments need to be known and shared to ensure transparency.

Job Analysis is the procedure through which you determine the duties for different positions and the characteristics of the people you hire for them. It is a detailed and systematic study of jobs to define the nature and characteristics of the people to be employed on various jobs.

Some of the definitions of job analysis are as follows:

1. According to **Michael Jucius**, *"Job Analysis refers to the process of studying the operations, duties and organisational aspects of jobs to derive specifications or, as they are called by some, job descriptions."*
2. According to **Edwin Flippo**, *"Job analysis is the process of studying and collecting information relating to the operations and responsibilities of a specific job."*

The study of these definitions reveals that job analysis is a process by which job, duties and responsibilities are defined and the information on various factors related to jobs are collected and compiled to determine the work environment, nature of work, qualities of persons to be employed on the job, position of the job, opportunities available and privileges to be given to the job etc.

4.3 Objectives of Job Analysis

Work Simplification

A job may be analysed to simplify the work and the methods involved in it. The purpose is to redesign the job, to enhance simplification and, in turn, enhance productivity.

Establishment of Standards of Performance

In order to enhance the quality of work by the personnel, and to determine in advance the standard of performance to which the employees can be expected to conform, job analysis helps to measure and establish the minimum standard of work expected from the employees.

Support to other personnel activities

The process of job analysis helps to facilitate the smooth functioning of recruitment, selection, training, performance management and job evaluation.

4.4 Uses of Job Analysis Information

1. Recruitment and Selection

Job Analysis provides information regarding the qualification, skills, knowledge and abilities required by the job. These are very important to measure in order to decide on suitable people to be attracted and selected for the job. The details provided through job description and job specification form the basis of effective recruitment and selection procedures.

2. Compensation

Organisations are able to determine the compensation in the form of base salary, bonus, and incentives and so on, on the basis of the information collected in terms of responsibility, accountability and position in the organisation structure through understanding of the knowledge, skills and abilities required for the jobs underlined.

3. Training

The job description lists the skills, knowledge and behaviour required for the various job positions and so, the Human Resource department is able to extend interventions in the form of training and development needs of the organisation. It is the base document to understand the competencies required to perform on the job effectively which in turn helps in finding the gaps for training.

4. Performance Appraisal

This process of evaluation determines and compares the employees' performance at various levels on the basis of expected standards and measures of performance as determined by the process of job analysis. Hence it provides the basis for control.

5. Discovering Unassigned Duties

A scientific and detailed job analysis reveals unassigned duties and functions of the personnel which may otherwise go unnoticed due to negligence. These get pointed out by the detailed process of job analysis. Take, for example, the common Human Resource personnel job of counselling. Among all the other functions, this seemingly unimportant but a very important job gets relegated to the side. A detailed job analysis may reveal the importance of this and get the HR personnel to deliberately take it up as an important though not fully measureable activity.

6. Safety and Health

The job analysis process uncovers hazardous and unhealthy environmental factors like heat, noise, fumes and dust. The management can take corrective measures to minimise the chances of various risks to ensure safety to workers and to avoid unhealthy conditions.

7. Employee Counselling

Job analysis provides information about career counselling and personal limitations. Such information is helpful in vocational guidance and rehabilitative counselling. Employees who are unable to cope with the demands of the job are transferred to subsidiary departments or advised to take premature retirement.

8. Labour Relations

Job analysis is helpful in improving labour-management relations. It can also be used to resolve disputes and grievances relating to work load and work procedures.

The process of Competency-based Job Analysis

The process of job analysis is a data collection process. The main steps involved are as follows:

1. **Organising and planning for the programme:** The first step in the designing of job analysis is to organise and plan the programme with a budget and a time schedule. The company must decide who will be in charge of the project and must assign responsibilities accordingly.

2. **Obtaining current job design information:** The job analyst should obtain the current design of the various jobs. For the purpose, current job description, job specification, procedure manuals and flow charts should be studied.

3. **Conducting research:** The job analyst should investigate changes and the revisions to be made in the current job descriptions and specifications as examined in the various documents, manuals and systems in the light of the changing paradigms, technology, new software, and new systems adopted by organisations. For instance, in the HR department, manual work of records and analysis has now been taken over by the HRIS (Human Resource Information Systems) and so the functional HR managers need to concentrate on skills like undertaking assessments, counselling, coaching and so on.

4. **Establishing priorities in the jobs to be analysed:** The human resource department working with various operational executives should identify the jobs to be analysed and the priority of each job analysis.

5. **Redesigning the job:** The next step is to redesign the job in the light of the changes in paradigms, procedures, systems and teams involved in the project. These are subject to constant change and so the analyst should reflect on the changing or transformational nature of jobs and revisit and review this.

6. **Preparing job description and job specification:** Job information which has been collected must be processed to prepare the job description form. This is a statement showing full details of the activities of the job. Separate job description forms may be used for various activities in the job and may be compiled later. The job analysis is done with the help of these description forms. These forms may be used as reference in the future.

7. **Developing job specifications:** Job specifications are also prepared on the basis of information collected. These take the form of a statement of minimum acceptable qualities of the person to be placed in the job. It specifies the standard by which the

qualities of the person are measured. The job analyst prepares such a statement taking into consideration the skills required in performing the job properly. Such a statement is used in selecting a person matching with the job.

The techniques of Job Analysis include Questionnaires, Observations, Interviews, and Records in the organisations, Critical Incidents, Job Performances, and related sources. Care must be taken to study each of these sources to include important features related to the various types of jobs and positions investigated and studied.

4.5 Job Description

A job description is an organised factual statement of job contents in the form of duties and responsibilities of a specific job. Some definitions of job descriptions are as follows:

According to **Edwin Flippo**, *"The first and the immediate product of job analysis is job description. As its title indicates, this document is basically descriptive in nature and constitutes a record of existing and pertinent job facts."*

According to **Pigors** and **Myres**, *"Job description is a pertinent picture (in writing) of the organisational relationships, responsibilities and specific duties that constitute a given job or position. It defines a scope of responsibility and continuing work assignment that are sufficiently different from those of other jobs to warrant a specific title."*

Writing of Job description

There is no standard format for writing a job description. However most job descriptions contain sections that cover:

1. **Job Identification**

This includes the job title, designation, functions included, unionised and non-unionised status and the desirable qualities of the job holder. It should be short, brief and suggestive of the nature of the job.

2. **Job Summary**

This describes the contents of the jobs in terms of activities or the tasks performed. The job summary should reflect the nature of the job. Primary, secondary and other duties to be performed on the job should clearly be indicated separately.

3. **Job Location**

Job location should be given in the description of the job. It means the place in which the job is to be performed, which means in which department or subsidiary location of the company.

4. **Duties and Responsibilities**

These include the major and the minor duties to be performed as related to the Job. It should underline even the expectations on the job by the employee performing the particular job. The responsibilities included should be training of peers and subordinates, counselling, sharing of skills with team members and such related responsibilities.

5. Machines, Tools and Materials

The machines, tools and other software and infrastructure required for the job should be included in this section. Each employee is required to work with these tools, machines and software and understand the complexity of the job through these media. Even the training requirements get determined through these appliances or software.

6. Working Conditions

The working environment in terms of heat, light, dust and job hazards should also be described. These help the employee to be prepared for any eventuality and to be trained for exigencies. Some jobs require silence, or an arrangement whereby the team members are present near one another for better understanding and work.

7. Nature of Supervision

The nature of supervision required should also be mentioned in the job description. There are some unskilled jobs done by subordinates or workmen which require supervision, and others which are performed by experts or skilled workmen, which do not require any sort of supervision, only a level of accountability.

8. Relation to other jobs

The jobs immediately above and below are mentioned. It gives an idea to understand the channel of promotion and the idea of a vertical work flow.

4.6 Job Specification

Job specification is also the product of job analysis. It specifies the type of person required in terms of educational qualification, experience, and aptitude on the job and so, assists in the selection of the appropriate personnel.

According to **Edwin Flippo**, *"A job specification is a statement of minimum acceptable human qualities necessary to perform a job properly."*

According to Dale Yorder, *"The job specification as such is a summary properly described as a specialised job description, emphasising personnel requirements and designed especially to facilitate selection and placement."*

Job specification should include the following:

1. Physical characteristics such as height, weight, chest, vision, health, voice and poise.
2. Psychological and Social characteristics like emotional stability, analytical ability, cognitive intelligence, pleasing manners, conversational ability and so on.
3. Mental characteristics such as memory, judgement, ability to concentrate and foresight.
4. Personnel characteristics such as sex, education, family background, hobbies and job experience.

Job Design

This is of comparatively recent origin. The human resource managers have realised that the design of the job has a huge impact on the performance and productivity of the employee.

Job design has been defined by experts as the process of designing and deciding on the contents of the jobs in terms of its duties, and responsibilities, on the methods to be used in carrying out the job, in terms of the techniques, systems and procedures and on the relationships that should exist between the job holder and his superiors, subordinates and colleagues.

Forms of Job Design

These include job rotation which is shifting of an employee from one job to another, job enlargement which is providing a variety of jobs, and training the employees to be more versatile and vibrant in the jobs themselves. Supplemented to this is job enrichment which involves horizontal and lateral expansions of jobs and an improvement in the quality of work in terms of its intrinsic worth.

Dejobbing

Another common term used nowadays is dejobbing which is defined as the broadening of the responsibilities of the jobs and encouraging employees not to limit themselves to what is on their job description. This is normally done through flatter organisations, work teams, boundary-less organisations, reengineering and so on. The work organisations of today are characterised by these new paradigms and shifts in working.

Discussion Questions

1. Why is job analysis important?
2. How is job analysis related to recruitment and selection?
3. What is the design adopted by modern day organisations?
4. Highlight the need for this activity today.

References

1. Anthony, Williams P. (1993) "Strategic Human Resource Management." N.Y. Dryden Press
2. Flippo Edward B. (1984) Personnel Management, New York, McGraw Hill.

3. Human Resource Management by Shashi Gupta, Rosy Joshi, Kalyani Publishers, 2010.
4. Human Resource Management, 12th edn, Gary Dessler and Biju Varkkey, Dorling Kindersley, 2011. Pearson Education, South Asia.

Chapter 5...

Equality and Diversity in the Workplace

Contents ...
5.1 Introduction
5.2 Diversity
5.3 Need for Diversity
5.4 Managing Diversity
- Discussion Questions
- References
- Recommended Readings

Objectives and Summary

The objective of this chapter is to help the reader understand the need for adopting diversity in the work culture and as an attitude for better working. It highlights the reasons for this need and elaborates on various forms of diversity. It also explains the benefits of diversity and how inclusive working has become a norm that takes in the fold all types of employees – women, physically handicapped, mentally challenged, with different sexual orientation and so on.

Diversity at the workplace is the new mantra today. More and more organisations are trying to incorporate diversity in terms of gender, looks, culture, nationality and sexual orientation, in order to reap the benefits of innovation and differences in perspectives. Diversity wheel speaks of differences in terms of age, gender, religion, culture, values and beliefs. The point is to celebrate these differences and learn new perspectives from different features. Diversity is a norm in organisations today and reflects itself in recruitment, selection, performance and so on.

Learning Outcomes:
1. Identifies the need for diversity policy in organisations;
2. Illustrates the benefits of diversity in all forms in organisations;

3. Explains the concept of diversity in various forms;
4. Elaborates the importance of diversity due to changes in the external and internal aspirations of the employees at work.

5.1 Introduction

Practising fairness at work is an underpinning value of human resource management. This is reflected in issues related to recruitment and selection in an organisation. Fairness has links with motivation and unfairness can mar the formal employment contract as well as the psychological contract alienating employees and reducing commitment (Greenberg, 1990). The focus is on designing workplaces in such a way that would ensure placing a lot of value in treating employees fairly and equitably. Such workplaces have been established and are known to developing a sense of commitment. Harassment at work and the exercise of power have been cited as the reasons that certain groups are able to treat others unfairly (Bachanan and Badhan, 2008). Thus, we need to consider the extent to which the persistence of inequality and disadvantage at work and also behaviour that impinges upon people's dignity are linked to abuses of power in organisations. Diversity has direct links with flexibility in organisations. Creating an employee force with a rich repertoire of experiences and perceptions lends unique and innovative solutions to problems. Research has amply indicated innovation, diversity and equality make an impact on performance and productivity.

5.2 Diversity

People are not alike. All are different. The diversity approach originated in the US way back in 1990 in response to the arguments from Americans that the equal opportunity approach to eradicate discrimination did not cover the minority groups or women in their ambit. Belbin (1993) in his research on what makes teams tick, shared insights on how culturally diverse work teams were far more productive than homogenous ones thus making a strong case for diversity as a policy to overcome challenges in motivating teams to differentiate and innovate. This provides an interesting business case for innovation and creation of an edge.

The characteristics of diversity cover visible parameters like age, sex, height, colour of skin, background, disability, working style and personality. The diversity argument is founded on the premise that harnessing these differences will create a productive environment in which everybody feels valued, where their talents are being fully utilised and in which organisational goals are met (Kandola and Fullerton, 1994). Thus the primary challenge facing employers and organisations today is to foster the spirit of equality and diversity and gain productive advantages from this.

Why Diversity?

In 2001, the UK government stated that "in order to become as high performance work place in the 21st century, with a flexible and highly skilled work force adaptable to change and able to compete in the global marketplace, employers need to be fishing in the widest possibly talent pool to ensure that they have access to the breadth and depth of skills available, which meet their business needs" (DTI, 2001).

To a large extent, demographic changes and globalisation provided the motives that drove equal employment legislation. Employers now have little choice but to willingly push for more diversity. In this context, diversity refers to the variety or multiplicity of demographic features that characterise a company's workforce - particularly in terms of race, sex, culture, national origin, handicap, age and religion. Globalisation has spurred on the employers to hire minority members with the cultural and language skills to deal with customers abroad. In short, it now seems to be a business imperative.

The business case for diversity and equal opportunities has become increasingly prominent. According to CIPD (2006) there are three main reasons for going beyond what is required by legislation and introducing diversity policies, people issues, market competitiveness and corporate reputation.

1. **People issues**

These include creating an open and congenial environment with empowerment for the workforce, a policy of inclusion, where people feel valued and are treated with dignity and respect. This consequently creates a climate of trust, commitment and productivity which in turn fosters innovation and creativity.

2. **Market competitiveness**

A diverse and passionate workforce can help to identify new product designs and services, create new market opportunities and help to enhance the market share of the organisation and make it overall more competitive.

3. **Corporate reputation**

Today with employer branding being primarily important to attract talent and a strong customer base, the policies of diversity, dignity and equality are at the core of making the work place ethical, transparent and these help in enhancing the corporate reputation of the organisation. Most organisations which are ranked as "Great Places to Work for" by the organisation of the same name, reflect the elements and character of dignity and diversity.

It appears from research that social justice and diversity are complementary because unless people are treated fairly at work they will feel less committed and will underperform.

Key features in Diversity and Equality

Given below is the impact of maintaining the status quo of inequality and forces that act towards a negative shift in attitude. Organisations need to investigate these features and take corrective actions by monitoring such behaviour.

1. Stereotyping and segregation

This includes stereotyping of people depending upon the groups they belong to and identify with. It is contended that subconscious stereotyping exists which results in discrimination of the workforce. For instance, women are considered to be very sensitive and emotional whereas men are considered to be more rational and objective. The truth may not be so. Thus for fostering diversity, organisations need to eliminate stereotyping and discriminatory employment practices.

2. Opportunity and Choice

Human capital theorists and rational choice theorists combine to form a set of arguments that are used to explain inequality of women and ethnic minorities in an organisation. Human capital is defined as the combination of skill, knowledge and attributes that a person possesses. Women, according to theorists, can be categorised as career focused, home focused and adaptive. It has been debated by theorists that the choices available to women are very limited as they are more domesticated; and even if they have a career they give it up to raise their children, only to return to it later. It has been debated that women have the opportunity for human capital development and high-level jobs but may choose not to exercise it. Avoiding such stereotypes is a challenge. Women might need to make a choice regarding childbirth. If and when they decide, the ways in which they evaluate their choices and options are different.

3. The glass ceiling

The term 'glass ceiling' refers to situation where the advancement of an employee within the hierarchy is limited. This limitation is based on some form of discrimination, most commonly being gender. Such discrimination also exists for different minorities and those with different sexual orientations.

4. Disability

It is known that disabled people remain disadvantaged in the workplace. It is considered wrong to focus on a person's disability and make wider judgements about their wider ability to work. It may be possible that the disability may not actually be linked to their capability or otherwise to work and secondly the individuals may be quite able to work if the employers were to make adjustments to working practices within the workplace. Employers are now expected to make adjustments for the disabled worker to work effectively in terms of rehabilitation, reallocation of duties, adjustments in working hours and so on.

As a case in point, an IT company in Pune, as an SME (Small and Medium Enterprise) has a large part of its workforce comprising of deaf and dumb employees who do the coding and testing of software applications. The owner has been quoted to be very happy with their sense of dedication and hard work. And in Chennai, the AACHI Group of Companies which manufactures AACHI MASALA products has provided employment to several hundreds of women and for over 40 differently-abled persons.

5. Age

This is an area where a lot of discrimination happens. Most advertisements to fill vacancies mention age bars. It appears that Indian organisations are conscious of not preferring older employees, especially those who are beyond their mid-40s and in their early 50s. However, many times due to the shortage of skill sets and competency gaps, companies are known to fill these with those in these age groups. An example is the changing demographics and workforce of WNS, the second largest BPO in India, where its CEO, Keshav Murugesh, believes in an eclectic mix of workforce and does not consider the limit to age as a barrier for securing the right skill base or mix.

6. Sexual Orientation

Sexual orientation refers to the sexual preferences of lesbians, gay and bi-sexual people, as well as transgenders. One of the challenges of organisations is to meld these in the working fabric of the workforce without any cruelty or discrimination or even ridicule.

7. Religious belief

It is considered unlawful under the terms of employment equality to discriminate on grounds of religious differences. Still, there are organisations which choose candidates also on the basis of their religious beliefs and ideology.

Equality and Diversity in the workplace

Man was born free, and he is everywhere in chains. One man thinks himself the master of others; but remains more of a slave than they.   **– Rousseau (1762), The Social Contract**

Why Equality and Diversity

The terms equality and diversity may be interchangeable in everyday use, but it is important that the HRM recognises that there are important differences between the two concepts. Equality is commonly regarded as sameness in relation to equal opportunity, equality of outcome in terms of equal pay. These terms are sometimes seen as a negative perception, because of which some organisations fail to comply with legal requirements and incur financial penalties rather than promote equality for business and social justice.

On the other hand, diversity has become more widespread in today's times. Diversity may be defined as valuing everyone irrespective of their differences as individuals – whether they are employees, customers or clients. The focus on diversity rather than equality has been advocated because of the benefits it brings to the organisation by enabling different perspectives on various aspects. But while the term 'diversity' and the concept have now been increasingly adopted by all organisations for enhancing innovation, understanding conflicts and managing them, it has been proved to be a differentiator in competition.

Why organisations manage diversity

Having considered the differences between 'equality' and 'diversity' and the different approaches, in terms of social justice and legal reasons for work place opportunities, why do organisations promote diversity and equality? A survey for the Chartered Institute for Personnel and Development in 2007 suggested that most organisations adopted diversity policies in response to legal pressures, and of course, to recruit and retain the best talent. Examples of some of the claims made by the UK employment tribunal on discrimination leading to unfair dismissal include discrimination on grounds of sex, disability, race, religion or beliefs, age and so on.

5.3 Need for Diversity

Organisations all over the world including in India are now acquiring and becoming more multinational with locations and acquisitions spanning the world. For example, Taj Resorts comprises 64 hotels in 45 locations across India with an additional 15 international hotels including The Pierre, the iconic landmark hotel on New York's Fifth Avenue, Taj Boston and the Blue Sydney. Take Bharat Forge, a Pune-based forgings company, has manufacturing operations across 11 locations, and 5 countries - 4 in India, 3 in Germany and 1 each in Sweden and the US and 2 in China. Its customers include the top five passenger car and the top five commercial vehicle manufacturers in the world. Bharat Forge became the world's second largest forging manufacturer after acquiring Carl Dan Peddinghaus, a German forging company. Its workforce includes Japanese, German, American and Chinese people. Or Dr. Reddy's Laboratories became the first Asia Pacific Pharmaceutical company outside Japan to list on the New York Stock Exchange in 2001. It acquired German generic pharmaceuticals company, Betapharma, which is one of the largest drug manufacturers, of Europe for a total enterprise value of $450 million - one of the largest deals by an Indian pharma company. It is one of the top pharma companies in India in terms of its turnover and profitability. Its products are manufactured globally, with a focus on India, the US, Russia and Europe.

Another rationale for embracing diversity is the social and political upheavals, which have led organisations to change the way they conduct business and encouraged their members to think globally. Globalisation in countries like India after the 1990s have spawned transnational companies like IBM, McDonald's and KFC to set up offices in India, while Indian companies like Tatas and Mahindras have set up locations all over the world. This has spawned the need to understand and be sensitive to the cultural differences around the world. Also with the new age workforce consisting of knowledge and millennial workers joining the workforce, their perspectives through social media and networking are transformational and are drastically changing the paradigms and values. Global companies like GE and IBM have not only opened offices but also started outsourcing much of their skilled knowledge-related work to companies in India. In turn, Indian organisations have also capitalised on their skill base and knowledge base and opened operations in many countries to extend their skills on software solutions. A report by Morgan Stanley suggests that India is expected to become the third largest economy of the world. In order to foster this interconnectedness with the world, expatriate managers, those who work in a country other than their own, benefit greatly from knowledge of cultural differences.

International executives are executives whose jobs have international scope, whether in an expatriate assignment or in dealing with international issues. Some of the key competencies required to learn from experience include integrity, insightfulness, risk-taking, the courage to take a stand, and the ability to bring out the best in people. International executives need to learn attributes like cultural adventurousness, flexibility, openness to criticism, the desire to seek learning opportunities, and sensitivity to cultural differences.

Apart from the cultural differences of other countries, in countries like India there is an enormous diversity of culture and hence the workforce needs to be sensitive to the cultural nuances of the different regions in the country. The ex-Chairman of Larsen and Toubro, A. M. Naik, reveals how he came from a small town in Maharashtra and could not even speak in English, and suffered a lot of ridicule due to this language handicap. Also hailing from a small town, he was very traditional in his mannerisms which created quite a stir. Over a period of time, he learnt to acquire the ways of the cities and imbibe the moral and modern fabric of the working organisations in transnational set-ups. Because workplace customs vary widely, understanding cultural differences becomes especially important for companies that are considering opening foreign offices. Carefully researching the information in advance help companies manage their foreign operations. Consulate offices and companies operating within a foreign company provide excellent information about national customs and legal requirements.

Cultural Difference and Work Related Attitudes

One key for any company competing in the global market place is to understand diverse cultures. Whether managing culturally diverse individuals within a single location or managing individuals at remote locations around the globe, organisations have to learn to cultivate sensitivity around different cultures among individuals either from different nationalities or different regions in the same country. Edgar Schein suggests that to understand an organisation's culture or even broadly any culture, one should dig below the surface of visible artefacts and uncover the basic underlying assumptions at the core of the culture. Micro-cultural differences, i.e. differences within cultures are keys to our understanding of the global work environment. Differences in symbols are extremely important. The thumbs-up sign, for example, means approval in the US, whereas in Australia it is an obscene gesture. Or many European countries do not use manila folders and therefore do not recognise the icons used in Windows applications.

Research studies indicate how cultural differences translate into work-related attitudes. The Dutch researcher Hofstede and his colleagues surveyed around 100,000 managers and employees working at IBM in different countries where it is located, to study the behaviour of individuals from different countries. The studies showed that national culture explains more differences in work related attitudes than do age, gender, profession or position in an organisation. Five dimensions of cultural differences were found by Hofstede which were classified and elaborated elsewhere. *(Details are mentioned in Chapter 15, on International Human Resource Management.)*

5.4 Managing Diversity

Managing Diversity means maximising the potential through increased cultural awareness and language skills, and minimising the associated problems like conflicts and misunderstandings due to bias, prejudice and stereotyping. Such a character is likely to undermine the performance and productivity of an organisation. A Diversity Management Programme facilitates blending the elements of diversity as a close-knit and it thus helps to generate productive results.

The following are the elements of a Diversity Management Plan:

1. ***Strong Leadership:*** Companies with reputations for embracing diversity in their employee fold usually have a strong leadership at the top that champions the cause for diversity in spirit. IBM is an example of such a championing leadership where a book called "Software of the Mind" has been written which is a compilation of IBM's active embodiment of diversity.

2. Any Diversity management programme starts with the organisation first assessing its focus on diversity, issues and challenges it faces with diversity as related to equal employment opportunity, retention issues, employee attitude or satisfaction surveys. Once these are assessed, the policies and values of the organisation may be further reinforced and embedded in all its policies and programmes to build on the diversity cause.

3. ***Impart Diversity Training and Education:*** After an assessment of the diversity-embracing culture in the organisation, which may not be perfect, the organisation should work on sensitising employees at all levels on the benefits of diversity and how the sidelining of issues of minorities may create problems of discrimination. The employer and the owners need to be aware of sensitising the minorities in their own language and culture, to make sure that they embrace the policies and the culture of

the organisation in which they are employed. All these issues can be covered as a training module conducted by trained personnel.

4. **Change and Management Systems:** The philosophy here is to recognise and respond to individual differences. These are quite contrary to the popular adage of treating everybody equitably. The employees at all levels should be sensitised to these changes and should act accordingly to reap the benefits in terms of productivity and efficiency through diversity.

5. **Assess the Diversity Management Programme:** It is very important to evaluate the Diversity Management Programme to measure its efficacy and leverage its benefits for enhanced productivity and efficiency.

What are the signs we need to look for to measure the effectiveness of Diversity Initiatives? They are as follows:

1. Are the turnover rates of women and minorities or differently abled employees higher than for the others?
2. Are international assignments accessible to all?
3. Are the women and other minorities reporting directly to senior managers?
4. Are the different sexually oriented employees still being ridiculed and alienated?

Strategy to Eliminate Discrimination

The starting point for eliminating discrimination is to formulate an Equal Opportunity Policy which should be mentioned in bold in the Employee Handbook as also be added to the list of the core values. These should not be just embedded in principle, but should be actively advocated and aligned with the behaviour of the line or functional personnel along with the HR personnel. The new age discrimination regulations have brought calls for employers to build integrated age strategies (Walker, 1999).

Another important responsibility of supervisors and managers at all levels is to foster the development of effective teams in which employees of all types and diverse cultures can work together to meet shared objectives. IBM is an appropriate example where the blending of skills from different cultures has become a major engine of human and corporate growth. False assumptions and prejudices about diversity issues in terms of age, gender and disability should be openly voiced and discussed to remove misconceptions; otherwise these remain closeted and dark in terms of a clearer understanding.

Cultural positivity is a method which is known to establish and facilitate collaborative working. It encourages an attitude shift from negativity, or pessimism, to one which builds a more positive and optimistic outlook. It also helps to acknowledge and celebrate cultural differences in order to build pride in self and ethnicity while addressing potential conflicts that are likely to occur when working with a culturally diverse workforce.

Work-Life Balance and Employment Flexibility

Employment flexibility and achieving positive work life balance represent important issues for employers when making the best use of a diverse work force, as is well established it affects participation in work. In India, according to the survey of companies which have been consistently ranked as Great Places to Work for, one of the common elements has been the thrust on the work-life balance for their various levels of employees. The philosophy of the organisations is to make sure that their employees work only the prescribed fixed hours, unless there are emergencies, and also that they take their eligible leave. Recently, even a nationalised bank like State Bank of India has issued a notice to all its employees, to compulsorily take leave, with the objective of achieving a better productivity at work. In companies like Infosys, it has been stated that the lights go off at 7 sharp in the evening, implying that if the employees are not able to complete their work till then, there is a problem with their efficiency and not an overload of work, as is made out to be.

Dignity at Work

The initiatives in the name of dignity at work have been launched to address equality, bullying, harassment and discrimination for all employees. The aim of many organisations is to change the working culture for everyone to make a more positive and supportive working environment regardless of employee demographics. To foster such an environment, employers work on providing training on valuing differences, positive energy and positive behaviour. 'Dignity at work' programmes need to ensure that as well as promoting the positive, they are also paying attention to negative behaviour.

Threading together

The following strong HR practices should be followed to promote diversity and equality among all levels of employees:

1. All employees understand their rights and obligations.
2. Managers have the skills and confidence to identify negative situations early and correct them before the damage is done.
3. A good formal complaint system where employees trust that their grievance will be settled amicably.
4. Regular feedback is sought from the employees to monitor the organisation's working environment positive.
5. Someone is appointed to track changes in the law and best practices.

Article excerpted from The Economic Times (Feb. 23, 2011)

Why gender equality stalled in the land of free

It is the 50th anniversary of the publication of the Berry Friedman's international best seller *The Feminine Mystique*. This has been widely credited by igniting the women movement of the 1960s. Readers who return to this feminist classic today are often puzzled by the absence of concrete political proposals to change the status of women. But the feminist mystique had the impact because it focused on transforming women's consciousness. In 1963, most Americans did not yet believe that gender equality was possible or even desirable.

Arguing that "the personal is political," feminists urged women to challenge the assumption at work and at home, that women should always be the ones who make the coffee, watch over the children, pick up after men and serve the meals.

Over the next 30 years, this emphasis on equalizing gender roles at home as well as in work produced a revolutionary transformation in American's attitudes. It was not instant. As late as 1977, two thirds of Americans believe that it was "much better for everyone involved if the man is the achiever outside the home and the woman takes care of the home and family. "By 1994, two thirds of Americans rejected this notion.

The Revolution Stalls

But during the second half of the 1990s and first few years of the 2000, the equality revolution seemed to stall. Between 1994 and 2000, the percentage of Americans preferring the male bread winner/ female home maker family module actually rose to 40 per cent from 34 per cent. Between 1997 and 2007, the number of full time working mothers who said that they would prefer to work part time increased to 60 per cent from 48 per cent. In 1997, a quarter of stay at home mothers, said full time work would be ideal. By 2007, only 16 per cent of stay at home mothers wanted to work full time. Women's labour force participation in the US also leveled off in the second half of the 1990s, in contrast towards continued increase in most other countries. Gender desegregation of college majors and occupations also slowed.

Women Inclusivity in the DNA of Punekars

Tech Mahindra in Pune hosted a social event on Jan. 9th 2012, to enhance awareness amongst its women employee on, how to 'Step Ahead' in their career. Women leaders from the industry participated and shared their views in a panel discussion with Sujitha Karnad, Head of HR and Quality of Tech Mahindra's IT arm.

Sujitha initiated the discussion with an overview of the current diversity practices in TechM. TechM has 10% women representation in Senior Management. She encouraged the women associates to make their own career choices, be aware of the difference in intensity of emotions they feel versus their male counterparts while handling various issues.

Beena Wankar, an Independent IT Consultant, inspired the audience with her story of success. She encouraged the women to be always at ease with themselves, know what they want and be willing to make a difference. An optimal combination of effort, ambition, drive is as important as navigating the organisation's dynamics.

Nikhila, the Dy. Chief (Results and Marketing) and head of NIE, promotes the use of social networking beyond the Facebook's and Twitters of the virtual world. She encouraged the audience to join and participate in networks that make them happy beyond their work. Some examples were the CII, Young Presidents Organisation (YPO), NGOs, Book and Adventure clubs etc. She stressed that networks help similar minded people to bond as they share.

Renuka Krishna, AVP Talent Acquisition at KPIT Cummins, helped the women understand that as a culture, women work twice as hard as their male counterparts, and hence are at risk of burnout, if they try to achieve all at once and be the BIG SUPERWOMAN. She encouraged the audience to set boundaries for themselves while they share their career aspirations with their family, friends and colleagues, people who really create the much needed support system for them. She emphasised the need to select supportive partners, so that a woman's career growth is not impeded due to issues like , "she earns more than me" or "is not there to support the kids and parents" etc. While the organisation supports young mothers through their various policies, the women themselves need to carve their own career path.

Sujitha concluded the session with a Q and A session along with the panellist's, and encouraged the audience to clarify their minds perceptions and myths, while taking note of suggestions to improve existing practices and policies. An dinner with women alumni, concluded the day on a high note of camaraderie for TechM, its processes, tools and people.

The session was hosted by the HR Operations team, in collaboration with the Diversity Council Members at TechM.

TechM launched the DIWA (Diversity and Inclusivity Winner's Association) community on their internal blog, Oie, for those who believe in Diversity and Inclusivity.

Case Study: Bringing international Diversity to build a global workplace (As narrated by KPIT in their own words..)

KPIT Cummins Infosystems Limited, a global IT Consulting and product engineering partner focused on co-innovating domain intensive technology solutions for corporations specialising in automotive and transportation, manufacturing and energy, and utilities, currently partners with 165+ global corporations including Original Equipment Manufacturers (OEMs), semiconductor companies and Tier-1 companies. With more than 31 offices in 16 countries the company today has a team of over 8000+ technology and business specialists.

The Business Need

With a majority of customers in North America and Europe we had embarked on a journey of transformation from being an India based service provider to a multinational technology partner to our customer industries. It was important in this scenario to bring in regional (global) diversity into the workforce. This was also the time when we were bringing in larger focus on our emerging markets strategy and therefore we decided to scout for Asian talent with global exposure.

The most critical driver in the IT consulting space is the human resource and the ability to attract, engage and retain talent. With the advent of global markets and global customers, a seamless ability to ensure the availability of the right resource for the job is critical for business success. It is not just the question of knowing the language of the customer but also the nuances of the culture, to be able to give comfort to the local customers and also understand and leverage local competencies.

It was essential to have resources from local markets , but with an understanding of the organisation's core values, culture and offerings be able to represent the company in local markets from both selling and delivery perspective. This is especially true of new complex, large markets like China, Japan, Korea, Brazil etc. where the way business happens is essentially different from the Indian way.

The Solution

Local hiring of the right resources for local markets, but with proper induction and necessary immersion into the organisation's values, processes, team structures and offerings.

Plan and execution:

We specially identified, after visits to relevant international schools, two highly self-motivated, innovative young Chinese management graduates. The choice of resources was critical as the plan for their deployment was special and they would need to have the same acumen as the company in executing this plan as their career choice.

Background

Both were schooled and educated in China for the initial years, then moved to an international top ranked B-school outside China for a Master's program, spending part of their semester in Europe for additional global market knowledge.

Plan

Post-hire, both joined the company at the corporate headquarters in Pune, India, for an 18 month immersion program, where they went through multi-function role allocations, to know and understand the way business happens in a multinational company headquartered in India and also connect with various key stake-holders and business leaders within the organisation.

Post this period, both were deputed in China as the territory to set up a local office in the country, manage necessary infrastructure and business development.

The plan has been very successful as post hire, in over a five year period, we have been able to establish an office, add clients, execute projects and look at future growth. Our local hires now are better aligned to company processes and values and the connect between offices is stronger as teams are known to each other. While an alternate of transferring candidates from India always existed, the cultural acclimatization would have been long drawn and acceptance by customers and markets would have taken more efforts, which was seamless now.

- From GLOBAL HR COMPETENCIES by Dave Ulrich, Wayne Brockbank, Jon Younger, Mike Ulrich, Publisher: Tata McGraw-Hill.

Discussion Questions

1. Why is diversity important today?
2. Explain how culture influences diversity.
3. Elaborate on the advantages of adopting diversity.
4. Give examples of diversity and their consequence in organisations.

References

1. Belbin M (1993) Team Roles at Work. Oxford. Butterworth Heinemann.
2. Buchanan D and Badham R (2008)Power, Politics and Organisation Change (2nd edn) London: Sage.
3. Greenberg J. (1990) 'Looking fair vs Being fair' Managing Impressions of Organisational Justice in B. Straw and L. Cummings (eds). Research in Organisational Behavior. Greenwich, CT, JAI Press, 111-57.
4. Kandola B and Fullerton J (1994).Managing the Mosaic: Diversity in Action. London: IPD.
5. CIPD (2006 e) Diversity: An Overview. Fact Sheet. London: CIPD.
6. CIPD (2007 e) Managing Conflict at Work: Survey Report, 2007 London: CIPD.
7. DTI (2001). Department of Trade and Industry. Diversity best Practice in the Corporate World: A Guide for Business. London: Women and Equality Unit.
8. Michael Carrel and Everett Mann "Defining the Workforce Diversity in Public sector Organisations, "Public Personnel Management, 24, No1, (Spring 1995) pp 99-111.

Recommended Readings

1. Human Resource Management by Sarah Gilmore and Steve William. Oxford University Press. 2009. UK

2. Human Resource Management. 12th edition. Gary Dessler and Bijju Varkkey. Prentice Hall, 2011.

3. Human Resource Management by Adrain Murton, Maragaret Inman and Nuala o Sullivan, 2011, Hodder ed:Great Britain.

Chapter 6...

Learning and Development

Contents ...
6.1 The Learning Organisation
6.2 Meaning of Education, Training, Learning and Development
6.3 Aligning Training with Strategy
6.4 On-the-Job Training
6.5 Job Instruction Training
- Discussion Questions
- References and Recommended Readings

Objectives and Summary

This chapter aims at understanding the various aspects of Learning and Development activities and systems adopted by organisations to hone the competencies and skills of their employees at various levels. It aims at understanding the process of identification of the needs of personnel and orienting the learning and development programmes to suit the requirements. It also discusses about new forms of learning like Coaching and Mentoring.

Also included in this chapter is understanding the need for learning and development, distinction between education, training, learning and development, process of employee boarding, competency models, identification of learning needs through performance analysis, informal learning and computer assisted learning techniques.

Learning Outcomes:
1. Elaborating on the various aspects of learning and development;
2. Developing process for identification of learning needs of the personnel;
3. Benefits of Coaching and Mentoring;
4. Implementation of the Management Development Programmes by organisations.

A journey of a thousand miles begins with a single step:
- Chinese Philosopher Lao Tzu

The competitiveness of any organisation today depends upon the skills, knowledge and capabilities of its people. Advances in technology and knowledge have increasingly focused the thrust on learning among personnel. This is an essential component for success in any organisation which wishes to survive and compete in this continuously changing world of technology, robots and knowledge. The advent of compulsory certifications like National Assessment and Accreditation Council (NAAC) for higher education, Quality certifications like the IS800 for structural design, and the Indian Society for Training and Development (ISTD)'s courses in training and development have focused on the area of learning and development, considered critical for organisations to be able to effectively compete in the market place. . Skills are increasingly seen as the key lever not only for the organisation but for the economy as a whole to compete internationally (Leitch, 2006).

There has been a range of initiatives in organisations to address the shortfalls in the skills levels and encourage employers to invest in the training and development of the workforce.

Apprenticeships

Apprenticeships have always been a traditional way of learning a trade in sectors like manufacturing in India for engineering and particular crafts. The term coined today is internship. The objective is to extend training across a wide range of sectors in order to plug the growing skills gap and to provide an alternative to the academic route. There are now Interns in all sectors from manufacturing to retailing, education, Information Technology and medical services. This is one of the most popular styles of development to train personnel for the lower and the middle levels in organisations. The Apprentices Act, 1961, was enacted by the Government of India to regulate and control training of apprentices. The act intends to achieve two objectives:

1. Promotion of new skills.
2. Improvement/refinement of old skills through theoretical and practical training in a number of trades and occupations.

Employers covered by this Act are under a statutory obligation to provide training to a prescribed number of people. However the employer is not bound to offer employment to the apprentice upon completion of training, nor is the trainee bound to accept any employment offer, unless the apprenticeship contract specifies it.

6.1 The 'Learning Organisation'

Such an initiative is aimed at encouraging a culture of life-long learning within an organisation. Senge (1990) introduced the concept of the 'learning organisation'. He was one of the first to write about the importance of continuous learning of employees. By that he meant an organisation which facilitated the learning of all its members for continuously transforming themselves. A learning organisation creates an atmosphere at work where learning is encouraged through everyday tasks. Sharing of ideas, letting people try out these ideas without fear of making mistakes and learning from each other is actively promoted as a part of the company strategy.

The late Rohinton Aga, who took over boiler manufacturer Wanson from his father-in-law and turned it into the environment and engineering major Thermax Ltd, was a passionate believer in this learning strategy.

Becoming a learning organisation often means changing people's thoughts and the way they work. It is also about getting people to realize that every task is a learning opportunity. Sharing such learning is a critical part of an organisation becoming a 'learning organisation'. This is possible through a regular feedback mechanism, teamwork and cross-functional teamwork so that personnel in different functions can benefit from one another's learning.

6.2 Meaning of Education, Training, Learning and Development

Education tends to be more formal and aims to develop people's intellectual capability, conceptual and social understanding and work performance through the learning process (Marchington and Wilkinson, 2008). The outcome is usually seen in terms of some sort of qualification or formal recognition, for example an MBA degree.

Training tends to be more specific. It is usually instructor-led and aims at developing a particular skill or changing a behaviour. For example, imparting training in how to use a new software package.

Learning focuses on the changes which take place within the individual. This may be in terms of skill, knowledge or attitude, and may have been brought about consciously through training or some other experience.

Development is a term which really covers both training and learning but tends to deal with the long-term changes which take place as a result of training and development.

Learning Theory by Kolb

Kolb argued that for learning to be effective, an individual needs to go through a cycle of learning:

Having an experience - observing and reflecting on the experience - concluding the experience - planning the next step and experimenting with new ideas.

The Training Process

Carefully selecting employees doesn't guarantee that they will perform effectively. Even high-potential employees can't do their jobs effectively without understanding the hows and the whys of doing the job, understanding the values, vision and culture of the organisation in which they are employed. For this, the HR department develops an orientation programme or a training programme to acquaint the employee with the "way to do things around here" or culture in an organisation developed by the top management with the inputs from all levels of personnel in the organisation.

The purpose of employee orientation or on-boarding:

Most organisations have an intensive orientation or on-boarding programme for new employees to familiarise them with the working environment, make them feel at home like a family and orient them towards the company's policies, programmes, culture, values, vision and mission. This helps familiarise the newly-inducted employee with the working of the organisation and educate him or her about the way things are done in the organisation, apart from the ethical use of passwords, infrastructure, leave policies, company facilities and so on.

IT organisations like Cognizant have a "buddy" system for newly-inducted employees at various levels. This mentor or buddy counsels the new employee, providing any clarification or assistance regarding any policy- or culture-related matter. Cadbury Kraft Foods adopts an on boarding system of learning to acquaint a newly inducted employee at any level with all the major activities and functions of the organisation. A minimum quorum of five is required to make conference-room presentations and then, over a fortnight, functional heads share with them the culture, working and how these would be related to the job and interactions of the new employee. Hindustan Petroleum Corporation Limited (HPCL) has designed a programme called "Samavesh" which is an award winning orientation and training programme. As a Fortune 500 oil refining and marketing PSU, the structured orientation and training programme is aimed at ensuring that the officer trainees are acclimatised properly to HPCL. It has three phases i.e. What is HPCL? How does HPCL work? And how does your SBU work? According to the company, the program helped to improve retention and engagement levels of the new officers. It was reported that attrition during the first six months got reduced from 55% in 2007 to 8% in 2008. The initiative included rigorous and continuous evaluation of learning and performance.

The Employee Handbook

Also called an Employee Manual, this serves as a blueprint or a written encyclopaedia for the employee who wishes to understand and get clarification and a deeper understanding of all employee benefits, policies, and processes and so on. For example, Mahindra Ugine Steel Company (MUSCO) has a detailed manual which serves as a reference book for an employee, at all levels, as it is like a ready reckoner to refer to for any company-related matter right from leave entitlement, allowance for outstation travel, training entitlement and so on.

The contents of the Employee Handbook also represent legally binding employment commitments. Therefore, employers often include disclaimers. These make it clear that statements of company policies, benefits and regulations do not constitute the terms and conditions of the employment contract, either expressed or implied.

Some Indian firms ask employees to sign an undertaking to work for a particular period before they can change jobs or demand that the employees deposit original certificates and documents with the company. Under Indian law, such one-sided contracts are not legally tenable. Also, forcibly holding a person on the job is illegal and a violation of fundamental rights under the Indian Constitution. Hence, many firms take an undertaking from an employee to serve a particular period, considering that the company has made investments in terms of training. If the employee decides to resign in between, then the company can claim compensation for the loss incurred.

The Spirit of the Murugappa Group

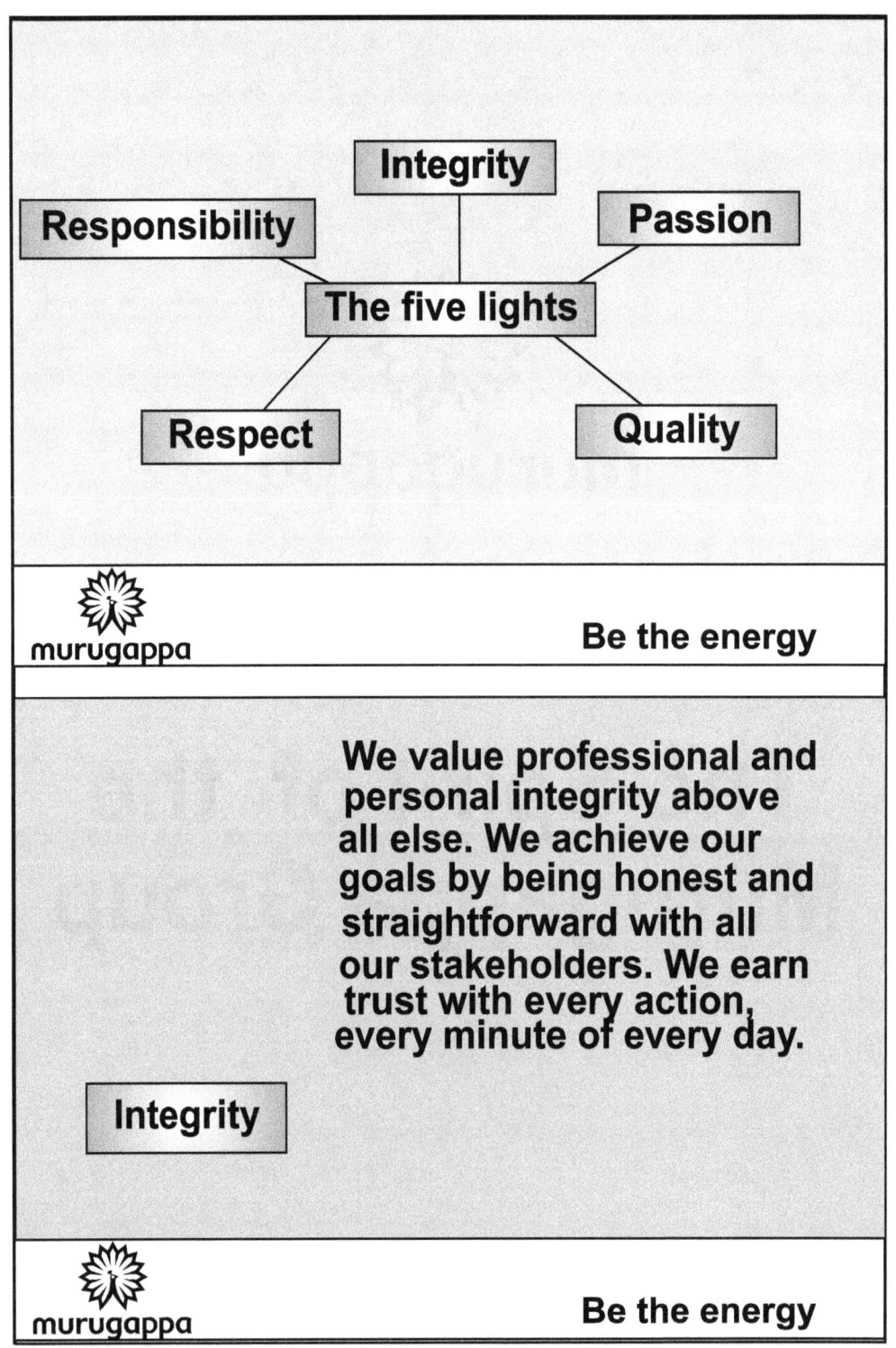

We play to win. We have a healthy desire to stretch, to achieve personal goals and accelerate business growth. We strive constantly to improve and be energetic in everything that we do.

Passion

Be the energy

Quality

We take ownership of our work. We unfailingly meet high standards of quality in both what we do and the way we do it. We take pride in excellence.

Be the energy

Respect

We respect the dignity of every individual. We are open and transparent with each other. We inspire and enable people to achieve high standards and challenging goals. We provide everyone equal opportunities to progress and grow.

Be the energy

Responsibility

We are responsible corporate citizens. We believe we can help make a difference to our environment and change lives for the better. We will do this in a manner that befits our size and also reflects our humility.

Be the energy

> **The spirit of the Murugappa Group embodies the core values and beliefs by which our people live.**

Informal orientation

Alongside the formal orientation, many organisations also attempt to introduce an air of informality. The informality helps newly hired people to open up and be relaxed. Many firms, including Infosys and TCS, have modelled their activities (in Mysore and Thiruvannthapuram respectively) where campus hirers join for orientation and initial training just like a university campus. Informal activities like get-togethers, celebrations, competitions, movie screenings, outdoor games and quiz competitions are held regularly. Informal meetings with the senior management are also arranged regularly in many companies like Cadbury Kraft Foods, Bosch and Philips.

6.3 Aligning Training with Strategy

More and more employers want to make sure that their training programmes are aligned with the organisation strategy in order to meet the firm's strategic goals. As Naushad Forbes, Director of Forbes Marshall, a power plant manufacturing organisation, said, "We underline the objectives of training very clearly and make sure we align the modules to meet the strategic goals and objectives. Every employee in our organisation is mandated to attend at least a week of training every year. The feedback is then taken."

For example, Bharat Forge has established an Institute to oversee all the training and development programmes. Kirloskar Pneumatic also has a University on the outskirts of Pune to oversee the top-level management's training and development activities.

The four-step training process:

ADIE (Analysis, Design, Implementation, Execution) a model outlining the four-step implementation process is normally adopted to undertake the training.

In the first, i.e. need analysis, you analyse the skills, knowledge and attributes of the employee in relation to the job and compare them with the employee's current level of skills, knowledge and experience, and thus identify the gaps to be filled by training.

In the design stage, specific and measurable training objectives are outlined including activities, budget, workbooks and exercises to be administered in the training.

The third step is to implement the programme by actually training the targeted employee group using methods like on-the-job or online training, simulation training, management games, lecture and classroom training, and so on.

Finally, in the evaluation step, the success or failure of the programme is evaluated by an immediate feedback after the programme and later a six-monthly review of the trainee is undertaken by an evaluation by their immediate supervisor to note tangible behavioural, skill and knowledge changes as observed by them. Cadbury Kraft Ltd adopts this pattern to measure the effectiveness of the training design and modules and ensure a perfect fit with the requirements of the job. In Cadbury, each line manager who nominates a subordinate for training is expected to closely observe the changes in the trainee and suggest modifications in the design and contents of the modules accordingly.

Competency Models

Many employers develop competency models for different jobs. The competency models are usually consolidated in one diagram, a precise overview of the competencies in terms of knowledge, skills and behaviour of someone who would do the job well. Companies like Aditya Birla Group, Mahindras have formulated a very comprehensive Competency Model Framework that underlines the detailed competencies required for every level of personnel. The following is the Competency framework for Mahindra Ugine Steel company (MUSCO).

I KNOW	I CAN OPERATE WITH ASSISTANCE / I CAN OPERATE INDEPENDENTLY	I CAN TEACH
Position: Department: Date:		
Skill		Required level
Technical		
	Operational skills	
1		
2		
3		
4		
5		
	Analytical Skills	
1		
2		
3		
4		
5		
	Equipment Handling	
1		
2		
3		
4		
5		
Competencies		
	Behavioural	
1		
2		
3		
	Managerial	
1		
2		
3		

Performance Analysis
Identifying the Current Employees' Training Needs

Performance Analysis is a very valuable process in identification and verifying if there is a performance gap or a deficiency and determining how training and learning could help to fill or correct such a gap or deficiency.

Generally in companies, the basis of deputing personnel for various types of training modules is the performance analysis. For instance, Kirloskar Oil Engines Ltd has a detailed method of performance analysis of each employee at all levels in order to determine the needs of training. So do Bharat Forge, Forbes Marshall, Thermax and so on. The Post-Apppraisal period in these companies determines the details of the various training modules to be developed and executed in accordance with the performance analysis. Apart from using this technique in identifying the training needs, some of the other methods used are:

- Job related Performance data (productivity, absenteeism, waste, grievance, late deliveries, product quality, consumer complaints).
- Observation of supervisor
- Attitude Surveys
- Individual employee detail diaries
- Assessment centre results

6.4 On-the-Job Training (OJT)

OJT means having a person learn a job by actually doing it. Every employee from the lower level clerk to the CEO gets on the job training when he or she joins a firm. In many firms OJT is the only type of training available.

Coaching and Mentoring Programme

The most popular OJT method is the coaching and the mentoring method. Here the supervisor is accountable, and his performance measure or a key performance indicator is, to what extent he has gone to train the subordinate and coach him for better performance and a positive attitude. Coaching helps the supervisor to motivate the subordinate and reduce hindrances in his productivity and efficiency by listening, sharing, empathising and creating an environment to generate confidence in the subordinate to make his own decisions. Nowadays coaching as a process for motivating, training, raising one's self esteem and mobilising solutions from the coachee i.e. trainee himself/herself is increasingly used for various levels of managers as well as vice presidents and CEO's in all types of organisations. Many organisations are employing the services of certified external coaches for their various levels of managers. Tanuja Baljekar is a certified Coach who extensively coaches women entrepreneurs as well as personnel from Thermax India and SKF Bearings Ltd, both from Pune. As a deep impact of the Coaching exercise over many sessions, Baljekar has seen noticeable differences in the coachees, she says. "Their sense of self-awareness is certainly raised. So, they start doing things better. Besides, to a large extent they are able to change their behaviour for the better."

Mentoring

This method is similar to 'train the trainer' where, as a snowball effect, the subordinates are trained to perfect their skills, gain knowledge on the job and thus become more innovative to improve their efficiency and productivity on the job.

Many companies like Nokia, Mahindras and Zensar Technologies are using the technique of reverse mentoring to train seniors who are not as exposed to the new technologies, social networking sites and the new world of youth. As a structured process, once a fortnight the senior supervisor has a meeting with the juniors or the newly-inducted employees and learns from them the new technologies that could be adapted in everyday working, or feedback related to the established processes; and in turn the junior learns from the senior's experience. For instance, in Mahindra group of companies the nomenclature given to this relationship is called a shadow board. As the name suggests, the newly inducted knowledge professionals form a part of shadow, in a board of directors meeting, and suggest or add new technologies and share the youth world and ideologies, as ideas are discussed. This is known to lend a young and topical touch to the discussions and enhance their relevance in the changing times. These are common OTJ training methods.

A new form of mentoring called Reverse Mentoring is for younger employees to mentor the company President and other senior executives in technology-based working. A Chief Executive, for instance, may not have the computer skills to create an Excel spreadsheet. A junior from the information technology department is detailed to train the boss on how to do this.

The following information is provided by Business Management Daily.com: http://www.businessmanagementdaily.com/5871/you-mentor-the-boss-not-so-crazy:

You? Mentor the boss? Not so crazy

You may not realise it, says executive coach Jenni Prisk, but your boss might love to have you as his or her mentor.

"All the time," Prisk says, "your boss is subliminally asking you: 'Do you think I did the right thing?' 'What would you do if you were me?'

"She's asking for your input all the time."

Learn how to give her the decisive feedback she needs...

Prisk should know: She was an administrative assistant for 26 years.

So, how can you parlay the boss's unstated need for professional and emotional validation into full-fledged partnership, under which she openly asks your opinion on important matters?

Approach the boss about what Prisk calls "360-degree mentoring." Here's what she means:

Lay some groundwork by speaking up whenever the boss expresses uncertainty about a decision or a problem.

Example: "This seems like a tough issue for you. Would another person's viewpoint be valuable to you?"

If the boss accepts, give him or her your honest assessment. Stay cautious, though; you don't want to scare the boss away.

Master the decision-making skills you need to make a bottom-line contribution at work... Plus, the facts and figures to show how you arrived at your choice, and justify why it's the best way to move forward.

Ask the boss to mentor you. This will show that you trust the boss: the first step toward inviting him or her to trust you.

Example: "I've always valued your input and honesty. I'd really like you to mentor me."

Suggest that you meet at least twice a month for 30 minutes or so. Use the sessions to ask the boss what he or she thinks you should be learning about the business. Review decisions you've made and problems you've faced since your last meeting.

Offer, during one of your mentoring sessions, to act as a "sounding board" for the boss. Hopefully, the boss now sees you as a thoughtful person who's interested in the business's best interests and who brings a valuable set of skills and decision-making abilities to the table.

If so, he or she will jump at your offer.

"In the middle of a busy week," says Prisk, "you're giving the boss time to think. That doubles your value. You'll become much more of a partner."

But if the boss declines, don't hang your head. Instead, look for chances during your one-on-one meetings to gently offer your opinion ... and watch the boss warm to the idea of you being a mentor.

Apprenticeship Training

This is a process by which people become skilled workers usually through a combination of formal learning and a long-term on-the-job training. It traditionally involves a learner apprenticeship study under the mentorship of a master craftsman.

The Apprentice Act, 1961, was enacted by the Government of India to regulate and control the training of apprentices. The Act is intended to achieve two objectives: promotion of new skills, improvement, and refinement of old skills through theoretical and practical training in a number of trades and occupations. Employers covered by this Act are under a statutory obligation to provide training to a prescribed number of people. However the employer is not bound to offer employment to the apprentice upon completion of training, nor is the trainee bound to accept any employment offer, unless the apprenticeship contract specifies it.

Informal learning

Although most organisations have formal learning as a structured process, informal learning is also encouraged through initiating and developing measures like learning from mistakes, using experience as a basis for learning, and learning from a close interaction with senior colleagues through informal get-togethers like parties, conferences, seminars, picnics and so on. Cadbury Kraft Foods combines most of its training and developing module sessions with get-togethers, bonding activities and art sessions which help to facilitate creative working and opening of the right brain which is relatively dormant, and thus stimulates competencies like intuition, spatial skills and so on.

CASE STUDY: *Art to build teams*

The use of the right brain by engineers and technical professionals, who are very good at analytics, numbers, reason-based problem solving etc. - which are typically called left-brain abilities – is also encouraged at two-wheeler and auto-rickshaw giant Bajaj Auto Ltd., which uses art as a means of bonding and promoting self-worth.

Called 'ArtEnergy', these workshops are conducted by Australian international artist and visual communicator Christopher Hogan, who describes the programme as "incorporating art and a little of art theory as a team-building exercise". The sense of ownership and worth created by exhibiting completed artworks in work spaces, he says, is similar to that in schools where children are encouraged to draw pictures which are then put up on the walls. "I encourage the artwork from my participants to be displayed in this manner," he says. "I have many fine examples globally of my art enrichment programme enhancing many public spaces as a collection."

According to Amrut Rath, vice-president –human resources at Bajaj Auto, it was a "very refreshing experience", with more than 200 people exhibiting "child-like curiosity" and exchanging good-natured banter within minutes. Several people surprised everyone (themselves included) with their paintings, which they gleefully held up at the end for the group photographs. The paintings now adorn the walls of the respective teams' offices. After the corporate collage was put up in a conference room, even senior members were seen identifying their paintings and showing them to their colleagues.

"Your painting on your office wall is a highly visible recognition that touches you deep inside," Rath explains. "The ArtEnergy workshops were conceptualised to stimulate creativity and lateral thinking, as part of our efforts on holistic development. There is a sense of pride, which says that this company values you and what you create."

Hogan, who has worked with large corporations and companies around the world, says his system teaches employees to "harness individual creative expressions into workplace synergy". The whole purpose of this unique employee engagement initiative is to promote team spirit while simultaneously giving an avenue for individual creative expression. "It is very impressive how an Indian company like Bajaj Auto is taking team building more seriously and focusing on initiatives that are in the best interest of all employees," Hogan says. "I have worked for many multi-national companies throughout the world and I am very pleased to say Bajaj Auto is the first company in India to take up my ArtEnergy."

Both Rath and Hogan describe the feedback from the 220 participants, drawn across functions and levels, as 'excellent'. Though most of the participants had not touched a paintbrush earlier, the format of the workshop unleashed levels of creative energy that produced paintings of which even trained painters would be proud. "I am enthused by the response from the management and staff of Bajaj Auto and I look forward to my continued association with this fine company in the future," says Hogan.

Adds Rath: "Participants found this to be a very refreshing, engaging and fulfilling experience. This workshop has broken barriers of inhibition and stimulates hobbies, self-expression and original thoughts. This was not just about a painting class, it was about finding out more about oneself and colleagues, coming together as a team and instilling a feeling that each one of us is capable of creating a masterpiece. We believe that 'out-of-the-box' development experiences offer a very rich source of learning."

Questions:
1. Elaborate on the learning emerging from this workshop.
2. How does the left brain potential and learning help better performance? What are the enhanced skills and capabilities developed among the personnel through such a workshop?

6.5 Job Instruction Training (JIT)

In this methodology, detailed step-by-step instructions are provided in order to undertake the job effectively. Jobs which require such logical sequencing can be learnt effectively by JIT. For instance, manufacturing processes are taught by supervisors to the workmen using this methodology. More commonly, sales jobs are taught by adopting JIT. In Godfrey Phillips India, an FMCG enterprise whose core business is cigarettes, sales personnel are taught the skill of selling cigarettes by using JIT where the new salesman or the junior supervisor works with the senior sales staff in the market and learns the process of selling step by step by observation and explanation by the senior.

Lectures

This continues to be the most popular and effective method in imparting training and learning. Lectures are used to share knowledge and experiences by experts and by providing a platform for an effective sharing of discussions and clarifications of doubts.

Some points which trainers take care are:

1. They make the sessions interesting.
2. They are alert to the audience and fit with their frame of reference.
3. They break long sessions into short ones.
4. They use presentations which are attractive or tell stories.

Programmed Learning

Programmed Learning or programmed instruction is a step-by-step self-learning method that consists of three parts:

1. Presenting questions, facts or problems to the learner.
2. Allowing the person to respond.
3. Providing feedback on the accuracy of the answers.

The main advantage of programmed learning is that it reduces training time. It also facilitates learning by letting trainees learn at their own pace, get immediate feedback and reduce their risk of error. With the wide use of e-learning as a component of e-HRM, IT companies like Cognizant, as well as manufacturing companies like Sandvik Asia, increasingly use this method to foster the process of continuous learning.

Audio Visual-based Training

Audio Visual-based training technologies like DVDs, films, powerpoint presentations, and audio tapes are widely used. The Ford Motor Company uses videos in its dealer training sessions to simulate problems and reactions to various customer complaints.

Thomas Cook India Limited (TCIL) and Jet Airways record actual calls made by customers to its call centres and uses the same for training purposes. Telecom companies like Airtel and Vodafone also record the calls made by customers and use them for training purposes. Business schools' faculty use video recording and playback as teaching aids in communication, negotiation and behavioural science classes.

The Audio Visual method is effective in the following situations:

1. When there is a need to illustrate how to follow a certain sequence over time such as when teaching machine repairs
2. When there is a need to expose trainees in events not easily demonstrable in live lectures, a visual tour of a factory or open heart surgery
3. When you need organisation-wide training and it is too costly to move the trainees from place to place.

Teletraining and Videoconferencing

With teletraining, a trainer in a central location teaches groups of employees at remote locations via televised hookups. Honda began by using satellite television to train engineers. Several distance education programs in Business Schools like Indira Gandhi National Open University (IGNOU) use teletraining to train students.

Videoconferencing allows people in one location to communicate in real time with people in another city or country, or with groups in several cities. This may simply involve using PC-based video cameras and several remote trainees or a dozen or more learners taking a class in a videoconference lecture room. Here, key pads allow audience interactivity.

Computer-based training

With computer-based training (CBT), trainees use interactive computer based and DVD systems to increase knowledge or skills. CBT is increasingly interactive and realistic. For instance, interactive multimedia training integrates the use of text, videographics, photos, animation and sound to produce complex training environments with which the trainee interacts. For example, medical students, faculty in higher education for common or professional courses are users of this technique for deeper understanding of complex syllabus.

Internet-based training

Internet or web-based training is rapidly replacing other types of training. Customer service personnel in many airlines receive much of their required annual training via the internet. This is fairly economical and reduces a lot of travelling time, besides exposing employees at higher levels, to receive expertise from the senior experienced personnel located in another country. For example, Wipro Technologies exposes its senior personnel to web-based training for making effective customer presentations, decision making techniques and so on.

Wipro widely uses this technique to train its middle- and senior-level managers. The top management encourages and uses online courses available to employees. Learning Portals are used to arrange with the employer's intranet website that offers employees online access to many or all of the training courses they need to succeed at their jobs. Most often the employer contracts with applications service providers (ASP). When employees go to their firm's learning portal, they actually access the menu of training courses that the ASP Company contracted with the employer to offer.

Voice and Accent training in BPOs

International call centres or customer contact centres in India required Indian employees to interact over the telephone with their international customers. However the Indian accent was different from the West, where the customers were based. Indian employees were trained to alter their accent to a neutral one, so that the customers could understand the conversation with ease. There were also words commonly used that an Indian call centre employee has to learn. Indian employees also learn about the customer's environment, style, and culture. There are specialized private agencies to conduct this training with the support of state governments, like Gujarat and Kerala, training centres have been established to train the youth.

On-the-job performance is closely monitored and those employees who are identified for improvement are sent for remedial training. As part of the training, employees also watch movies or TV Serials like the TV show 'Friends'.

Off-the-job managerial training and development Programmes

The Case Study Method

The case study method presents the trainee with a written description of an organisational problem. The participants as trainees discuss the problem in detail through an interactive session. Most of the time, the cases are live or related to real-life issues. Participants are formed into groups and made to brain storm and discuss relevant issues and make a presentation of the same. This gives them an opportunity to dissect the problems in detail, provide an insight into the minds of others, and understand different perspectives to common issues. This medium provides a valuable technique for their growth and learning.

Management Development Programmes

The objective of Management Development Programmes (MDP) is to expose employees at all levels to acquire and apply the skills of management and leadership. In order to impart these skills, organisations have adopted a multitude of ways to do the same. For example, companies like Wipro, WNS, a BPO Company, and Bank of America have tied up with management education universities, which send their faculty to the premises of companies to hold lectures on weekend's .These follow the model of an academic pattern, with regular attendance, tutorials, assignments and exams. Employees' students here are awarded certificates, on the completion of the course and a good assessment. Another model followed by organisations is to tie up with renowned institutes and depute their personnel on weekends to these institutes for education and training. For example, Kirloskar Oil Engines have a tie up with Welingkar Institute of Management in Mumbai. In order to motivate students to enrol for these courses and participate effectively, companies even tie up the promotions and job rotations, sought by the employees, on the basis of their attendance and performance in these MDPs.

Some organisations like Infosys, Bharat Forge, Goenkas, have designed their own Universities for employees. These have a structured curriculum catering to the requirements of the industry and aimed at gearing their employees to develop the understanding and skills related to the business that they work for. Another area being focussed upon as a component of a management development programme is a Leadership Development

Programme. These modules are considered necessary by organisations to develop a pool of leaders in the pipeline and also to engineer a succession planning model. Mahindra group of Companies has a special Leadership Development programme at its Nasik training centre. Also Infosys Technologies has a special Leadership Development Training centre at its Mysore campus. The chief aim is to impart skills of leadership to all levels of employees and generate the benefits of risk taking abilities, innovation, motivation, people skills and so on.

The following is the common list of competencies underlined by firms for their C suite and middle level managers.

Competencies	1	2	3	4	5
Vital Competencies					
Analysis and judgement Seeks all relevant information; identifies problems, relates relevant data and identifies causes; assimilates numerical data accurately and makes sensible interpretations; work is precise and methodical, and relevant details are not overlooked; makes decisions based on logical assumption that reflect factual information.					
Product and job knowledge Ability to understand the business goals and objectives end keeps abreast of developments in the concerned area, both in the organization and external market.					
Result-oriented Sets demanding goals for self and for others: is dissatisfied with average performance.					
Planning and organising Plans priorities, assignments and the allocation of resources; organises resources efficiently and effectively, delegating work to the appropriate staff.					
Customer orientation Actively seeks to understand customers' requirements. Actions anticipate and pre-empt requests fat, service, based on well-developed relationships.					
External awareness Has extensive knowledge of issues and changes within the external environment and is able to identify existing or					

Competencies	1	2	3	4	5
Vital Competencies					
potential strengths, weaknesses, opportunities and threats to the organization. Understands the effects and implications of external factors on own decisions.					
Negotiation skills					
When negotiating, communicates proposals effectively, identifies a basis for compromise and reaches an agreement with others through personal power and influence.					
Communication					
Effectively assimilates information points and ideas clearly, is enthusiastic and lively, tailors content to audience's level of understanding, listens dispassionately and conveys the clear impression that key points have been recalled and taken into account.					
Team Building					
Gives clear direction and leads from the front whenever necessary. Fosters effective team working by involving subordinates' and adopting the appropriate leadership style to achieve the team's goals. Effectively monitors and evaluates the results of subordinates' work and provides feedback and advice whenever possible.					

CASE STUDY: **Behavioural Competency Frames at HPCL**

Individual Contributor Frame

An individual was assessed on five competencies under the Individual Contributor Frame as shown in Table 6.1.

Box 6.1: Competency Model - HPCL

Sr. No.	Competencies
1.	Dynamic Customer Focus
2.	Active Learning and Agility
3.	Co-operative Teamwork
4.	Enduring Commitment and Initiative
5.	Drive for Excellence

Process

Six tools were used to assess the individuals on the given five competencies. Each competency was assessed through two or more tools and each tool measured more than, one competency. The tools used were psychometric test, group discussion, in-basket interviews, team, simulation, simulation presentation, role play and competency-based structured interview. There were 3 : 1 assessors. The competency profile was shared with each and every employee in a one to one session. This was followed by the Individual Development Plan (IDP) Form.

Each employee was supposed to have selected at least two competencies from the opportunity/development area. The list of possible projects to be undertaken was discussed in the group along with VIPCL officers. The Individual plans and projects were also discussed with the employees and were laid down at the time of individual sessions. A sample report is shown which summarizes Competency Profile along with opportunity areas and areas of development in Table 6.2 and Individual Development Plan Form in Box 11.4.

Table 6.2: Competency Profile - HPCL

Competency						
Dynamic Customer Focus	Active Learning and Agility	Co-operative Teamwork	Enduring Commitment and Initiative	Drive for Excellence	Overall Rating	
						D
						D+
						C
						C+
						B
						B+
						A
						A+

Introduction

This report provides a description of the strengths and developmental needs as observed during the Developmental Need Identification Programme in New Delhi.

It is important for HPCL to grow and develop leadership talent internally. Therefore, in order to keep the leadership pipeline at HPCL, such reports are designed and seriously monitored.

Table 6.3: Individual Development Plan Form (A Sample)

1. Name of the Participant   :
2. Designation   :
3. Location   :
4. Name of the Supervisor   :
5. Supervisor's Designation   :
Developmental Tools that I will use to build upon competencies.

Name of the Competency:					
Development tools	Action steps to be taken by employee	Target completion date	Progress indicator/Result	Others involved	Nature of support needed from others

Signature of Participant

Date: _____

Definitions Used

Overall Score:

A +: Demonstrates excellence in all competencies with a very high frequency/consistency.

A: Demonstrates very strong capabilities in most behavioural strong indicators of all competencies.

B+ : Demonstrates strong capabilities in several behavioural indicators of most competencies and is considered the 'right fit' for the current role.

B: Demonstrates well developed capabilities in some behavioural indicators of several competencies.

C+: Demonstrates well developed capabilities in some and above average capabilities in remaining competencies in a consistent manner.

C: Demonstrates average capabilities in most competencies in a consistent manner.

D+: Demonstrates average capabilities in most competencies but not in a consistent manner.

D: Does not demonstrate expected behaviour across most/ all competencies of the current profile.

HPCL has so far successfully integrated the Competency Mapping process to the following areas of HR:

(a) Recruitment/ Absorption ion process/Performance Appraisal of Officer Trainees.

(A Sample)
Competency: Dynamic Customer Focus

Definition: Demonstrates concerning meeting changing customer needs in a manner that provides customer satisfaction.

D	D+	C	C+	B	B+	A	A+

His work pace should facilitate his ability to champion or deliver customer-focused initiatives and activities. His assertive nature should help him to effectively advocate customer-focused initiatives and activities. His interest in analyzing people should help him to recognize their perspective and adapt his approach to better influence them. This should help him to align business offerings with customer needs.

Demonstrated evidences:

In-Basket (Tool 1)

He demonstrated the concern for meeting customer needs that lead to customer satisfaction by giving high priority to the leper of complaint.

Creativity (Simulation Presentation) (Tool 2)

He symbolized pictures well. He could have demonstrated analysing data on customer needs and awareness of the market trends and competitors information. His approach is traditional.

Role Play (Tool 3)

He should have listened and acted on suggestions and feedback of the colleagues. He gathered and analyzed data on customer dissatisfaction. He could not demonstrate awareness of the market trends and competitors' information.

Somewhat cautious and skeptical in his view of others, he may not trust customer intentions. Concerned that they may take excess advantage, he may be reticent to suggestions and feedback given by customers.

(b) Behavioural/Technical Trainings
(c) Multi-rater feedback system
(d) Promotions from Non-Executive to Executive cadre

CASE STUDY II: *Meeting a Critical Need*

Ashwin Ramakrishnan was so happy being called into his company's Board meeting one more time, after almost 12 months. They wanted to 'raise a toast' to him, the CEO, Rajan Mookerjee, had told him over phone in the morning. The company's dramatic turnaround and its increased market-share were being touted as benefits of a strategic HR initiative that Ashwin had led.

And to imagine that just a year ago, facing the same Board, Ashwin knew he was up against an impregnable wall! As HR Head, on that earlier occasion, he had an important budget to demand and present to the Board. The annual Training, Learning and Development budget of ₹ 1.23 Crore. The company he worked for, Alchemy Inc, manufactured chemical intermediates for the global paints industry. Owing to the recession and certain domestic market conditions, including restrictive government policies, the company's topline had dropped 13% in the previous fiscal. Profitability had dropped sharper by 23%. The Board was clear – all departments had been advised to shrink and embrace austerity. The CFO Vinod Dangle, in a pre-Board review, had told Ashwin that he was not getting anywhere with his budget. "It will be shot down summarily," the CFO had ominously predicted.

Ashwin remembered his presentation with a certain confidence that even amazed CEO Mookerjee. Ashwin said: "Consider the quality reports and the customer feedback. Quality complaints have risen 33% this past year. Product rejections have gone up a whopping 24%, up 80% from the previous year. The loss we have incurred on account of defective and rejected product alone could have added 14% to our bottomline. The principal reason why we are facing these problems is that our aging workforce continues to make product without understanding what the market expects from us. They have no customer insight. They don't see value in following quality processes and confirming to global best manufacturing standards. Not because they are pig-headed. But because we have done nothing in the last 10 years in this direction. My proposal is to put our entire workforce, from CEO to the last factory hand, including key contract labour, through an intensive year-long Programme on 'Customer Sensitisation, Quality Appreciation and Best-In-Class Manufacturing'. This Programme will address employee attitude, employee skills and employee accountability in the raw material to finished goods cycle. This Programme will include Sensitisation Workshops, Customer Visits, On-the-job Training both at our plants and in customer locations, Internal Quality and Manufacturing Seminars led by experts and a special Rewards and Recognition plan that will celebrate Programme champions contextually. Our demand for this seemingly avoidable expenditure is not to fulfill a mere HR whim or want but to meet a critical organisational need. Without quality and customer, Alchemy is dead. Without a concerted Training, Learning and Development effort, that needs urgent sanction and immediate kick-off, we are not going to focus on quality or customer in a long, long time." Ashwin, of course, used data and graphs extensively during his presentation.

The Board members were silent for several minutes after the presentation. The CEO thought Ashwin's logic and demand were unputdownable. But it was the Chairman Harish Talwar who spoke first, applauding and approving the budget. All eleven members of the Board, including the independent directors, followed suit raising no objections at all.

The CFO, Vinod, over tea, tapped Ashwin on the back and said, "Huzoor, chhaa gaye aap! You simply mesmerized them!"

Questions:
1. Why was Ashwin so convincing? Was it his personal aura or was it data?
2. Why did the Board unanimously approve the budget without any caveats especially when it is so common, in a downturn, to slash Training, Learning and Development costs?
3. What's the other outcome that is possible and how could Ashwin have prepared to deal with it?
4. What would have been the future like for Alchemy Inc if the Board had rejected Ashwin's demand and proposal?
5. What are the learnings for your company?

Discussion Questions

1. Explain the need for learning and development.
2. How are Competency Models useful in Learning and Development?
3. Explain the various forms of Computer assisted learning.
4. What are the advantages of having a structured Employee Boarding?

References and Recommended Readings

1. Nisha Nair, Niharika Vohra, T. V. Rao and Atul Srivastava "Induction and Orientation", HR best Practices: Manufacturing Sector in India, New Delhi, SAIL, 2008, pp 90-96.
2. Kotter, "Leading Change" pg 85.
3. Leitch S. (2006) Prosperity for all in the Global Economy- world class skills. HM Treasury.
4. Marchington M, Wilkinson A (2008) Human Resource Management at Work. London: CIPD.
5. Senge P. (1990) The Fifth Discipline: The art and Practice of the learning organisation. London : Century
6. Human Resource Management by Adrian Murton, Margaret Inman, Nuala O Sullivan, Hodder Education, South Asia
7. Human Resource Management 12th edition, Gary Dessler and Biju Varkkey, Pearson, 2011.
8. Competency Mapping Models adapted from the Handbook of Competency Mapping by Seema Sanghi.

***

Chapter 7...

Performance Management and Appraisal

Contents ...

7.1 What is Performance Management?
7.2 Performance Management Process
7.3 Performance Appraisal
7.4 Graphic Rating Scale
- Discussion Questions

Objectives and Summary

This chapter explains in detail the nature of performance management, its features and importance, the appraisal process, types of appraisal, biases in appraisal and the need to be creative in designing the appraisals. The appraisals are appropriately designed in order to optimise the performance of the employees and motivate them to enhance their efficiency and productivity. The chapter stresses the importance of performance for survival and growth in organisations.

Performance management is related to creating systems of training, mentoring and developing a climate of experimentation and freedom for the employees to extract the best performance from them. Good performance does not happen in a vacuum. Employees at all levels need to be consciously counselled, mentored, trained and encouraged to innovate without fear of making mistakes and taking risks. There are various scales designed to measure and compare their performance. Appraisals are very important motivators for employees to put in the best in their work and surpass expectations in performance. Care should be taken to design and conduct appraisals which are free from prejudices and biases. There are many forms of appraisals apart from the traditional ones involving the superior with the subordinate, like the 360-degree feedback instruments.

Learning Outcomes:
1. Highlighting the importance of a performance management system to optimise employee performance;
2. Underlining the various measures for appraising performance;
3. Designing the performance appraisal system.

Introduction:

Recruitment and Selection of good-quality personnel does not guarantee that they will perform well. Employees need to know the details of what the job entails and what is expected of them in terms of functional expertise and behavioural attributes. These are called standards of performance and these too change as the organisation adopts new technology and adapts to new systems and strategies. Besides, the employees at all levels do not always perform according to expectations. At various times, they need training, support, guidance and motivation to achieve their best performance and ultimately for delivering high organisational performance. The term 'performance management' is often mistakenly used to refer to performance appraisal, or a practice which revolves around measurement and objective setting. While these are integral components of managing performance, however, performance management should be viewed as a holistic and integrated approach to managing the business. It is a comprehensive process which starts as soon as an individual joins the organisation and incorporates every HR activity like recruitment, selection, induction, training, performance appraisal and capability procedures. Most organisations today including the small and medium enterprises (SMEs) have a formal Performance Management Process for most of their employees at all levels.

The role of performance is a complex one. It is a mixture of inputs based on an individual's knowledge, skills and actions combined with the available organisational resources and support. For example, in a call centre the quality of output, in terms of promptness and accuracy in handling customer queries and reducing complaints depends upon the knowledge, skills, content expertise and behaviour of the employee or associate. These factors determine the quality of performance. In a similar vein, a student's performance is fairly determined or considered depending on one, the teacher's ability to teach and share valuable information; and two, the degree of patience demonstrated in solving the doubts of the students.

Performance Management is a complex process, often misunderstood, considered as an area of interpersonal conflict and difficult to implement effectively (*Latham et al, 2007*).

7.1 What is Performance Management?

There is no one widely accepted definition of performance management that describes its key features.

Armstrong and Baron (*2005, p2*) describe performance management as a natural process of management which contributes to the effective management of individuals and teams in order to achieve high levels of organisation performance. As such it establishes shared understanding about what it is to be achieved and an approach to leading and developing people which will ensure that it is achieved.

It can also be described as a continuous process of identifying, measuring and developing the performance of individuals and teams and aligning performance with the strategic goals of the organisation (*Aguinis, 2009*).

The objective of performance management is to encourage, support and sustain high performance at the individual, team and organisation level.

Performance management is strategic initiative and it consists of a shared understanding of how to improve organisational effectiveness. A well-designed performance management system is flexible and enables the organisation to respond to the changing economic and competitive environment. It is a holistic approach to managing people and brings together many interrelated HR activities to help and support effective performance such as induction, training and development, reward and recognition, performance appraisal and capability procedures. Line managers at various levels need to constantly manage and monitor the performance of their employees, have informal discussions about progress and problems, and provide feedback regularly instead of waiting for the end of the year at the time of the appraisal.

7.2 Performance Management Process

The framework of a Balanced Scorecard developed by Kaplan and Norton (1992) is widely used in organisations and translated into performance measures for individuals at every level in the form of Key Result Areas and Key Performance Indicators.

The balanced scorecard assesses performance on four measures or perspectives: the customers, financial, learning and innovation, and internal processes. All the processes are equally weighed and integrated. The balanced scorecard approach avoids overemphasis on the financial aspects of performance and allows managers to make connections between changes in one area with their impact on another.

The Performance Management Cycle

At the beginning is the induction process in a performance management cycle. The induction process is very important after the recruitment and selection processes. Even for the qualified and competent candidate, induction is important as it educates the new employee about the company culture or 'the way we do things around here'. The inducted employee needs to feel familiar with the socialising process in order to avoid isolation as the need to network is also significant glue that binds employees in the induction process, often accompanied by a buddy or a mentor, for at least a six-month period. The objective here is to educate the inducted employee with the strategic objectives, policies, programmes, standards of performance, career planning and overall expectations from him or her. Research studies show that maladjustment among the newly inducted employee is the cause for them exiting the organisation in a few months after joining.

Apart from the familiarisation process for the employees through a mentoring or buddy system, all the employees need to go through a formal and an informal process through regular meetings, feedback, project reviews, formal reviews, annual events, training and development, social gatherings and so on.

7.3 Performance Appraisal

This is an important component of Human Resource Management (HRM). Most organisations including MNCs, Service Providers and Manufacturing organisations have a formal appraisal process in place and conduct appraisal meetings. Such meetings are conducted as an ongoing process with the objective of monitoring and evaluating the performance of employees at all levels. One of the desired outcome from such meetings is strategising the need to leverage the capabilities of the personnel to raise the organisational performance standard. Most Appraisal Systems have components relating to targets or key result areas and competency mapping or commonly stated key performance indicators. These criteria help to appraise the functional areas as well as the technical expertise of the personnel so necessary in raising productivity and efficiency of the personnel and ultimately of the organisation. Organisations like Godfrey Phillips India, Cadbury Kraft Foods and GTL Limited have a detailed once a year performance appraisal design including key result areas as well as key performance indicators or competency mapping with a common ratio of 70:20 weightage for measurable targets and competencies respectively.

Why Appraise Performance?

The following are the main reasons for appraising performance:

1. From a compensation point of view, even today most employers still base pay and promotional decisions on the employees' appraisal.
2. The appraisal points out the gaps for the appraisee and helps to develop a plan to reduce the same and reinforce the things the subordinate does right.
3. This path or approach serves a useful career development purpose. It provides an opportunity to review the employee's career plans in light of his or her established strengths and weaknesses.
4. Performance Appraisal provides a blueprint for the performance management process and helps identify, measure and develop the performance of individuals and teams and aligning their performance with the organisation's strategies and goals.
5. The PMS also serves as an information base of the employee and provides valuable data for supplying current employee information.

Realistic Appraisals

While reviewing the process of appraisal and reviewing the various tools used, the approach that needs to be adopted according to experts should be that of candour and authenticity. GE's former CEO, Jack Welch, once said, "There's nothing crueller than telling someone who's mediocre that he or she is doing well." Someone who might have had the chance to correct bad behaviour or find a more appropriate vocation might find himself in a dead end situation. Hence as far as possible, in the long-term interest of the employee as well as for the organisation, a realistic appraisal is necessary.

Steps in Appraising Performance

The steps involved in the appraisal process involve the following:

1. Make sure that the detailed job functions and the performance standards are clearly spelt out and the measurable components are discussed and understood by the subordinate after a discussion with the supervisor.
2. Compare the actual performance with the expected standards of performance and point the deficiencies if any.
3. Finally, discuss the ratings between the supervisors and the subordinates and counsel or reinforce the performance depending upon the gaps existing in the performance of the subordinate. The following is an example of a rating Scale of an FMCG Company designed for their level of managers and Supervisors in sales.

7.4 Graphic Rating Scale

[(Sample rating scale reproduced here)]

Sr. No.	Area of Responsibility	WT	ACHMT	% Of KRA Achmt	Factors impacting performance +ve/-ve	Total % Achmt	% of KRA Achmt	Other factors that influenced the % Achmt	Increase / Decrease in % achieved due to external factors	Total % Achmt
					(Self)	(Self)	(MGR)	(MGR)	(MGR)	(MGR)
1	Delivering Business Result	30		115	Constant Monitoring of the team helped in surpassing the target	3450				
2	Financials	25		102		2550				
3	Train & Devel	15		102		1530				
4	Cigars	20		100		2000				
5	Candy	10		101		1010				
		100				10540				

Overall Achievement By Appraisee:

Total Weighted Performance	% of overall Achievement
100	

10540	105.4
100	

HUMAN RESOURCE MANAGEMENT   PERFORMANCE MANAGEMENT AND APPRAISAL

Sr. No.	Competencies	Functional Weight	Level Weight	Expected level of Performance	Total Expected Score	Self Rating	Manager Rating	Self Total	Manager Total	Manager Comments	
		A	B	C	A*B*C	D	E	A*B*D	A*B*E		
1	Managing Environment(EF)	1	3	100	300	125		375			
2	Customers Delight (EF)	2	3	100	600	120		720			
3	Delivery Busi results (EF)	2	3	100	600	130		780			
4	Strategic Thinking (IF)	2	3	100	600	125		750			
5	innovation &Creativity (IF)	2	3	100	600	120		720			
6	Effective Communication (IF)	2	3	100	600	135		810			
7	Continuous Improvement (IF)	1	3	100	300	120		360			
8	Systematic Approach (IF)	1	3	100	300	125		375			
9	Enterprise (IF)	1	3	100	300	120		360			
10	People Development (PF)	1	3	100	300	130		390			
11	Team Play (PF)	1	3	100	300	125		375			
12	Passion for Winning (PF)	2	3	100	600	125		750			
					5400			6765			
	SELF RATIO	TOTAL COMPETENCY RATIO --			TOTAL WEIGHTED PERFORMANCE SCORE						
					TOTAL EXPECTED SCORE						
					6765				*	100	125.28
					5400						
	MANAGER RATIO										
	OVERALL RATING (APPRAISAL *COMPETENCY COMBINED)										

7.7

The Graphic rating forms typically measure some of the prominent job relevant dimensions.

As denoted in the figure, some of the dimensions measured are as follows:

(a) Generic job dimensions such as team working, motivation and morale building, creative skills depiction, tolerance and promotion of leadership skills among the subordinates or all. As in the above example, the competencies of a sales manager in an FMCG company are measured using a rating scale of 100.

(b) Apart from the generic job dimensions, other dimensions as key result areas include points like sales of various brands of products, targets achieved as underlined, market share enhanced as predetermined and so on.

Such rating forms assess several things: the employees' performance relating to both the competencies and the measurable targets and objectives. There are columns dedicated to be filled by the employee or the appraisee, the supervisor as well as the reviewer or the manager. The aim is to provide a multi-perspective view of the appraisee in order to reduce the bias or the prejudice of the rater and give a fair chance to the appraisee as in most organisations, promotions, increments and even employee retention are based on the consequences of the ratings in an appraisal process.

Paired Comparison Method

The paired comparison method helps to make the ranking method more precise. For every trait (quantity of work, quality of work and so on) you pair and compare every subordinate with every other subordinate.

For instance, suppose you have five employees to rate. In the paired comparison method you make a chart of all possible pairs of employees for each trait (Gary Dessler, pg 324).

Critical Incident Method

In this method, the supervisor maintains a log book and records in it every dominant incident, good or bad, involving the subordinates. As a result, the subordinate is being assessed throughout the year rather than only at the end of the year when only the recent incidents remembered by the supervisor act as a basis for appraisals and introduces a bias in the process of assessment. The list of critical incidents provide examples of what specifically the subordinate can do to eliminate deficiencies. However, this method is not too useful for comparing employees or for salary decisions.

Otherwise too, it is useful to collect incidents to justify the reasons behind the employee ratings.

Behaviourally Anchored Rating Scale (BARS)

This is an appraisal tool that anchors a numerical rating scale with specific examples of good or poor performance. Organisations that use this scale say it provides better, more equitable appraisals than any other tool used.

Developing a BARS typically involves the following steps:

1. Write critical incidents: Record the critical incidents or specific instances of good or poor or not so effective performances of the job holders own as well as those provided by the supervisor.
2. Develop performance dimensions: All these incidents can be grouped or classified into different performance dimensions related to his or her core job functions.
3. Reallocate incidents: To further validate these groupings, have another group or team members to arrange the same critical incidents or events related to the job holder according to the performance dimensions. Then whichever are repeated, these dimensions remain.
4. Scale the incidents: The second group then rates the behaviour described by the incident as to how effectively or ineffectively it represents performance on the dimension.
5. Develop a final instrument: Choose about six or seven of the incidents as the dimension's behavioural anchor.

Computerised and Web based Performance Appraisal

Employers are increasingly using computerised or web-based performance appraisal systems. These enable managers to use or keep computerised notes on the subordinates during the year and then to merge these with the ratings of employees on several performance traits. The software then generates written text to support each part of the appraisal.

Dealing With Performance Appraisal Problems

Interviews with several employment agencies owners and those with the HR departments of organisations reveal maximum attrition in the post-appraisal period. Much of this can be attributed to 'surprises' for the employees post appraisal, where the feedback and the ratings do not match with the employee's self-appraisal and so the element of an unpleasant surprise drives them to leave the organisation. Employers are increasingly aware of the pitfalls in the process and highlight some of the common potential appraisal problems:

1. Unclear standards: Many a time the standards defined in the performance appraisal are ambiguous and the interpretation of the terms differs. This is so especially for terms like 'good', 'bad', 'fair', 'poor performance' and 'creativity', 'innovation', or 'quality of work'. This problem can be fixed by using more descriptive phrases to define and explain as to what quality or behaviour would mean good and what would be average i.e. those would be like expected standards of performance clearly mentioned in the appraisals.

2. Halo effect: Halo can be defined as "the influence of a rater's general impression on ratings of specific rare qualities". For example, an unfriendly or reserved employee is often rated low on most scales and not only on the scale of 'unfriendly employee'
3. Central tendency: Some supervisors or HR specialists often stick to the middle path and rate employees typically on an average rating between 3 and 5. This tendency often distorts the real picture and does not reflect the correct evaluation of the employee for the purpose of providing increments, promotions, transfers and job rotations. Many employers are now using the ranking method or a descriptive method in order to reduce the errors in this type of rating.
4. Leniency or Strictness: There are some supervisors or HR specialists who consistently rate their employees or subordinates too high or too low. These extremes are often adopted due to a sense of casualness in approach or strictness or a leniency problem of the rating supervisor due to his behavioural demeanour. These too can be controlled by using descriptive information to justify each of the phrases and validating the ratings by using instances.
5. Recency Effects: The recency effect means letting what the employee has done recently which affect or influence the ratings at the time of appraisal. This limitation can be minimized by maintaining a log book and recording significant incidents of the employee throughout the year to influence the rating process.

Bias: There are various forms of bias during the process of appraisal. It appears many times during the process of appraisal, and reflects more of the personality of the appraiser rather than that of the appraisee. This can be minimised by using a multi-rater system and a calibration meeting where the supervisors discuss among themselves their reasons for points or appraisals which they give their subordinates or peers.

Appraisals and the law

Bias and prejudices and incorrect handling of appraisals can cause legal problems for the employer and top management. In India, government organisations, both central and state, cannot withhold any information relating to appraisals which earlier were kept confidential. Now, under the Right to Information Act (RTI), an employee can insist upon the employer and the supervisor to disclose the rating and the detailed comments made and also the methodology used for basing increments and promotions respectively.

Who should do the Appraising?

Some of the main agencies doing the appraisals are as follows:
1. **The immediate supervisor:** The supervisor's ratings are the heart of most appraisals. In all appraisals, the supervisor is the most necessary component in the process of rating as he is always closely associated with the subordinate and closely trains and monitors the performance.
2. **Peer Appraisals:** In order to reduce the element of bias in the performance ratings of the subordinates by their immediate supervisors and with the widespread use of self-managed teams and cross-functional teams, it is now slowly becoming a norm to use peer appraisals for appraising colleagues and working team members of their

group. These are justified with instances or examples as a critical incident method. The perception of the peer group members is valuable to note the behavioural traits of their peers as well as performance efficiency and contribution in terms of innovativeness, organising skills, decision-making skills and so on.

3. **Self appraisals:** This is a method where the employees rate themselves. For this process to be effective, it is necessary that the employees are trained effectively to rate themselves so that the figures on the rating scale are not inflated to satisfy their egos. There is a human tendency to always rate oneself on a higher than expected scale. The use of a log book helps to balance this method and provide a more realistic approach to this strategy. The main advantage in this process is that the self rating allows the assessee to be actively involved in the rating process and be personally accountable and responsible for the functions to be performed effectively. However, the rates or points provided should be interpreted with care to avoid self-rater bias, which is a common error in organisations using the self rating approach.

For the benefit of learning, here's an appraisal format of a company called GTL Ltd. which is engaged in providing telecom services

Performance Appraisal Forms of GTL

PERSONNEL RATING FORM

(TO BE FILLED IN BY THE REPORTING OFFICER IN CONSULTATION WITH THE DEPT. HEAD)

PERIOD OF APPRAISAL: Last one year

NAME: _____ **DEPT.:** _____

DESIGNATION: _____ **REPORTING OFFICER:** _____

FOR DEVELOPING THE SUBORDINATES, THE REPORTING OFFICER MUST SPEND SUFFICENT TIME IN APPRAISING AND COUNSELLING.

Remarks of the Reporting Officer on the performance during the year (Particularly about achievement of KRAs):

Signature of the Reporting Officer

Guidelines:

(a) This is a confidential document and will be sent by the Head of the Department to HOD (PIR-HRD).
(b) Please note that this is an important instrument in development an employee's career. It is essential that you do the assessment BEFORE _____
(c) It is advised to have a joint meeting of all the Reporting Officers with the Departmental Head while filling the forms of the Department.
(d) Please make in box at the point of scale that gives the best assessment of employee.
(e) Recall instances typical of employee's work and ways of working during the whole period. Do not judge solely on the most recent instances.
(f) Be sure you will be able to justify your ratings objectively if called upon to do so by Reviewing Committee during review discussion.
(g) Scale Points given inside may be interpreted as below.

"5" Indicates Outstanding i.e. Exceptional Performance/Quality for surpassing expectations.
"4" Indicates Very Good i.e. Performance/quality which is definitely better than normally expected, which exceeds the requirement of the position producing result.
"3" Indicates Good i.e. reasonable performance/quality which consistently meets the requirement of the position.
"2" Indicates Fair i.e. marginal performance/quality which hardly meets the requirement of the position.
"1" Indicates Unsatisfactory i.e. Poor, Inadequate performance/quality, much below expectation.

JOB PERFORMANCE RELATED FACTORS

A. 1	Target fulfillment	Weightage	Scale Points	Factor Score = Weightage × Scale Points
	Achievement of targets w.r.t. assigned jobs	5	1 2 3 4 5	

A. 2	Quality of Work	Weightage	Scale Points	Factor Score = Weightage × Scale Points
	General Excellence of output, Methods and systems.	4	1 2 3 4 5	

A. 3	Cost/Time Control	Weightage	Scale Points	Factor Score = Weightage x Scale Points
	Optimum utilization available Resources/time.	3	1 2 3 4 5	

A. 4	Job Knowledge	Weightage	Scale Points	Factor Score = Weightage × Scale Points
	Thorough knowledge of his and Related jobs regardless of Complexities	4	1 2 3 4 5	

MANAGERIAL ABILITY/SKILLS FACTORS

B. 1	Planning & Organising	Weightage	Scale Points	Factor Score = Weightage x Scale Points
	Ability to anticipate work needs And match them with plans of Action.	0.5	1 2 3 4 5	

B. 2	Problem Analysis and Decision Making	Weightage	Scale Points	Factor Score = Weightage × Scale Points
	Ability to identify problems and Take consistently sound timely and optional decision.	0.5	1 2 3 4 5	

B. 3	Inter-personal Skills	Weightage	Scale Points	Factor Score = Weightage × Scale Points
	Ability for effective lateral Co-ordination vertical relationship And promote co-operation and understanding	0.5	1 2 3 4 5	

B. 4	Communication Skills	Weightage	Scale Points	Factor Score = Weightage × Scale Points
	Quick grasp and clarity of thought At all times sharing and giving feedback of relevant information with all concerned.	0.5	1 2 3 4 5	

B. 5	Self Motivation/Initiative	Weightage	Scale Points	Factor Score = Weightage × Scale Points
	Ability to provide thrust by Personal example and expert and time guidances.	0.5	1 2 3 4 5	

B. 6	Commitment	Weightage	Scale Points	Factor Score = Weightage × Scale Points
	Dedication to work & Company objective. Reliability to complete Assigned tasks.	0.5	1 2 3 4 5	

B. 7	Responsiveness to change/Innovation.	Weightage	Scale Points	Factor Score = Weightage × Scale Points
	Skill to quickly interpret and adjust to new situations and openness to new ideas.	0.5	1 2 3 4 5	

B. 8	Developing Sub-ordinates	Weightage	Scale Points	Factor Score = Weightage × Scale Points
	Ability to guide, counsel and develop sub-ordinates on a continuous basis.	0.5	1 2 3 4 5	

B. 9	Management of Human Resources:	Weightage	Scale Points	Factor Score = Weightage × Scale Points
	Positive utilization of sub-ordinates, ability to integrate employees into teams and motivate them to high levels of performance.	0.5	1 2 3 4 5	

B.10	Safety consciousness and positive discipline	Weightage	Scale Points	Factor Score = Weightage × Scale Points
	Effective leadership in contributing To safe work environment and positive discipline in the company.	0.5	1 2 3 4 5	

C INTEGRITY

ABOVE BOARD	OPEN TO DOUBT	SUPPORTING EVIDENCE IF OPEN TO DOUBT.

D What are the strengths and weaknesses of the appraisee?
(Please be descriptive)

Strengths:

Weaknesses:

SIGNATURE OF THE REPORTING OFFICER

SIGNATURE OF THE DEPARTMENTAL HEAD

Name: _____ Designation: _____

The periodicity of Performance Appraisals has changed over the years. From an annual feature, where there were surprises at the end of the year as a feedback, organisations have now realised the need to increase the frequency of the appraisal to reduce the element of surprise at the end. Companies like GTL Limited have a bi-annual performance appraisal, one in April and another in September every year. Raman Iyer, HR Manager, explains the process: "We have designed Appraisal Forms for all levels of personnel and these are administered by their respective superiors. We have tried to measure the Key Result Areas and the competencies in the ratio of 70:30. This means that the ratio of KRA and competency is 7:3. The objective is to base our increments and promotions on these areas which are discussed with the various levels of personnel beforehand."

Computerised and Web-based Performance Appraisal

Employers are increasingly using computerised or web-based performance appraisal systems. These allow the managers to use computerised notes on the subordinates throughout the year and then to merge the information on these ratings on several competencies or KRAs outlined. Most of the popular appraisal software combines several of the basic methods such as graphic ratings plus critical incidents or BARS.

IT companies like Wipro use online performance appraisals. A menu of more than a dozen evaluation dimensions including communication, fairness, and leadership attributes, judgement, are mentioned. Within each of these dimensions, there are several performance factors again in the menu form. Also in the companies of Aditya Birla Group, an intensive competency mapping exercise is undertaken. For all the levels of positions, details of competencies under several heads like in communication, team building, technical expertise, learning and development, leadership, management, empathy and emotional intelligence, are underlined and the appraisees as well as potential candidates are mapped against these competencies to be eligible for increments as well as promotions.

Performance Appraisal and Employee Engagement can be done through a social gamification platform called EMEE, developed by Persistent Systems. This innovation is considered as a forerunner by *Harvard Business Review*. eMee helps to engage employees by gifting them virtually and also warning them if their performance is not up to the mark. The hanging banana skin, at the social platform, reminds them of the consequences and hence goads them to pull up.

The following are the experiences at Persistent:

eMee was born in the summer of 2010 at Persistent as part of the company's efforts to bring a revolutionary change in the way employee appraisals were done. The company wanted to do away with the lengthy, inefficient and stressful end of year appraisals, and instead bring in fun and excitement to the process, and ring in a continuous assessment and mentoring culture. eMee has now transitioned to a full-fledged engagement and gamification platform for enterprises.

Now in its third year, the results have been stunning. Attrition dropped by 350 basis points, customer ratings have consistently gone up and employee satisfaction scores are higher than ever before. Regular feedback and mentoring have ensured that employees have a constant motivation and opportunity to tackle their weaknesses, participate in social goals, and see their performance improve long before the end of the year is upon them.

While it is difficult to attribute these improvements to eMee alone, it is clear that the new appraisal regime is leading to huge efficiencies. At a conservative estimate, the elimination of the lengthy end of year appraisal process will save the company of 7000 plus employees at least 30,000 person hours, by reducing, and in many cases, completely removing the need to sift through emails and fill lengthy appraisal forms.

Today, employees and managers have a single window into all aspects of an employee's performance such as KRAs, competencies, training needs, certification, and social participation. It is an invaluable advantage.

Part of Persistent's product portfolio, eMee has now grown into a full-fledged platform for serious enterprise gamification.

video: http://www.youtube.com/watch?v=kRBDbB3ta80]

Discussion Questions

1. What is a performance management system?
2. What are the various measures adopted for measuring performance?
3. What is performance appraisal? What are the limitations of a supervisor driven performance appraisal system?

Chapter 8...

Compensation: Establishing Pay Plans

Contents ...
8.1 Introduction
8.2 Job Evaluation
8.3 Types of Pay
8.4 Employees Benefits
- Discussion Questions
- References

Objectives and Summary

This chapter aims to explain the components of compensation, the various factors influencing the determination of compensation, the elements of job evaluation and the various forms of variable pay designed by organisations to motivate employees at various levels so as to achieve productivity and efficiency at work.

Compensation is the value in terms of money as well as non-monetary benefits accorded to an employee for the services rendered by him in an organisation. Research shows how compensation is one of the biggest motivators for retaining an employee at any level, as well as driving him or her to peak performance. Employers today are conscious of determining the compensable factors like knowledge, skills, competencies and working conditions required to optimise each employee's job performance and determine the compensation accordingly. A process of job evaluation also needs to be done in order to structure the compensation depending upon the nature and the importance of the job. More and more organisations are designing compensation elements depending upon the status and the preferences of the employees.

Learning Outcomes:
1. Identifying the components of compensation;
2. Designing a compensation plan for employees at all levels;
3. Describing the methods of job evaluation;
4. Deciding the components of fixed pay and variable pay in an employee's total CTC (cost to company).

8.1 Introduction

The employment contract is about an exchange relationship by which a specific quantity of labour power is traded for various rewards - a basis for all motivation theories. The conservative and the traditional approach to motivation emphasize economic rewards linked to productivity. The human relations approach emphasizes non-monetary rewards as a prime motivating factor while the human resource approach suggests that workers are motivated by many individualised reward systems.

For most employees, rewards as monetary compensation are the most important. The other major extrinsic reward is job security. Most employees prefer secure employment in view of their personal and family commitments or at least a sufficient notice period should their employment be terminated due to some reason like recession or a cost-cutting strategy of the organisation, or a conflict, or a poor display of performance.

At the 146-year-old Balmer Lawrie, as in most other public-sector organisations, job security is the big motivator. As HR Director P.P. Sahoo says, "People stay because of the comfort of a PSU. The pay that our 3,400 permanent employees get is not great, but it is mostly comfortable – especially down the line. It is much better up to the manager level than right up at the top. An average workman costs the company ₹ 4 lakh a year against about ₹ 30 lakh for the MD: those are the ratios with which we operate." This has obviously worked, with no lateral-level recruitment: most of the senior most people, including him, joined as management trainees. "People who have been here for more than five years do not leave," he observes. "This is because your identity gets subsumed in that of the organisation."

Intrinsic rewards are those that form part and parcel of the working day. These include issues such as recognition from peers and superiors, job satisfaction levels, celebrations on attainment of goals and a sense of belonging in a community. The importance of such intrinsic rewards should not be understated.

The reward that a worker or an employee gets from his efforts indicates whether his or her behaviour is appropriate, and is sufficiently compensated. Organisations must work towards achieving the right balance of rewards to keep the personnel motivated. Overall the system of rewards and punishment are used to immediately link different types of behaviour and their consequences.

Employee compensation refers to all forms of pay going to employees and arising from their employment. The elements and components include direct financial payments including wages; salaries, incentives, commissions and bonuses, and indirect financial payments like leave travel concession and employer-paid insurance.

Several factors determine the design of any pay plan: legal, union, company strategy and policy, equity and so on.

Most employee compensation systems in the world are guided by the framework of legislation. Fair compensation at work is an integral component of "Decent Work "as defined by the International Labour Organisation (ILO). In India, various laws influence the structure, computation and payment of compensation. Wage legislation in India is covered for non-managerial levels of employees and a section of workers from the informal sector. These are Central Acts, but the States have the freedom to make suitable amendments without diluting the essence of the Central legislation. Among the various laws in India related to wages and compensation, some examples are: Minimum Wages Act, 1948, Payment of Wages Act, 1936, and Equal Remuneration Act, 1976. There are separate laws which are enacted to cover bonus payments, retirement benefits, and social security benefits.

(Check the topic on Labour laws which include the wages and legislation)

Financial Rewards

Base Pay: This is the amount of money which is paid for a particular job. It is often called payment by time, where an individual is paid for a specific amount of time at work. This can be based on an hourly rate or as a weekly or monthly salary. There are many different types of pay structure but they tend to fall into two categories, spot pay and graded pay.

Spot rates involve payment of a single rate of pay per period of time and type of job. There is usually little opportunity for pay progression other than via a general increase in all rates often related to inflation. A spot rate pay system is simple to administer and is easy for everyone to understand. The minimum wage set by the government is a form of a spot rate.

The other main type of pay format is a graded structure. Jobs are assessed according to their worth and put on a "scale". Typically, the scale will be divided into grades or bands in which similar groups or jobs are placed. There is a variety of types of graded structures, but the most commonly used are the broad bands, job families and the narrow graded pay structures. Broad-banded structures have four or five grades within each band, whereas narrow-graded pay structures consist of a sequence of narrow grades, perhaps ten or more. Job family structures are when groups of jobs with similar characteristics are each divided into levels. The levels between jobs families may differ depending upon the going job rate. The salary of the employee will depend on where his or her job is placed within the band or grade.

Although this type of pay arrangement rewards experience and is relatively cheap to administer, it provides little incentive to do a job well as the payment will be the same however much effort to put in. Each year an employee stays in the job, he or she move up one more point on the salary scale. This can result in "grade drift" where organisations that have many long-serving employees: all end up at the top of the scale. Once they have reached the top within their pay structure, their salary will not rise unless they get a promotion.

8.2 Job Evaluation

In order to decide where a job should be placed in a pay structure, job evaluation has become a widely used method of assessing its worth. Job evaluation helps to determine or measure the true worth of a job. This is a formal and a systematic comparison of jobs to determine the worth of one relative to another. It results in showing the pay rates of a job or various types of jobs. For instance, one principle is that jobs that require greater qualifications, more complexity, and more responsibilities should receive higher pay than jobs with less such requirements. The basic procedure is to compare the jobs in relation to one another. Salary surveys help to price key benchmark jobs and then use job evaluation to determine the relative worth of all the other jobs in the organisation relative to these.

Compensable Factors: These are focused on factors that allow comparison of one job with another. For example, the factors commonly adopted for comparison include knowledge, skills, effort, responsibility and working conditions. In some organisations, knowledge, accountability, problem solving and responsibility are considered as compensable factors for comparison.

The identification of compensable factors plays a key role in the process of job evaluation. The factors to be included depend upon the level of a job. These will differ if the job is that of a cleaner, an office assistant, or a manager.

The various methods of Job Evaluation are:

1. Job Ranking

In this method, after the process of job description and analysis of the various jobs in different departments, the compensable factors are chosen for the basis of comparison to rank the jobs. The ranking is usually done department-wise rather than having one single rank.

This is one of the simplest and easiest methods of job ranking and it usually takes less time than others.

2. Job Classification

In this method of job classification or job grading, jobs are classified according to their level of difficulty or on the basis of comparison of the compensable factors. The groups are called classes if they contain similar jobs or grades in terms of complexity or difficulty levels. One of the ways to categorize jobs is to write the grade description or class description and place jobs into classes or grades based on how well they fit these descriptions. Alternatively, one can write a set of compensable factor-based rules for each class in terms of judgement, skill, and physical effort and so on. Then categorise the jobs according to these rules.

The classification method has several advantages. The main one is that most employers usually end up classifying jobs into classes regardless of which method they use to evaluate jobs. They do this to avoid having to work with and price dozens of jobs separately. The disadvantages are that it is difficult to write the grade or job descriptions and considerable judgement is required to use the method.

3. **Point Method**

This is also one of the most common methods employed to evaluate jobs. Here the several compensable factors are counted in degrees of their presence. For example, if the factor is responsibility, then degrees of responsibility for a particular job are counted on a total point scale. Further, assume you assign a different number of points to each degree in each factor. Then the total number of points is calculated by the evaluation committee depending upon the degree to which each compensable factor is present.

4. **Factor Comparison**

This is an extension of the ranking method. In the ranking method you treat each job as a separate entity and rank the jobs on the basis of the compensable factors for each division or department. In the factor comparison method, the same job is counted several times on the basis of the ranking for each compensable factor separately. For example, if the compensable factor is skill, then on the basis of this factor it will be counted. Then, if the other factor is responsibility, it will be counted again, and so on. Then, the total points are calculated and the ranking or the numerical rating is done. This is quite an extensive exercise.

5. **Computerised Job Evaluation**

The using of quantitative methods is quite time consuming and it involves consensus judgements. Computer-aided job evaluation streamlines the process. Most of the computerised streams have two main components. There is, first, a structured questionnaire. It contains items like details of the job complexities, the number of reporters for the superior and so on. This information is then statistically analysed through the customised computer programmes, and the jobs are priced automatically. Parameters like benchmark jobs, current pay are all incorporated to calculate the pay.

8.3 Types of Pay

Variable Pay

When pay varies according to performance, contribution, skill, experience, effort, or is paid as a cash bonus, it is described as 'variable pay' (*Armstrong, 2007*). This type of pay is based on the assumption that those who are motivated by money will work harder as they will get paid more. A bonus is usually a lump-sum payment either to individuals or to groups. Wright (*2004, 135*) lists the different types of variable pay:

1. Sales commission or sales incentive designed to increase the performance of the sales force;
2. Bonus payment related to the output of the team or business unit;
3. Executive increments that may be related to the success of the business unit;
4. Piecework where individual output may be measured and paid for accordingly.

Payment by Results

Performance-related pay is a form of payment by results, which usually makes up a part of the employee's pay. In cases where the output is more important than the input and the employees are pressured to achieve targets and adhere to the customer deadlines and promises, this form of pay is a big driver for the employees to achieve results and retain customers by adhering to the schedules promised. Most companies which have such an arrangement prefer to design a performance-related component of pay.

In India, IT and ITES companies like Wipro, Infosys, SAP, Accenture and Cap Gemini have a major component, sometimes even 30 per cent of their base pay component, as variable or performance-related pay. However, the actual percentage of the salary which is related to the performance varies for various organisations and types of jobs.

Merit based Pay

Performance Related pay in the form of merit-based pay too is increasingly becoming common to incentivize employees who perform jobs which have a specific target, or produce work which cannot be quantitatively measured. Here the employees receive a bonus over and above their regular pay. The bonus component varies, and acts as motivation to boost their productivity.

For this system to be effective, it is very necessary that the Human Resource division clarifies the expectations of the job from the employees and designs a transparent method to measure and determine the parameters of their performance, which are mutually agreed upon.

Employee Appraisal Ratings are a common form of determining how much bonus an employee should receive.

Employee Stock Option Plans or Share Ownership

There are many schemes in operation which encourage employees to have a financial stake in the employing organisation. These have become particularly popular after the 1990s when tax incentives were introduced by the government. Today many private companies as well as MNCs have some form of scheme related to the financial stake share or a share ownership scheme of the company.

In India, such schemes became extremely popular when media coverage led to the publicity of such a scheme of share ownership to all categories of employees at Infosys. The buzz around Infosys, which achieved a resounding success in its quarterly results and in the share market, saw even their chaiwallas becoming millionaires. Company founder N. R. Narayanamurthy's driver, for instance, sold a part of his shares to buy a flat!

Subsequently, many IT and ITES companies, as well as other private companies like banks have floated such schemes, especially among their middle and top-level managers. For instance, HDFC Bank has such a scheme of share ownership. The condition here is that the personnel need to abide by the lock-in period of a minimum of three years before they are allowed to transfer the shares in the market. Still, reports of such employees earning windfall gains from such schemes have been rampant in the media.

Although such schemes motivate personnel to stay in the organisation and promote enhanced performance and loyalty, the flip side is the market volatility. There are many factors influencing the prices of shares and not just the profits of the organisation. These factors may create a feeling of disillusionment among employees who expect a consistent gain from their shares.

Competency based Pay

Traditionally, as seen in the job evaluation programmes, the employee is paid according to the relative worth of the job and internally equitable pay rates are assigned for each job. It means that the pay rate principally depends on the job itself, and not on the one who is doing it.

In a competency-based pay system, the company pays for the employee's range, depth and types of skills and knowledge rather than the job title that he or she holds. These are variously called competence, knowledge and skill-based pay.

Different organisations define competencies in different ways. The US Office of Personnel Management uses competencies similar with knowledge or skills or abilities required to do a particular job. Another approach is to define competencies as demonstrable knowledge, skills, and types of behaviour that enable performance.

Normally, competency-based pay includes two basic types of pay programmes – namely, pay for knowledge and skill-based pay. Pay for knowledge is known to reward employees for learning organisationally relevant knowledge while skill-based pay tends to be used more for workers with manual jobs or technical expertise related jobs. Experts give reasons for pay based on competencies rather than on job duties. First, paying for competencies enables companies to encourage their employees to develop competencies which are needed for the achievement of the strategic aims of the company. For example, in Wipro, team-based competencies are preferred as most project outcomes are based on the team performance.

Secondly, paying for measurable and influencable competencies provides a focus for the employees' performance management process. For instance, at Canon, this might mean focusing the hiring, training and appraising activities on employees achieving higher levels of functional competencies.

Competence-based pay in practice

In practice, any skill, competency, knowledge based pay programme generally contains five main elements which are based on:

1. A system for defining specific required results;
2. A process for tying the person's pay to his or her skill level;
3. A training system for employees to extend the required skills;

4. A formal skills competency testing system;
5. A work design that lets employees move among jobs to encourage work design flexibility.

8.4 Employee Benefits

These are those aspects of the rewards which are made by the employer or the top management in addition to the overall basic pay given to the employee as compensation for the job undertaken. Benefits make up the remuneration package of the employee or the Cost To Company (CTC) as normally referred to by employers.

The type of benefit paid to the employee depends upon the philosophy of the organisation and the relative worth of the value of the benefit as perceived by the employee. These may include the following: Pension plans, Training and Development, Paid leave, free tea/coffee, Diwali party/lunch, child care crèches, onsite parking, life assurance, enhanced maternity and paternity leave and so on.

Organisations can compete on basic pay but it is often the benefits package which makes the organisation more or less attractive than its competitors. Those companies which need to compete for the best employer in the face of challenges of talent retention and talent acquisition adopt the basket of benefits package to make themselves attractive.

There are organisations which are quite creative in designing the benefits package and therefore manage to secure the retention of employees at all levels. For example, according to the survey of companies which ranked in India as "Great Places To Work For" have benefits like a concierge to run personal errands for employees, offer a chauffeur-driven car for the employee and the spouse to celebrate birthdays and anniversaries, a paid holiday to some foreign destination, a gymnasium at the office, subsidised food in the canteen, petrol allowance, discount coupons, meal card vouchers, leave sabbatical for higher education or pursuing some hobby and so on.

Flexible benefits

Many organisations provide flexible benefits to employees at various levels and tailor the benefit package according to their requirements. For instance, a benefit for a married couple may not be suitable for those who are not married or a benefit for children may not be suitable for those who do not have children. Sometimes the employees may take the benefits like pension or paid holidays or leave, for granted. The objective is to raise the awareness of the real value of the benefit and trade it for some other benefit. However, the administrative cost of this may be quite high and hence only companies with a work force of a high number of employees, crossing 1000, may extend such flexibilities.

Non-Financial Rewards

It should be understood that rewards do not always have to be financial in nature. Research has shown that organisations are also increasingly adopting non-financial rewards too as the basis for motivation and are increasingly adopting the same to secure retention of the employees.

Some of these are:

1. Recognition

Organisations adopting this kind of reward believe that this too works wonders. It may take a form of performance feedback such as praise by the manager or public recognition in some common function. Even simple praise can go a long way in motivating an employee and building his confidence. Some organisations have Employee of the Week/Employee of the Month recognition systems. Organisations like WNS, a BPO, have different performance targets set for most of their processes, and an employee achieving these is recognized by offering him or her team a meal, or a small souvenir after an appreciation party. This, according to the personnel at WNS, is known to take them a long way in terms of morale boosting and confidence. In Godfrey Phillips India, the organisation provides appreciation of good performance among the junior sales force, by putting up the achievers' photographs in the department. All such initiatives go a long way in boosting the confidence of the employees.

2. Opportunities to develop Skills

Organisations increasingly believe that providing employees at various levels with opportunities to develop expertise and skills, helps to facilitate their self-learning and skill enhancement, as well as fostering a belief that the company is assisting them in their life-long career planning. Organisations like Cisco, Unilever, Proctor and Gamble and Mahindra's have tie-ups with Universities abroad and the IIMs in India to extend learning and training to their various categories of personnel. This initiative is also very valuable to secure employee retention and confidence, and enhances the spirit of loyalty among employees. Such companies speak about reduction in attrition thanks to such measures.

3. Career Opportunities

This is also an important area which companies are adopting to track their employees' career moves and learning curves. Today with organisations becoming flatter unlike in earlier times, where the hierarchies were more vertical - which makes promotions fewer - employers and Human Resource personnel are helping employees to move across locations and functions to understand the work better and allow them more versatility.

4. Work Life Balance

For people in various stages of their career and personal life, some may value the availability of flexible hours to tend to their old parents or give time to their young children who need their nurturing, or even attend parent-teacher meetings at their schools. The retention of such employees is driven by the organisation's sensitivity to their work-life balance needs. Organisations like Infosys and TCS have a very strong philosophy towards work-life balance and they insist that their employees, unless absolutely necessary, do not spend long hours at work.

Total Reward

This is the term used for the combination of rewards, which include the base pay, benefits, allowances and rewards.

Armstrong (2007) suggests the benefits of the total rewards:
1. Creates a long-lasting impact on motivation and commitment of employees;
2. Allows for flexibility to meet individual needs and so employees are bound more strongly to the organisation;
3. Can serve as a key way for attracting people to work for the organisation as they become the "employer of choice".

Organisations need to be careful to create a right mix of their rewards to enhance the value for the employees. Many organisations offer a benefits package, but not many are good in showing how the range of benefits is integrated in a total reward structure and then communicating this to their employees.

Case Study: Non-financial Rewards

A manufacturer of electronic instruments located in Beaverton, US, has "You Done Good Award," notecards for employees to document and send "Thank you" notes to others in the company.

A Philadelphia-based leisure services company organises a day of appreciation for a deserving employee. The day and the reason for the celebration are announced in advance. The employee being honoured is treated specially.

In a financial services firm in Blue Bell, Pennsylvania, junior salespeople are bought a new suit when they first reach their sales goals.

PepsiCo headquarters in Purchase, NY, has a full-time concierge to help its 800 employees with personal errands such as booking restaurant tables and theatre seats, arranging events for children, and household repairs.

At the Office of Personnel Management in Washington, DC, a beautiful engraved plaque is given to the division's special performer by peers. A recipient can keep it as long as he or she wants, or until he or she discovers another special performer. The award is passed on with a grand ceremony and lunch.

At Singapore Airlines, the Managing Director's Award is given each year to those staff members whose actions demonstrate the airline's commitment to total quality service. Winners are celebrated, photographed, interviewed, published, wined, dined and praised. No special monetary award is offered.

At Levi Strauss & Company, based in San Francisco, employees nominate one another for an award recognizing initiative, risk taking, cost-saving initiatives and creativity. Winners receive a plaque and a cash prize at an annual ceremony.

In a temporary staffing agency, every time a temporary employee exceeds a client's expectations, he or she is eligible for a draw of prizes.

A car rental firm, headquartered in St. Louis, posts financial results of all its branch offices and encourages healthy competition. In this way, employees are motivated to perform at their best at all times.

On the occasion of every major success, employees at an Atlanta-based marketing services company, set off a siren to let all their co-workers know about it.

Vice presidents at a Denver-based food distribution company conduct regular employee appreciation lunches where they cook and serve the food. As employees pass through the serving line, the vice presidents tell them how much they are appreciated.

(Excerpted from www.humancapitalonline.com)

Case Study 2

The Chief Executive of a Multinational Corporation in paper and packaging explains that every company formulates its own guidelines on how to hire and what the compensation philosophy should be. This is top down and with a global approach in most of the MNCs. Local HR then works closely with the India-centric policy and then on the local philosophy.

Many MNCs have their roots in the country with a single representative office, and the first recruit is found either through the company's network and/or an existing Indian-origin employee abroad who wants to relocate to India for a short stint. Nowadays it is also important to have India experience on your CV, and hence many take up assignments in India. The salary is essentially a special expat package.

Post that, the first few recruits are hired without any real compensation philosophy, on an earlier-emoluments-plus basis. After few years the administration person becomes the HR head, and then it gets further confused as he does not have any scientific background on compensation.

Once the organisation reaches 50+ people, the need for a proper policy comes into play. People hire consultants and do the gradation etc. But this is not a long-lasting solution - it is more like first-aid treatment for postponing the main operation.

"In all my experiences the jobs were not comparable to a particular industry. In my earlier company, although we were in the bracket of FMCG, we did not operate in that environment. We hired people from FMIC (fast moving industrial consumables) businesses or pharmaceuticals where the salaries were more on incentives, whereas in FMCG the salary structures are very high. Keeping all this in mind, we made decisions on creating a grade-wise package in a range. We worked on a matrix combination of existing salary and fitting into a grade. This created hierarchical problems after a year.

"I am certain that no salary compensation package is transparent, well designed and scientific. I also believe that the marketing within the organisation has to be hyper in order to give a general message that things are scientific and transparent.

"Generally in a growing market, like everyone I also believe in :

1. High variable component to fixed (up to 40%) for sales, service and marketing guys, paid for the full year if on the payroll for the entire year and partial year if they join in between. Those who leave in between don't get any of this.
2. 20% variable to finance, HR, logistics and manufacturing. The same conditions of length of service apply.
3. Health insurance for family and one set of parents.
4. Car (leased) above a certain level.
5. No housing.

The common philosophy is to pay 75% of the benchmark industry your company falls in."

Discussion Questions

1. Why is compensation important today?
2. What are the various components of compensation?
3. What are the methods of evaluating jobs?
4. What are the various forms of variable pay? Explain monetary as well as non-monetary elements of the same.

References

1. Human Resource Management: Adrian Murton, Margaret Inman, Nuala O Sullivan, published by Hodder Education, South Asian edition, 2011, Chennai.
2. Armstrong M. (2007). Employee Reward Management and Practice. London: CIPD.
3. Human Resource Management: A Case Study Approach by Muller-Camen, Croucher, Leigh. Jaico Publishing House, 2008, Mumbai.
4. Ledford: 'Three Case Studies on Skill Based Pay' Compensation and Benefit Review, March/April 1991, pg12; Skill based Pay and Skill Seeking, Human Resource Management Review, 10, No 9, 2000, pp 271-287.
5. Human Resource Management-12th edition, Gary Dessler and Biju Varkkey, Pearson Prentice Hall, 2011.

Chapter 9...

Talent Management

Contents ...

9.1 Introduction
9.2 Career Management: Developing Talent Over Time
9.3 Career Development Initiatives
- Discussion Questions
- References

Objectives and Summary

The aim of talent management is to acquire, select, train, develop and retain employees who show exemplary performance through their unique combination of knowledge, skills and attitudes. It is essential to design systems and processes enabling talent to be retained in organisations. This chapter aims at understanding the need for succession planning, and the use of various diagnostic tools and features to be adopted to facilitate a conducive working environment for talent.

Talent retention is the biggest challenges confronting organisations today. Research has shown how the only differentiating factor among competitors is people and their talent. Organisations need to scientifically create assessment tools, diagnostic tools and monitoring systems to secure the right fit and develop personnel by designing an ambitious career plan for them. Succession planning is another process that organisations need to monitor, to avoid vacuums created by the exit of talent due to various reasons. Organisations also need to concentrate on creation of an employee-centric climate to retain manpower and provide avenues to promote them.

Learning Outcomes:

1. Explain Succession Planning;
2. Identify personnel for talent management initiatives;
3. Design Career Planning systems;
4. Create an Employee Value Proposition.

9.1 Introduction

Talent Management is the automated end-to-end process of planning, recruiting, developing, managing and compensating employees throughout the organisation. Because talent management involves recruiting, hiring, and developing high potential employees, it requires coordinating several high human resource activities - in particular, workforce acquisition, assessment, development and retention. In the simplest terms, talent management refers to "the process of attracting, selecting, and training, developing and promoting employees through an organisation". The main thing about driving the talent management movement is the availability of new talent management information systems; these integrate talent management related system components like succession planning, recruitment, learning and employee pay to enable seamless updating of data among them.

Talent management is in a sense career management from the employer's point of view. The employee wants to align his or her skills training, performance feedback and development in such a way so as to have a successful career. The employer for its part wants to integrate the same functions to ensure that it is using its corporate talent in the best possible way. One survey of CEOs of large companies said they typically spent about 20 per cent or 40 per cent of their time in talent management issues.

The idea that organisations 'compete through people' highlights the point that the success of an organisation depends upon its ability to encourage talent or human capital. The term 'human capital' is known to describe the economic value of employees' knowledge, skills and capabilities. Although the value of these assets may not show up directly on an employers' balance sheet, it still has a tremendous impact on an organisation's performance. As Jack Welch, Chairman, General Electric Company, said, "An organisation's ability to learn and translate that learning into action rapidly is the ultimate business competitive advantage."

Changing Attitude towards Work

Employees today do not equate their personal success only with financial gains. Personal fulfillment, self-expression and a work-life balance are the new key complex components in their attitudes. Research studies show that though most people still enjoy work, and want to excel at it, they tend to be focused on finding interesting work and may pursue multiple careers rather than being satisfied by just "doing a job".

9.2 Career Management: Developing Talent over Time

Authors on talent management point out, that regardless of whether talent relates to recruitment, transferring, developing, deploying or developing people, it needs to be considered within the long-term talent retention of the human capital. Integrating career development with other HR programmes creates synergies in all aspects of HR which reinforce each other. If career development is to succeed for the talent retention, it must receive the complete support of the top management. In the best possible way, the senior manager as well as the HR department needs to work together to design and implement a career development system. The system should reflect the culture and the goals of the organisation and the philosophy of the HR should be woven throughout. The HR can provide a clear set of directions and expectations for their career development. In order to achieve this, management should be trained in all areas of job design, performance appraisal, career planning and counselling.

The talent on their part should have clear knowledge of the organisation's immediate goals, technology and change. While talent management integrates a number of related HR activities, those who direct the process have to keep a steady watch on the needs and requirements of the organisation. This involves an analysis of competencies required for jobs, the progression among related jobs and the supply of ready and potential talent to fill those jobs.

In competency analysis, the know-how is broken down into three types of job knowledge, technical, managerial and human relations. These also include the competencies of problem solving and accountability. It appears that career development of talent can reap the following benefits: an increase in at least one skill area in one new assignment, and experience of assignment in different functional job areas. Earlier, career development and planning systems were primarily focused upon promotions and hierarchical advancements. However, in today's flatter organisations, and a more dynamic work environment, an individual's career advancement can occur along different career paths- transfers, demotions, exits and promotions. HR policies have to be flexible enough to adapt as well as helpful enough to support the career change.

Proactive organisations focusing on talent management emphasise personal mentoring plans that assign a mentor to employees who are recommended for upward movement. GE, for example, selects the top 25 per cent of its employees and allows these people to choose their own mentors based on the list of executives provided. Under a good mentor, learning focuses on goals, opportunities, expectations, standards and assistance in fulfilling one's own potential. Organisations with formal mentoring programmes include Johnson and Johnson, Shell International, Accenture and Hindustan Unilever. For example, interns in Goldman Sachs, India, become fully contributing members of the team and gain valuable work experience as they develop and demonstrate their skill in the financial industry. They work alongside the leaders within the industry as well as the top performers in the organisation who value the firm's commitment to excellence. The organisational objective of such an endeavour is to offer the type of responsibility and experience that will provide valuable guidance as they make important career choices.

There are various forms of mentoring. For example, Infosys Technologies invited school students of Standards 9 and 10 to join the organisation and learn about its nature and the various functions. This would inculcate a sense of understanding and help them realise their career dreams after they finish their plus-two levels. Talent management initiatives have become common place in organisations today. These are known by different names. For example, in Deloitte India, it is called 'Career Gallop'. For the ambitious achievers, there is a separate career path, which leads them to various upgrade levels as they achieve their objectives related to each level. According to company officials, such moves help to motivate the overly ambitious personnel and retain them, as there is appreciation and promotion as they achieve each level.

9.3 Career Development Initiatives

Although career management involves a good deal of analysis and planning, it should provide tools and techniques that help employees gauge their potential for success in the organisation. Informal counselling by HR staff and supervisors is used widely. Many organisations also give their employees information on education assistance, company policies, salary administration and job requirements. Career planning workbooks and workshops are also popular means of helping employees identify their potential and the strength of their interests.

In a recent study undertaken by Drake Morin, the six most successful career management practices by organisations are as follows:

1. Placing clear expectations on employees so that they know what is expected of them throughout their careers with the organisation.
2. Giving employees the opportunity to transfer to other office locations, both domestically and internationally.
3. Providing a clear and thorough succession plan to employees.
4. Encouraging performance through rewards and recognition.
5. Giving employees the time and resources they need to consider short-term and long-term career goals.
6. Encouraging employees to continually assess their skills and career direction.

Organisations need to be aware of some of the barriers for career development of employees:

1. Lack of time, budget and resources to plan their career and undergo training and development;
2. Rigid job specifications and lack of leadership support for correct management and short-term focus;
3. Lack of career opportunities and pathways for employees within the organisation.

Talent Management Systems

While employers have long 'managed their talent' without computerised systems, talent management today is usually information technology-based. Several software providers offer specialised talent management suites. The suites include and integrate underlying talent management components such as recruiting, training, performance reviews and rewards.

A talent management system is a set of procedures and processes that translate an organisation's talent creed and strategy into a diagnostic and implementation programme

for achieving organisation excellence. Most successful talent management systems consist of the following four components:
1. Assessment tools,
2. Multi-rater assessment,
3. Diagnostic tools,
4. Monitoring processes.

Assessment Tools

This is an important infrastructure of human resource systems and processes and the reasons cited for failed organisations is typically an incoherent mosaic of unconnected, incomplete, missing and inconsistent assessment tools and methods. Assessment tools include performance appraisals, assessments of potential, competency evaluations, career planning and replacement planning. The disconnect gap increases as the cost of implementing these programmes as separate and distinct is low, the time expenditure is high, credibility is low and the employee dissatisfaction is pervasive.

Successful organisations use a talent management model that contains the five assessment tools or building blocks.

For instance, the Competency Assessment, which serves as a building block of a talent management system, consists of behaviour, skills, knowledge and other types of stated expectations that are crucial to the success of each employee and to the success of the entire organisation. Competencies used for every assessment are expected to include the organisation's creed. Research indicates that organisations use between four and ten competencies in their talent management process.

Performance Appraisal

In a Talent Management System, the performance appraisal system is designed to include areas for which the employee is held accountable and the competencies are deemed critical to the job and the organisation's success. The competencies incorporated in the performance appraisal system should be consistent with the ones outlined in the competency mapping of the various positions and responsibilities in the organisation.

Potential Forecast

A potential forecast is a prediction of how many levels (organisation/job) an employee can progress within an organisation based on his or her past or current performance appraisal, training and development needs, career preferences, and actual and projected competency levels and positions that represent a realistic future job opportunities. Like any forecast, an individual's potential is subject to periodic evaluation, and is heavily influenced by the quality of the input provided by different assessor groups and by a variety of situational factors associated with job conditions at different moments in time. Researchers collectively have highlighted three critical attributes which can be used to assess potential no matter what assessment process or rating system is used. These attributes are as follows:
1. How does an individual set his or her business agenda right?

2. How does the person take others with him or her?
3. How does the person present herself or himself as the leader?

It would be reasonable to assume that periodic multi-rater assessments based on these attributes could generate a reasonable forecast or potential.

Measurement Scales for Performance and Potential

Most organisations in some type of successful talent management process showed that the vast majority use a simple five point scale to measure performance and potential. The most common scale for performance measurement is as follows:

Greatly exceeds expectations (5), exceeds expectations (4), meets expectations (3), below expectations (2), greatly below expectations (1). The most common scale for potential assessment is: high potential (5), promotable (4), lateral or job enrichment (3), marginal (2), none (1). The above scales are straightforward and they achieve credible results.

Succession Planning

In the broadest sense the process that seeks to identify replacement candidates for current incumbents and potential future job openings and to assess the time frames in which they can move to these positions.

Career Planning

This process identifies potential next steps in an employee's career and his or her readiness to move to new positions. Career Planning merges the organisation's assessment of employee growth readiness, employee career preferences and the likelihood that positions in a career path will become available.

Organisations as a part of their talent management strategy needs to publicise the extraordinary performance attributes required for any position, to facilitate and enable employees to plan their career and advancements in positions accordingly.

Extensive research has been conducted on competencies over the past 20 years. It is established that competencies are in relative high supply in the labour pool like Drive for Results, and those which are in short supply are dealing with Ambiguity. It must be reiterated that competencies are most related to performance at the various stages of career development.

Competencies can be grouped into unique combinations that are used to define success for a particular context. These particular competency models are often referred to as competency success profiles. Common applications of success profiles include the following:

1. Role-specific success profiles based on job analyses are often used to create job descriptions, guide behaviour-based interviews, generate development plans, aid in selection for assignments, and promotions, and generally inform workforce planning activities.
2. Position-level specific success profiles are often used to enhance career planning and development.

3. Core organisation competency profiles reflect the set of critical competencies required throughout the firm to shape the organisational capabilities and culture required to achieve the strategic intent.

An accurate competency success profile represents the ideal leadership texture for a particular context. It describes those people who perform well and deliver results in that particular context, the people who are deemed competent. Those who most closely mirror the competencies in the success profile will be considered the most competent, the star performers. They will deliver the highest value to their organisations, and to the extent that they perform in a meritocracy, they will receive rewards that reflect their results.

Other leadership competency competencies such as Conflict Management, organising, interpersonal savvy and organisational agility are very important for success even for individual contributors in the most technical of positions. While people in these positions are often hired for functional-technical competence, they are far more likely to have performance problems, even derail, because of deficiency in other leadership competencies. For senior executives, functional technical competencies typically contribute very little to leadership effectiveness.

Competency Success profiles can be created by analysing data from several sources:

1. Research and empirical studies and normative data that indicate what's most important for a defined role, such as that of a Chief Financial Officer, or for a defined context such as a turnaround situation.
2. Executives or executive leadership teams who typically with the assistance of a competency expert have identified the competencies that most closely map to business-specific factors such as strategy, mission, vision and values.
3. Subject matter experts who are exemplary performers in the targeted role led by a skilled facilitator.

It is common to use a combination of these methods and any of them will likely result in placing competencies into one of at least two classifications. 'Price of admission' competencies are those important for the context but in high supply in the target population.

Regardless of the method or combination of methods used to create a success profile, it's a best practice to have a team of key stakeholders validate it through a group process facilitated by a skilled competency practitioner. This helps achieve buy in and support from key leaders who are in a position to promote it in the organisations.

An ideal Performance Appraisal Management System

It includes the following:
1. Organisational Competencies (Behaviour Component)
2. Job Family Competencies
3. Key Job Responsibilities
4. Goals/Major Projects

How to Create an ideal Performance Management System
1. Get the top management actively involved.
2. Establish the criteria for an ideal system.
3. Appoint an implementation team.
4. Design the form first.
5. Build your vision, mission, values and competencies into the form first.
6. Ensure an ongoing communication.
7. Train all appraisers.
8. Orient all appraisees.
9. Use the Results.
10. Monitor and Revise the Programme.

Creating an Effective Employee Value Exchange (EVE)

Sibson has redefined the traditional definition of employee value exchange to include the expectations of the employer. Simply put, the EVE examines the balance between the rewards employers offer and the expectations they set in exchange for those rewards. This is done using Sibson's Rewards of Work Model which examines the proposed suite of rewards an employer offers its employees.

In this model there are five types of rewards:
1. **Affiliation:** The sense of feeling of belongingness to an admirable institution that shares the employees' values.
2. **Compensation:** The money employees receive for their work and performance.
3. **Benefits:** Indirect compensation including health insurance, retirement, and time off.
4. **Career:** Employees' long term opportunities for development and advancement.
5. **Work Content:** The satisfaction employees receive from the work they perform.

Each of these factors affects current and potential employee decisions concerning their employment, especially whether to move to a new job or stay in the current one.

From the organisational perspective, the following factors are important:
1. **Performance:** The specific levels of discretionary efforts required, and the desired objectives needed to achieve the organisation's stretch goals and deliver superior performance.
2. **Three Cs of team work:** The coordination, collaboration and communication of organisational performance that is expected of individuals within and across business units and teams.
3. **Engagement:** The knowledge of what the priorities are and the motivation to attain them.

4. **Behaviour:** The acceptable/desired behaviours required of individuals to support the desired culture and achieve results.
5. **Retention:** The level of retention that is desired of individuals and required to support the overall business strategy.

All these are in the form of the organisations' expectations from their various levels of manpower.

Employees need to understand the value exchange process with their organisations and its expectations from them. All in all, the desire is to match the two and align the expectations of each in order to drive the desired results.

What Keeps Talent?

These are the factors influencing job satisfaction, and commitment:
1. Exciting, challenging and meaningful work.
2. Supportive manager, great boss.
3. Being recognised, valued and respected.
4. Career growth, learning and development.
5. Flexible work environment.
6. Job security and stability.
7. Fair pay.
8. Job location.
9. Working with great coworkers and clients.
10. Pride in the organisation, mission and product.
11. Fun, enjoyable work environment.
12. Good benefits.
13. Loyalty to my co-workers and boss.

(**Source:** *Love 'em or Lose 'em: Getting Good people to Stay. Berrett-Kochler. Publishers: Beverly Kaye and Sharon Jordan-Evans; 4th edition (January 2008).*

Retaining Talent

As one head of talent at a multinational company expressed it, "It's not much good if you have a succession plan and the talent you need has left." The objective of talent management is to recruit people who are likely to stay and adapt to the changing roles in an organisation rather than hiring a person who is likely to fit in a particular role. It has been echoed by practitioners that understanding the dynamics of how long a talented employee is likely to stay in the organisation is very important. When an employee quits, the costs associated with recruitment, selecting and training replacements often 100 per cent of the annual salary. The costs associated would also include loss of succession planning, costs associated with allowing the talented employees to make mistakes and learn from them and the cost of the full focus by the managers on them rather than on the average performers (*Cascio 2006; Mitchell et al, 2001*). Talented employees are also more likely to be people with extensive relationship networks in the organisation; losing them has a particularly strong negative impact on the business (*Shaw et al, 1998; Shaw et al, 2005*). It has also been observed that many a time, the talented employees, when they leave, take many other already employed talented employees with them, to other organisations. For instance, when Ramesh Sobti, VP, ABN Amro Bank, left the bank to join a private player like Indusind Pvt Ltd, he took many top personnel with him to join the private bank. Today, he and his team are known to have secured a turnaround in the bank. Many Indian companies are known to follow this trend of the talented employee taking with him more talent from the same organisation.

The obvious question is: What makes employees quit? There appear to be many reasons, but it appears to be that pay is not anywhere near the top of the list (*Griffeth et al, 2000*) nor job dissatisfaction (*Lee et al, 1999*) but having a sense of decreased opportunity is. So, it makes sense for employees to try to identify and promote opportunities for employees. Some of the ways of classifying opportunities are:

1. **Blue Sky:** This is a medium to distant future, dependent on a platform, of changes not directly applicable to individuals.
2. **Medium term:** Emergent from existing plans and strategies, relevant to employees with specific aptitudes with track record.
3. **Short term:** Known changes of role or position, for which candidates will be sought in the next few months.

Research into employee retention tells us that people who stay tend to be those who are most embedded in the organisation (*Mitchell et al, 2001*). Embeddedness is related to fit and links and sacrifice. Fit is the value match, links are the networks we build with colleagues, sacrifice is the employers' perception of what the employees are likely to give up if they leave the organisation in terms of perks, status, promotion, work location, convenience and status.

Creating an Environment for Alignment

Apart from the various features mentioned above, it is important to note that talented employees should be encouraged to investigate areas that interest them and to share their learning. For example, companies like Google give employees a percentage of their time to follow their noses on ideas they choose (*Smith and Paquatte, 2010*). Although there is no empirical evidence on the impact on their core role, evidence suggests that there is no negative impact on their performance in terms of quality and quantity of output.

Nowadays with the workforce comprising more of Generation Y or Millennial talent, James et al (2008) found that gen Y regards works differently to Baby Boomers – less as a means to live than as an important part of their social life. They expect to be trusted to work from home most of the time. They also place a high value on learning from peers and mentors. They expect to be valued for their strengths and given the opportunities to use their strengths. They exert their own individuality and do not wish to be stereotyped. They are also more likely to quit if they do not feel aligned to the organisation and its culture, or if there is a poor leadership. Here transparency and a proper systematic process of talent growth is required to retain talent and facilitate an environment in the organisation through trained leadership where they put in their best efforts and are motivated to learn and grow.

In today's times, it is important for the organisations to think beyond the traditional models of career and expand their thinking to an overall career development and growth strategy that focuses on three critical groups: the organisation, the manager and the employee. To begin, we need to ask a lot of questions. Investigate what's happening in your organisation to discover the truth about the development culture (Talent Management Handbook).

Case Study

Never hire someone who knows less than you do about what he's hired to do.

– Malcolm Forbes, Former Publisher of Forbes

"How true!" remarked the CEO of a leading advertising agency as she came across a similar situation in her own office. In a service business like advertising having the right kind of human resources is critical for the company's success and hiring the right one an important decision. New employees bring in a fresh prospective and infuse the organisation with vigour and enthusiasm. Especially for a business that thrives on newness, hiring the right people is paramount as it brings in innovative ideas, concepts, learning and trends and sets the course for the business's future. Being a prominent agency the company had always attracted good talent and was known as an agency that always reinvented itself and consistently achieved success, but now managing that talent was appearing to be a new ball game altogether.

A young member of the agency who had joined a few months back walked up to the HR manager with her resignation. When asked why she wanted to quit, her answer was that she had not expected advertising to involve such hard work. In another case a bright copy talent, who had recently joined the firm and was just turning out to be a good performer, decided to put in her papers as she wanted to be with her partner abroad. The CEO thought that there must be something more to what meets the eye and wanted to check the reasons for all the exits in the company in the last one year. As expected, she indentified a trend, a pattern emerging which had to be acknowledged.

The following were her observations:

She realised that there are two kinds of professionals. The first kind is very hardworking, driven, ambitious and willing to switch jobs at the drop of a hat. They do not want to hang on to an organisation for more than 15 months. Facebook and other social networking sites have a large role to play. Since everybody is connected to everybody else the pressure to conform and appear cool is very high.

The second kind has an entitlement mentality, which translates to wanting everything on a platter. They think work is a relaxed affair where they don't need to push very hard. They do not like to work beyond 6.30 pm and actually quit a job saying they did not expect it to be so strenuous. They are a part of an entire generation of soft people, who do not have the wherewithal to handle some obstacles and hardships. Despite explaining the job profile in detail, at the first sign of difficulty they want to rethink their options.

Most of them are from upper-middle-income families with good English-speaking skills and many attend tony schools. They do not know what a corporate life actually entails and confuse it with the easy-go fantasy lifestyle they concoct. Misleading TV shows, films and pop culture, where professions like Media & Advertising are portrayed in a very glamorous manner, have led to this sad state of affairs and miscued view of the corporate world. On the flip side the findings were that people from smaller towns and lower middle families are more hungry and focused and willing to put in long hours and build their careers.

Another noticeable trend was that the promise shown during the interview by prospective candidates did not really translate into action when the company actually hired them. An internal analysis showed that interviews were a woefully inadequate technique to gauge the actual potential of prospective employee and fell flat when it came to hiring somebody on a long-term basis. The CEO felt that interviews are soon losing relevance and they need to be backed up with written tests, group discussion, situation analysis test etc.

The CEO observed how the youngsters of today are also confused and a plethora of options is the real culprit. They do not know what they want to pursue. After showing a lot of promise in the first year they suddenly decide to chuck corporate life completely and start writing scripts, or pursue dance. Of course they discover all this after the organisation has taken great efforts to train them and just when they are showing promise – and they decide this is not what they want to do at all.

She felt that the young professional of today is intelligent, confident and has good exposure. What he needs is focus, a good work ethic, perseverance and ability to learn. This gap has to be addressed at school level as by the time a student graduates he knows how much work he needs to put in to get by. He has to realize that 'A rolling stone is not going to become an expert at anything'. Although his salary will keep on rising he will lack knowledge and will not possess the required depth to go to the top echelons of management.

So what should be done, was the big question.

The CEO thought a consistent and continuous effort was required to resolve the issue.

First, the recruitment process had to change, a deeper understanding of the prospective employee was required. Thus it was decided that henceforth a more practical assessment would be employed, with group discussions, situational understanding and problem-solving skills put to use.

A weekly meeting would be held where employees would be asked to present their views on:

- What should we start doing?
- What should we stop doing?
- What should we keep doing?

Efforts would be taken to promote team work and recognise the efforts of employees and team leaders would be asked to assess their team members on a regular basis and try and identify any signs of dissatisfaction or decreasing confidence if any.

Questions:
1. How important is attracting and managing talent for the organisation?
2. Do you agree that a more holistic approach should be employed for employee retention and contingency planning?
3. How should a leader handle such a situations if it does arise?
4. Do you agree with the steps taken by the CEO to resolve the crisis? What would you have done if you were in her place?

CASE 1
The Glass Case

The Background: A Container Glass company was undergoing capacity expansion plans and enlarging its market reach. With 24% CAGR over the past 5 years, the company was the 2nd Largest Container Glass Player nationally. It catered to 80% of the container glass business customers across industry segments. The company was an SBU of a multi-sectoral 1000+ crore enterprise. The manufacturing facilities are located at Hyderabad and Bhongir, which is 50 kms away from Hyderabad.

The Recruiting Challenge: The Chief of Marketing was close to super annuation. Hence, the company had to identify the 'right' marketing professional so that the transition could be smooth and complete. The number of suitable candidates available within the industry was limited.

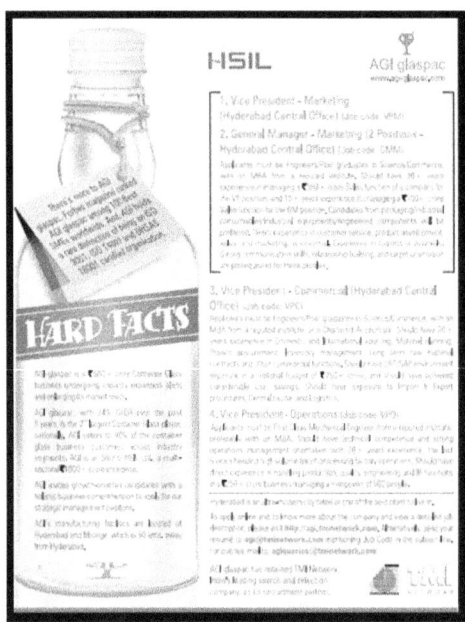

Recruiting Insight:

The Target Group and Source Map were expanded to Cement, Steel and so on. This resulted in a diverse list of applicants engaged in comparable business and comparable marketing challenges (Like profits of clients, Rupee value of business and Just-in-Time supplies).

Since the position was very crucial for the company, a quarter page advertisement was released in a business newspaper, a business magazine and a national daily. A phenomenal 177 resumes that arrived made assessment a veritable nightmare. In order to trim the long list down to a shortlist of 43 candidates (which itself was a fairly daunting number for a senior position), extensive assessment and coordination efforts went in. Detailed additional information (apart from resume) was sought from the applicants. A set of three senior executives reviewed every applicant spending several man-days each. In short, eliminating candidates itself is time consuming and an elaborate process.

- T. Muralidharan, Chairman TMI Group of Companies.

CASE 2
Article on Talent Management (Practices in Organizations)

Talent Sourcing and Development has been a big challenge for HR Managers in growing companies. How to develop, nurture and retain high-potential talent is a key concern for CEOs and HR heads. Retaining such employees also helps a business to preserve organisational knowledge. Perhaps the greatest challenge that business leaders face today is how to stay competitive amid constant turbulence and disruption. Today's marketplace is incredibly competitive in every industry around the globe.

This is perhaps what led the India-born CEO of PepsiCo Indra Nooyi to comment: "The difference between success and failure is talent, period." One of the documents by the global consultancy firm, McKinsey, brought out a few years ago mentioned that 'War for Talent' will become a differentiator.

Organisations are keen to build a leadership pipeline to grow their current businesses and to address growth opportunities - through new markets, new products and newer geographies. This often leads the HR Director, COO and CEO to identify high-potential candidates to prepare the leadership to take on higher and strategic roles to drive the firm's growth.

Traditionally FMCG companies like ITC and HUL have undertaken this task by identifying high-potential candidates. Many organisations have set up their own leadership development initiatives to develop talent, like the Tata group's TAS (Tata Administrative Services), the Aditya Birla group's Gyanodaya and the Infosys Leadership Institute.

The New Delhi-based Leadership Development consulting firm Organisation Development Alternatives (ODA) has been helping identify, train and coach high-potential candidates in several Indian firms from the Engineering, Pharma, FMCG and Telecom sectors.

ODA conducts a one-year leadership development programme that has three workshops spread over a period. These workshops are:

1. Leading Self;
2. Leading others;
3. Leading Systems and Innovation.

Says Santhosh Babu, founding managing director of ODA: "Creating a talent pipeline that is ready to take on higher roles is one of the biggest challenges organisations face. One way to prepare a cadre of people is to take them through an integrated learning journey."

ODA's clients EIL (Engineers India Ltd), pharmaceutical companies Merck and Novartis, and telecommunications service provider Vodafone, for example, were preparing their leaders to take on higher and bigger roles. EIL has taken 40 of its people through a year-long leadership development journey. Max Life Insurance has also taken its 120 leaders though an Integrated Leadership Development Intervention that has classroom sessions, one-to-one coaching and workplace projects.

Identifying talent practices adopted by some of the organisations in which ODA is training employees, Santhosh Babu lists

1. Assessment and Development centres;
2. Competency frameworks and balanced scorecard;
3. High-potential identification and development.

[From the soon-to-be-published book A Complete Reference to Acquisition of Indian Talent by T. Muralidharan and Anu Srinivasan]

Discussion Questions

1. What are the various initiatives to retain talent?
2. What is career planning?
3. Why is succession planning important?
4. What are the measures adopted to create an employee-centric climate at work?

References

1. Human Resource Management by Scott Snell, George Bohlander and Veena Vohra. Cengage Learning. 2011. New Delhi.
2. Larry Cambron, "Career Development Pays" Far Eastern Economic Review, 64, No 42 Oct., 25, 2011; 83.
3. Cascio W.F. (2006). The economic impact of employee behaviours on organisational performance. California Management Review, 48 (4), pp 41-60.
4. Griffeth R. W., Hom, P. W. and Gaertmer S. (2000) A meta analysis of antecedents and correlates of employee turnover: updates, moderator tests and research implications for the next millennium. Journal of Management, 26, 463-88.
5. James A. Bibb S, and Walker S. (2008) A summary report of the "Tell it how it is" Research talentsmoothie, Newbury, www.talentsmoothie.com.
6. Lee T. V. and Hill J. W. (1999) The unfolding model of employee turnover: a replication and extension. Academy of Management Journal, 42, pp 450-62.
7. Shaw J., Delery J. Jenkins G. and Gupta M (1998). An organisation level analysis of voluntary and involuntary behavior. Academy of Management Journal, 41, 511-25.
8. Smith Sand Paquette S (2010). Creativity, Chaos and Knowledge Management, Business Information Review, 27 (2), pp 118-23.
9. The Talent Wave: Why Succession Planning fails and what to do about it. David Clutterbuck. Kogan Page 12. Britain.
10. Talent Management Handbook: Creating a Sustainable Competitive Advantage by Selecting, Developing and Promoting the Best People, 2nd Edition. Lance Berger and Dorothy Berger. Tata McGraw Hill. Edn. (2011). New Delhi.

Chapter 10...

Law and HRM

Contents ...
10.1 Universal Human Rights in Employment (Ethical Perspective)
10.2 Laws and Amendments
10.3 The Trade Unions Act, 1926
10.4 The Payment of Bonus Act, 1965
- Discussion Questions
- Bibliography

Objectives and Summary

This chapter introduces the reader to the various forms of legislation related to the protection of rights, duties and responsibilities of the employees at all levels. It includes the minimum wages and forms of compensation to be paid to the employees. It also discusses the limits on the working conditions, minimum welfare facilities and bonus payments. In short, it is a compendium of laws enacted from time to time governing the working conditions of the employees at various levels.

Law is very important for HRM. Whether related to ethics, culture or corporate governance, all aspects in an organisation are controlled by legislation. Today there is legislation in India related to even the employment of a diverse workforce like women, minorities, differently sexually oriented and otherwise enabled employees to protect them and induce them to achieve better performance in organisations.

Learning Outcomes:
1. Understanding the various forms of legislation relating to collective bargaining, wages and working conditions of the workers;
2. Getting to know about the need for legislation and the origins of laws in the world and in India;
3. Understanding corporate governance, culture and the law.

Introduction

Employees have the right to form organisations for the purpose of seeking to improve their working conditions, wages, hours and benefits. These employee-created organisations, called unions, seek to manage their working environment primarily through a process called collective bargaining. When there are no unions, employers usually set employment terms and conditions unilaterally, i.e. without consulting the employees, within the constraints imposed by market conditions and the law. Collective Bargaining allows employees to participate in setting terms and conditions of employment through their unions. Through collective bargaining, the company and the union bilaterally addresses many of the HRM policies.

Historical Context

Developments that have affected labour unions have been due to the influence of the economic, political and social environment. Labour, on its part, has also influenced the development of society and has secured work place privileges and protections, which all started in the U.S.

The first American Trade Unions, formed in the 1700s, were primarily craft guilds in occupations such as shoe-making and carpentry. Their goal was to control the price of skilled labour that they provided by limiting apprenticeships, demanding uniform rates and setting quality standards. Later, in the 1850s and 1860s, the Industrial Revolution saw the rise of new unions in industries such as railroads and printing. The American Federation of Labour (AFL) was organised in 1886 by the leaders of a group of craft unions. The AFL emphasised collective bargaining about bread-and-butter issues as a means of improving working conditions for skilled workers, and set the stage for contemporary unionism.

The continued expansion of mass production created entirely new industries that employed a large number of workers in large industrial facilities. The AFL found it difficult to organise the skilled workers in these facilities but was opposed to organising the masses because that violated the principles of craft unionism. The Congress of Industrial Organisations (CIO) was formed in 1935 to fill this void. Industry unions organise on the basis of industry regardless of skill. The CIO sought to create one umbrella union for each major industry and to include all workers from the most highly skilled to the unskilled. Within a couple of years, the CIO helped create the United Auto Workers, United Steel Workers and several other such unions.

The Legal Context

For many years, unions and union members had few legal rights and were actively persecuted by employers and the courts. This began to change around 1933. At present the two main laws that regulate the employers and the unions are The Railway Labour Act of 1926 and The National Labour Relations Act.

10.1 Universal Human Rights in Employment (Ethical Perspective)

Employment is more than a contractual relationship involving contractual rights. It is more than a legal relationship involving statutory and perhaps Constitutional rights. Employment is a fundamental human relationship and therefore necessarily implicates fundamental human rights. But just what are the human rights which are at stake in employment? The International Labour Organisation (ILO) has been struggling with this question since it was founded in 1919. Today the ILO is a part of the United Nations and seeks to advance worker rights and conditions of work around the globe.

A major milestone in the movement for global human rights occurred just after World War II with the founding of the United Nations and the adoption of the Universal Declaration of Human Rights in 1948.This declaration was founded by an United Nations Human rights accord, which recognises the concept of worker rights as a subset of human rights. Human rights are deemed acquired by virtue of one's humanity and ought not be dependent upon, or compromised by, any act of government or anyone else. In turn, employment rights are those acquired by virtue of employment and ought to exist independently of employer whim, government effectiveness or stage of economic and political development. Within the UN framework of human rights, the ILO has adopted nearly 200 conventions addressing standards for employment rights. Over the years, eight of these conventions have come up to be seen as fundamental. They are as follows:

1. Forced Labour Commission (No.29)
2. Freedom of Association and Protection of the Rights to Organise (No. 87)
3. Right to Organize and Collective Bargaining Convention (No. 98)
4. Equal Remuneration Convention (No. 100)
5. Abolition of Forced Labour Convention (No. 125)
6. Discrimination (employment and occupation) Convention (No. 111)
7. Minimum Age Convention (No. 138)
8. Convention of the Worst Forms of Child Labour (No. 182)

In 1998, the ILO adopted a Declaration on Fundamental Principles and Rights at Work that declares that all member states, even if they have not ratified the conventions in question, have an obligation to respect the Principles concerning the Fundamental rights that are the subject of those conventions.

Ironically, the United States, which considers itself a bastion of human rights, has one of the worst records in the world in terms of ratification of the fundamental worker rights conventions. It has ratified only two of the eight - only conventions 105 on forced labour and

182 on elimination of the worst forms of child labour (this will require amending the Fair Labour Standards Act of 1938 to bring it into compliance in agriculture). Only four of 177 member nations have ratified fewer.

10.2 Laws and Amendments

The given below are some of the laws and amendments in relation to Workmen's Compensation, Injuries, Bonus, Leave, Working Hours and Trade Union Rights and Responsibilities.

Amount of compensation

For a Workman, whose injury results in death

When the injury to a workman results in his death, the amount of compensation payable to his dependents is an amount equal to 50% of the monthly wages of the deceased workman multiplied by a figure ranging from 228.54 to 99.37 (depending upon the age of the deceased workman) or an amount of ₹ 80,000, whichever is more. However, if the monthly wages of the deceased workman exceed ₹ 4,000, his monthly wages for the purpose of calculating the compensation shall be deemed to be ₹ 4,000 only.   S.4(1)(a)

Deduction from the amount paid to the deceased workman as ex-gratia payment

There is a total bar against any deduction to be made by the employer for any payment made by the employer out of Court so as to reduce the corpus of the compensation payable in case of death of a workman.

Compensation to a workman when his injury results in his permanent total disablement

When the injury of a workman results in his permanent total disablement, the amount of compensation he is entitled to receive is an amount equal to 60% of the monthly wages of the injured workman multiplied by a figure ranging from 228.54 to 99.37 (depending upon the age of the injured person) or an amount of ₹ 90,000, whichever is more. However, if the monthly wages of the injured workman exceeds ₹ 4,000, his monthly wages for the purpose calculating the compensation shall be deemed to be ₹ 4,000 only.   S.4(1)(b)

Note: By Amendment Act of 2000 the minimum amount of compensation for permanent total disablement has been increased from ₹ 60,000 to ₹ 90,000 and the deemed maximum monthly wage of the injured workman is enhanced from ₹ 2,000 to ₹ 4,000.   S.4(1)(d)

Time for payment of compensation

Time limit for payment of Compensation and the Result of a Default

The employer must pay compensation as soon as the injury is caused to a workman. He cannot falter that it falls due when it is settled by the Commissioner. If he delays the payment of compensation beyond one month from the date it fell due, he may be charged simple interest at the rate of 12% per annum or at such higher rate not exceeding the maximum of the lending rates of any scheduled bank on the amount of compensation plus penalty up to 50 per cent of the amount of compensation. S.4-A

Workman who is awarded penalty under Section 4-A(3)(b) claims grant of interest on the amount of the penalty

Section 4-A underlines the compensation as "arrears" and empowers the Commissioner to direct payment of interest thereon when any employer is in default in paying the compensation within one month from the date it fell due. The amount of penalty underlined by Section 4-A(3)(b) is a distinct head and hence the law does not contemplate grant of interest on penalty. The demand for grant of interest on the amount of penalty is not supported by any provision of Section 4-A.

The method of payment of compensation in the case of fatal accidents

Payment of compensation in respect of workman whose injury has resulted in death is not to be made directly to the dependents of the workman. In such case the employer is expected to deposit the amount of compensation with the Commissioner for Workmen's Compensation. The Commissioner will then apportion the amount among the dependents of the workman.

Claims for compensation

Procedure for claiming compensation payable under the Act

The procedure for claiming compensation payable under the Act may be explained as follows:

An application for claiming compensation payable under the Act has to be made to the Commissioner for Workmen's Compensation in the prescribed format

Before filing the application, the workman has to give notice of the accident to the employer mentioning the details of the accident.

Before filing the application the workman has also to undergo a medical examination if he is required to do so by the employer.

The application has to be made within 2 years of the occurrence of the accident or within 2 years from the date of death.

If any applicant is poor, the Commissioner may exempt him from paying the application fees.

The Commissioner can take the assistance of any person possessing special knowledge of any matter relating to the case for deciding the application.

The Commissioner can recover the amount payable by any person under the Act as an arrear of land revenue. Ss. 8,10,11,19

A Workman, who is residing at Shillong in the State of Meghalaya, may file a claim petition under the Act for the accident that took place in the State of Maharashtra, before the Commissioner for Workmen's Compensation, Meghalaya

Section 21 of the Act, as amended by Act 30 of 1995, enables the workman to file the claim petition either before the Commissioner for the area in which the accident took place or before the Commissioner for the area in which the workman ordinarily resides.

10.3 The Trade Unions Act, 1926

The Trade Unions Act, 1926, is one of the old enactments in the field of labour laws, but it is a conservative piece of legislation which deals only with the registration of trade unions and the legal status of registered trade unions.

The Constitution of India confers on all citizens a fundamental right to form associations or unions. The right to form unions is thus doubly recognised in India, by the Constitution of India and the Trade Unions Act, 1926.

The Act needs a drastic revision to make it a complete enactment.
The amendments to the Act carried out as far back as in 1947 and again recently in 1982 are yet to be brought into force.

The aim of the Trade Unions Act

The object of the Act is to provide for the registration of trade unions and to confer on registered trade unions certain protection and privileges.

The meaning of "Trade Union"

As understood "Trade Union" means a body formed for the purpose of regulating and controlling the relations between workmen and employers. The definition of "trade union" given in the Trade Unions Act, 1926, includes a combination formed for the purpose of regulating the relations not only between workmen and `employers but also between workmen and workmen or between employers and employers. S.2(h)

Registration of trade unions

The procedure for the registration of a trade union

(a) At least seven members of the trade union have to make an application in the prescribed form and accompanied by the prescribed fee to the Registrar of Trade Unions for the registration of the trade union. The application must be accompanied by a copy of the rules of the trade union and should give particulars about its name and address, its members and its officers.

The Registrar, if he is satisfied that the trade union has complied with all the requirements of the Act, will register the trade union and issue a certificate of registration to it.

The certificate of registration will be conclusive evidence that the trade union has been duly registered under the Act.   Ss. A 5, 8 and 9

Note: By Act No. XXXI of 2001 the number of members required to make an application for registration is at least ten per cent or one hundred of the workmen, whichever is less, subject to a minimum of seven.

- **Supervisory Officers and Managers form a Trade union**

Supervisory Officers and Managers in an industry can form a trade union and the same can be registered. Under the definition of workmen under the Act, all persons employed in trade or industry is included. It is not restricted as in any other labour legislation. When the act itself provides for definition and for a wider meaning, the court cannot narrow it by its decision.

Note: The Government of Maharashtra by a notification dated 13-12-2001, has revised the fees payable under the Bombay Trade Unions Regulations, 1927 as under:

			₹
(1)	(a)	Registration of a Trade Union with a membership of 1,000 or over.	600
	(b)	Registration of a Trade Union with a membership of less than 1,000.	400
		Duplicate certificate of registration	50
		Registration of alteration of rules	25
		Inspection of register of Trade Unions maintained by the Registrar	50
		Inspection of a document in the possession of the Registrar	50

Compulsory registration of a trade union

The Trade Unions Act, 1926, does not make registration of a trade union compulsory. But it is advisable to get a trade union registered under the Act because the Act confers many rights and privileges on a registered trade union.

Trade Union required to have a certain minimum membership

Section 9-A requires that a registered trade union shall at all times continue to have not less than ten per cent or one hundred of the workmen, whichever is less, subject to a minimum of seven, engaged or employed in an establishment or industry with which it is connected, as its members.   S.9-A

Legal status of registered trade union

Legal status of a registered trade union

A registered trade union is a body corporate. having a perpetual succession and a common seal.

It has power to acquire and hold both movable and immovable property and to enter into contracts.

It can sue and be sued by its own name.

Its office bearer or member cannot be prosecuted for criminal conspiracy for following its legitimate objects.

No legal proceedings can be filed in any Civil Court against it in respect of any act in furtherance of a trade dispute even if such act (i) induces some other person to break a contract of employment, or (ii) is in interference with the trade business or employment of some other person, or (iii) is in interference with the right of some other person to dispose of his capital or of his labour as he wills.

Any agreement between its members is not void or voidable even if its objects are in restraint of trade. Ss. 13 & 17 to 19

Cancellation of Registration

Circumstances for the registration of a trade union to be cancelled

The Registrar of Trade Unions can withdraw or cancel a certificate of registration of a trade union if:

the trade union applies for its cancellation;

the Registrar is satisfied that the certificate has been obtained by fraud or mistake;

the trade union has ceased to exist;

the trade union has wilfully contravened any provision of the Act. S.10

Note: By Act No. XXXI of 2001 the Registrar of Trade Unions is empowered to withdraw or cancel the registration of any trade union of workmen if it ceases to have the requisite number of members.

Registration of trade unions

Withdrawal or cancellation of registration of trade unions.

Sanction of prosecutions for the offences committed under the Trade Unions Act, 1926.

Ss.8, 9, 10 and 33

Minor to be admitted as a member of a registered trade union

If a person has reached the age of 15 years, he can be admitted as a member of a registered trade union provided that there is no prohibition in the rules of the trade union on admitting any minor as its members. S.21

Rights of members

The rights of a member of a registered trade union

Every office bearer or member of a registered trade union has a right to inspect the books of accounts and also the list of members of the trade union at such times as may be provided for in the rules of the trade union. S.20

Rights of Unions

Permission for a Trade Union to constitute a political fund apart from its general fund

It is permissible for a registered Trade Union to constitute a separate fund for the promotion of the civic and political interest of its members. Contribution to the fund will be optional and no member will be compelled to contribute to the fund. Consequently, a member who does not contribute to the fund shall not be deprived of any benefits of the Trade Union. S.16

Trade Union changing its name

A registered Trade Union can change its name with the consent of not less than two thirds of the total number of its members and after following the procedure prescribed under section 25 of the Act. Ss. 23 & 25

Time and Method of Payment

Requirements of the Act in respect of time of payment of wages

The following are the requirements of the Act in respect of time of payment of wages:

Wages must be paid on a working day and not on a holiday.

Establishments employing less than 1,000 persons must pay wages before the expiry of the 7th day of every month and other establishments must pay wages before the expiry of the 10th day of every month.

When the employment of any person is terminated, the wages earned by him must be paid before the expiry of the second working day from the day of termination. S-5

Requirements of the Act in respect of method of payment of wages

Wages must be paid in current coins or currency notes or in both and not in kind. It is, however, permissible for an employer to pay wages by cheque or by crediting them in the bank account if so authorised in writing by an employed person. S.6

Note: In the State of Maharashtra in certain circumstances, a certain percentage of bonuses can be paid by investment in a prescribed manner.

Q. What is the provision of the Act regarding deductions from the wages payable to an employed person?

A. The Act prohibits all kinds of deductions except those which are authorised by or under the Act. S.7

10.4 The Payment of Bonus Act, 1965

The Payment of Bonus Act, 1965, gives the employees a statutory right to a share in the profits of his employer. Prior to the enactment of the Act some employees used to get bonus but that was dependent on the will of the employers.

The Act enables the employees to get a minimum bonus equivalent to one month's salary or wage (8.336/o of annual earnings) whether the employer makes any profit or not. But the Act also puts a ceiling on the bonus and the maximum bonus payable under the Act is equivalent to about 2 1/2 months' salary or wage (20% of annual earnings).

It is to be noted that employees drawing salary or wage exceeding ` 10,000 per month are not entitled to get any bonus under the Act.

Object of the Payment of Bonus Act, 1965

The object of the Act is to maintain peace and harmony between labour and capital by allowing the employees to share the prosperity of the establishment reflected by the profits earned by the contributions made by capital, management and labour.

Employee entitlement to get bonus on the basis of his entire salary or wage

If an employee is drawing a salary or wage not exceeding ₹ 3,500 per month, he is entitled to get bonus on his entire salary or wage. If an employee draws a salary or wage exceeding ₹ 3,500 per month, but not exceeding 10,000 per month, the bonus payable to him is to be calculated as if his salary or wage were ₹ 3,500 per month. An employee getting a salary or wage exceeding ₹ 10,000 per month is not entitled to get bonus.   S.12

Amount be deducted from the bonus

(1) If in any year the employer has paid any amount to an employee as customary bonus, then he can deduct such amount from bonus payable to the employee for that year.

(2) If an employee is found guilty of misconduct causing financial loss to the employer, then the employer can deduct the amount of loss from the amount of bonus payable to the employee for the year in which he was found guilty of misconduct.   Ss. 17 and 18

Meaning of customary bonus

Customary bonus is that amount which is being paid by way of tradition or custom at a uniform rate over a number of years and which has no link with profit.

Fixing Minimum Wages

Procedure the Government has to follow for fixing and revising minimum wages

A. The Government has to fix and revise minimum wages either–

- by appointing one or more committees and sub-committees consisting of representatives of employers and employees and also of independent persons to hold necessary enquiries and by taking into consideration the advise tendered by the committee or committees; or
- by formulating and publishing its proposals and taking into consideration the representations received in response to the proposals.   S.5

Obligation of Employers for Payment of Wages

Obligation of the employer in respect of payment of wages under the Minimum Wages Act, 1948

Where minimum wages are fixed and enforced under section 5 of the act in respect of any employment covered by the Act, the employer is bound to pay to every employee engaged in that employment wages at a rate not less than the minimum rate so fixed and enforced. S.12

Number of hours which constitutes a normal working day for the employees covered by the Act?

A normal working day prescribed for the employees covered by the Act is of 9 hours. 5.13 & Mah. Rule 24

Employees' entitlement to overtime wages

A If an employee covered by the Act works for more than 9 hours on any day or 48 hours in any week, he is in respect of overtime work entitled to wages at double the ordinary rate of wages. 5.14 & Mah. Rule 26

The Equal Remuneration Act, 1976

The Equal Remuneration Act is a gift of "the International Women's Year' to women workers. It is enacted to give effect to the provision of Article 39 of the Constitution of India which contains a directive principle of equal pay for equal work for both men and women. The Act provides for the payment of equal remuneration to men and women workers for the same work or work of a similar nature and for the prevention 01 discrimination on the ground of sex against women in the matter of employment. The main provisions of the Act are as follows.

Equal pay for equal work

No employer shall pay to any worker employed by him remuneration at rates less favourable than those at which remuneration is paid by him to the workers of the opposite sex for performing the same work or work of a similar nature. S.4(1)

No discrimination to be made while recruiting men and women

No employer shall make any discrimination against women while making recruitment for the same work or work similar nature.

Exceptions

The provisions of the Act shall be inapplicable when special treatment is given to women under any law or when special treatment is accorded to women in connection with the birth of a child. S.15

The Central Government or a State Government may make a declaration that in a particular establishment or employment the difference in regard to the remuneration of men and women is based on a factor other than sex and on such declaration being made any act of the employer attributable to such difference shall not be deemed to be a contravention of any provision of the Act. S.16

Claims and complaints

Complaints with regard to the contravention of any provision of the Act and claims arising out of non-payment of wages at equal rates to men and women workers for the same work or work of a similar nature shall be heard and decided by an authority appointed by the appropriate Government. An appeal shall lie against any order of the authority to an appellate authority appointed by the appropriate Government. S.7

Monies due from an employer arising of the decision of the authority or the appellate authority can be recovered by making an application under Section 33-C(1) of the Industrial Disputes Act, 1947. S.7(8)

Penalties

If any employer (a) makes any recruitment in contravention of the provisions of the Act, or (b) makes any payment of remuneration at unequal rates to men and women workers, for the same work or work of a similar nature, or (c) makes any discrimination between men and women workers in contravention of the provisions of the Act, he would be punished with fine upto ₹ 10,000/-. S.10

Maintenance of register

Every employer shall maintain in the prescribed form a register in relation to the workers employed by him. S.8 & R.6

Industrial Dispute and Existence

A dispute or difference between workmen and the employer which is connected with the employment or non-employment or the terms of employment or with the conditions of labour of any person is called an industrial dispute. An industrial dispute comes into existence when a demand is made by the workmen on the employer about any matter connected with the employment or non-employment or the terms of employment or with the conditions of labour of any person, and the employer refuses to concede the demand. The demand need not necessarily be made in writing. It need not necessarily be made directly on the employer.

Strikes

Stoppage of Work due to Strike

When a body of persons employed in any industry stop their work acting in combination (to coerce the employer to accede to some demand they are said to be on a strike. S.2(q)

Lock-outs

Meaning of a Lock Out

When an employer temporarily refuses to continue to employ a body of persons (i.e., without effecting a termination of their service) (to coerce them to his point of view and to accept some demand) he is said to have effected a lock-out. S.2(1)

Note: The Act treats strikes and lock-outs as synonymous. The provisions of the Act relating to strikes and lock-outs are, therefore, almost the same. The same circumstances, as those which make a strike illegal, make a lock-out illegal.

Relationship of employer and employee come during the period of a lock-out

The relationship of the employer and the employee continues to exist during the period of a lock-out.

Bibliography ...

1. John R. Commons et al, History of Labour in the United States, 2 Vols (New York: Macmillan) 1918.
2. ibid, chap 16
3. ibid, chap 19
4. Managing Human Resources: Shaw and Fisher
5. Employer's Guide to Labour Laws: S. R. Samant, Labour Law Agency, Mumbai, 2009
6. Managing Human Resource, (India Edition), Cynthia D. Fisher, Lyle Schoer Feldt, James Shaw, Cengage Learning. New Delhi, 2006.

A new law to clean up India's Corporate Governance

(excerpted from The Economic Times, Jan 5, 2013)

India's corporate culture is about to witness a shake-up. A new law will make it mandatory for most Indian Companies to separate the role of the chief executive and the chairman of the board. The shift, already the norm in the UK but long resisted elsewhere, should help to narrow India's governance discount.

This change is far from cosmetic .The CEOs of about half of India's top 50 listed companies double up as Chairmen.

Those that want to continuously combine the roles will need the explicit approval of their shareholders.

The country's securities regulator is also getting into the act. The SEBI's proposed governance norms for the public by traded companies are actually tougher than corporations face in more advanced economies.

For instance, India may require independent directors resigning their position to publicly disclose the reason for their departure and personal reasons would not be considered a satisfactory answer if the directors are only giving one of the multiple directorships.

The regulator also wants to explore the viability of requiring companies above a certain size to appoint at least one independent director from among the small shareholders. The rules are no guarantee of future good business behaviour. Even boards that boast of independent leadership can do better.

Discussion Questions

1. Explain the various measures of legislation related to wages and working conditions of the workers.
2. Compare legislation of India and other countries in general.
3. Explain the origin of law and HRM.
4. Describe law in India in relation to HRM.

Chapter 11...

Collective Bargaining

Contents ...

11.1 Introduction
11.2 Features of Collective Bargaining
11.3 Significance of Collective Bargaining
11.4 Functions of Collective Bargaining
11.5 Collective Bargaining in India
• Discussion Questions
• References

Objectives and Summary

This chapter shares the understanding of the working of manufacturing and service companies, which employ a large workforce. These companies have a need for a worker representative on one hand and a management representative on the other hand, to sort out any issues related to the workforce. This chapter explains the role of trade unions in collective bargaining with the management, their force and power in influencing decisions related to workers and for the workers, functions of collective bargaining and the various types of dispute resolution.

Collective bargaining is a process which is very important for the goodwill as well as the smooth working of the workers and the management together. The management, especially in manufacturing companies with a large workforce in the factories, is very conscious of the necessity to maintain smooth relations with the workers, and understanding and solving their issues before these storm into a strike. The recent Maruti strike at Manesar and the whopping loss of man days and financial loss, speak of the dire need for maintaining harmonious relations with the workforce. Today apart from the trade unions of workers, employees at all levels even in IT and ITes companies are conscious of uniting to put forth their demands and facilitate a shared understanding. Recently even managers have started forming unions like the one at Cummins. It was formed earlier and was soon dissolved by the intervention of the HR.

Learning Outcomes:
1. Outlining the need for collective bargaining and the process for the same.
2. Highlighting the benefits of collective bargaining accrued to the employees as well as the top management.
3. Sharing various forms of legislation related to employee bargaining and fair practices.
4. Outlining the various types of collective bargaining in India.

11.1 Introduction

A cordial settlement of disputes is very necessary to improve the industrial relations in the organisation. The rise and growth of trade unions evolved a device of collective bargaining to resolve their disputes by negotiations between the two parties without the intervention by the arbitrator.

Collective bargaining has been considered as a form of industrial democracy and as a facilitator of workers participation in management.

Collective bargaining is concerned with the representation between the trade unions (collective workers' participation) and management (representatives of employers).

Different authors have defined collective bargaining as follows:

1. According to **Michael Jucius**, *"Collective Bargaining refers to a process by which employers on the one hand and representatives of the employees on the other, attempt to arrive at agreements covering the conditions under which employees will contribute and be compensated for their services."*
2. According to **Encyclopaedia of Social Services**, *"Collective bargaining is a process of discussion and negotiation between two parties one or both of whom is a group of persons acting in concert. The resulting bargain is an understanding as in terms and conditions under which a continuing service is to be performed."*

11.2 Features of Collective Bargaining

1. **Group and Collective Action:** It is a group process in a number of ways. Firstly, the workers unite and discuss common issues related to their benefits and wages. Secondly, the collective action includes a joint negotiation with the top management to settle their issues amicably.
2. **Strength:** The point of view is made on the basis of an egalitarian philosophy. Both the parties sit across the table and discuss the issues to the mutual satisfaction of both the interests.
3. **Continuous process:** It is not a one-time affair. The process of collective bargaining is related to issues not directly related to compensation alone. It may include issues like features in the working environment not conducive for them, superiors' behaviour which may be tyrannical, benefits like clean drinking water, mess facilities may be inadequate and so on. The process, therefore, is a continuous one where monitoring also is overseen apart from the joint negotiation.

4. **Flexible:** It is assumed that the process of collective bargaining begins with a flexible stance on both sides and not a rigid viewpoint. It starts with a case of perhaps divergent views and concludes after a round of mutual negotiation with an amicable settlement, most of the times, much to the satisfaction of both the parties.
5. **Voluntary:** The entire process of collective bargaining is absolutely voluntary. The main objective is to have a meaningful and valuable dialogue between both the parties - the labour or the employees and the top management - to discuss issues with an aim to amicably settle differences to the benefit of both.
6. **Dynamic:** The process of collective bargaining is undergoing a transformational change over the years. In the earlier times in India, there has been a record of a turbulent and a vitriolic relationship. The Datta Samant-led strike of the 1970s by textile mill workers in Bombay is an appropriate case in point. The environment then was a hostile relationship between the workers and the management. The premise of the agitation was built on how the management was exploiting the skills of the workers and underpaying them to save costs and earn more for themselves. In today's times, the relationship is based more on the spirit of trust and objective and rational arguments where both the parties are concerned to forge a win-win situation.
7. **Power relationship:** The basis of collective bargaining and discussion is the power relationship shared by both the parties. The management wants to retain its stance and extract the best from the workers; and the workers, in their position of influence through their unified representation, want to extract the best from the management. The unfortunate case of the Maruti Manesar strike and the subsequent killing of the HR manager is a case in point.
8. **Bipartite process:** In most cases, unless there is no headway, the two representative parties meet face to face without any third-party intervention. There have been solitary occasions when an arbitrator or a third party has been called in to settle a stalemate.
9. **Two-way process:** It is a mutual two-way process and not a 'take it or leave it' attitude. The objective is to discuss the issues mutually and not have either side adopting a condescending approach.

Objectives of Collective Bargaining
1. To maintain cordial relations.
2. To settle disputes.
3. To protect the interests of the workers.
4. To ensure the participation of trade unions in the industry.
5. To resolve the differences between the management and the workers.
6. To avoid the need of Government intervention.

Types of Collective Bargaining
In India, the process of Collective Bargaining can be classified under the following broad categories:

1. Settlements under The Industrial Disputes Act include the negotiation by unions and the representing officers during the course of the discussions and the proceedings involving both the parties.
2. Agreements which are settled and discussed by both the parties themselves without the intervention of the Conciliation Officer of the Government Office.
3. These include agreements which are voluntarily settled by both the parties in cases where the issues are subjudice, and have been submitted to industrial tribunals, labour courts or labour arbitrators for incorporation into the document as parts of awards. These are known as Consent Awards.
4. Agreements which are drawn up after direct negotiations between labour and management and are voluntary in nature. These depend for their enforcement on moral force and on the goodwill and cooperation of the parties.

11.3 Significance of Collective Bargaining

According to the **National Commission on Labour**, *"The best jurisdiction for collective bargaining is that it is a system based on bipartite agreements and as such superior to any arrangement involving third-party interventions in matters which are essentially the concern of employers and workers."*

Thus collective bargaining is important for the following reasons:

1. It results in better cooperation and understanding between the workers and the top management or the employers. The employers or the top management get a detailed insight into the problems and the difficulties of the workers in relation to their wages, working conditions and relations with their superiors. As far as the workers' unions are concerned, they are better able to understand the constraints of the employer, market complexities and exigencies in the organisation's environment which precludes them for paying high wages as expected by the workers. Companies like Forbes Marshall have regular meetings and discussions with the workers and arrive at mutually agreeable solutions. Perhaps this is one of the reason why this organisation is considered a 'Great Place to Work', consecutively for the last few years. Being a manufacturing company, this award is unique in itself.
2. It facilitates a measure for an organisation's adaptation of the technological, political and social conditions and thus extends it to mutual agreement with the top management and the workers to thus settle disputes amicably.
3. It is a democratic set-up without any need for compulsive action, except in rare cases where the voluntary process of negotiation or discussion does not work without intervention by a third party or arbitrator.
4. An industrial jurisprudence is created through this medium where the employers or the top management cannot act in an arbitrary manner. It pushes both the parties to create a mutually discussed code of conduct and set standards of performance and environment features for better performance by the workers. It also establishes a code of conduct by the top management or the employer, detailing the action and behaviour standards expected from the workers.

5. It is one of the most important relations between the labour unions and the employers, and sets the standards of conduct and performance from each of the parties.
   6. The ultimate purpose of collective bargaining is to share the benefits of both the performance and the economic and competitive environment, acting as a medium for mutual gain and thus promoting mutual wellbeing.

11.4 Functions of Collective Bargaining

According to Arthur Butler, Collective Bargaining has three important features:
1. Technique of long-run social change;
2. Peace treaty between two parties in continual conflict;
3. System of industrial jurisprudence.

1. Long-Run Social Change

Collective bargaining is not just confined to developing economic relations between the workers and the employers. According to Selig Perham, "It is a technique whereby an inferior social class or group exerts a never-slackening pressure for a bigger share in the social sovereignty as well as more welfare, security and liberty for individual members. Collective bargaining manifests itself equally in politics, legislation, court litigation, government administration, religion, propaganda, religion and education.

2. Peace Treaty

Collective bargaining is like a peace treaty between the two parties, employers and workers. It is like a compromise situation where both the parties don't stick to their individual stand but learn to relent and compromise.

3. Industrial Jurisprudence

Collective bargaining creates a system of industrial jurisprudence. It is a method of introducing civil rights in the industry. It is like a compulsive requirement on the part of the management to be more objective or impartial rather than arbitrary.

11.5 Collective Bargaining in India

In India there were no special labour laws until about 1930. Employers were not required to engage in collective bargaining with employees and were virtually unrestrained in their behaviour towards unions. Most union weapons, even strikes, were considered illegal.

In India the Trade Unions Act was passed in the year 1926 where both employers and employees could join to register a union. Later legislation like the Industrial Disputes Act 1947, and the Factories Act 1948 came into force. The Industrial Disputes Act laid down the framework for resolving the conflicts between employers and workers or unions.

Collective bargaining was introduced in India in the year 1952 and it acquired significance and importance through the various years. According to details released by the Labour Bureau, the practice of determining the rates of wages and the conditions of employment have been applied to all sectors of the Indian industry. Data show that a large number of disputes too have been resolved by this medium.

From the year 1955, a huge number of plant-level agreements have been reached. These include the following: Bata Shoe Company Agreement, Modi Spinning and Weaving Company, Tata Iron and Steel Company Ltd, Bhilai Steel Plant and so on. What followed in the 1960s and the 1970s was a rise in trade union activity, leading to strikes and lock-outs. Though the imposition of Emergency in 1975 led to the suspension of trade union rights and a sudden fall in the trade union activity (many prominent Opposition-party trade union leaders like George Fernandes were jailed during Emergency) union activities picked up after it ended. Under pressure from the trade unions, the Industrial Disputes Act was amended in 1976, making it mandatory for firms employing more than 300 workmen to take prior government permission before retrenching workmen.

At the industry level, the mills at Mumbai and Ahmedabad are a strong example focusing on members' requirements. There has been a voluntary settlement of various disputes and equal distribution of bonus. Soon, the need to achieve productivity gains and the need for maintaining a healthy bottom line were realised by both the employers and unions. The effects of competition and market forces became obvious to both. The focus also shifted to building a positive work culture and enhancing skills. There was a marked shift towards adopting a collaborative approach rather than a confrontationist approach.

The next phase of economic reforms introduced in 1992 focused on the opening of the economy and integrating India with global economic forces. The Voluntary Retirement Scheme (VRS) became a legal option for firms to separate excess employees on mutual agreement. The National Renewal Fund was established in 1992 to help firms adjust to the new economic realities. Currently many traditional unions both in the public and the private sector have recognised the significance of the market forces and competition and are prepared to work with the management to increase competitiveness. While the industry and investors demanded reforms in the labour laws to introduce more flexibility and the right to hire and fire, much progress could not be made due to opposition from national unions.

The emergence of the IT/ITES sector saw firms where labour union activity was absent. Employees focused on career and professional growth showed antipathy towards unions and their employers went ahead to ensure good conditions of work. Union of Information Technology Professionals (UNITES Pro) based in Bangalore has been campaigning for employee rights but its acceptance levels are low. However the rising job insecurity in the IT/BPO sector has changed the outlook of knowledge workers, who are generally not inclined to unionism and its method of asserting their rights. Confronted with withdrawal of job offers, the prospective employees of Satyam computers attempted unionisation. Non-union firms have also become a norm in traditionally unionized sectors like manufacturing and services. The examples are the private banks which are completely trade union free.

Impasses, Mediation and Strikes

In collective bargaining, the impasse occurs when the parties are not able to move further towards a settlement. An impasse is usually because one party is demanding more than the other will offer. Sometimes it can be resolved through a third party - a disinterested person such as a mediator or an arbitrator. If not, the union may call a work stoppage, or strike, to put pressure on management.

Third-Party Involvement

Negotiators use three types of third party interventions to overcome an impasse: mediation, fact finding and arbitration. With mediation, a neutral third party tries to assist the principals in reaching agreement. The mediator usually holds meetings with each party to determine where it stands regarding its position, and then uses this information to find common ground for further bargaining.

Arbitration

Arbitration is the most definitive type of third-party intervention, because the arbitrator often has the power to determine and dictate the settlement terms. Unlike mediation and fact-finding, arbitration can guarantee a solution to an impasse. With binding arbitration, both parties are committed to accepting the arbitrator's award. With non-binding arbitration, they are not. Arbitration may also be voluntary or compulsory (in other words, imposed by the government agency).

Strikes

A strike is a withdrawal of labour. There are four main types of strikes. An economic strike results from a failure to agree on the terms of a contract. Unions call unfair labour practice strikes to protest against illegal conduct by the employer. A wildcat strike is an unauthorised one, occurring during the term of a contract. A sympathy strike occurs when one union strikes in support of the strike of another union.

Some of the common examples of grievances are: absenteeism, working hours, wages, transfers, work assignments, overtime, vacations, incentive plans, holidays, irrational plant rules and insubordination by an employee. A grievance is often a symptom of an underlying problem. Problem employees are yet another underlying cause of grievances. These are individuals who, by their nature, are negative, dissatisfied and prone to complaints. Discipline and dismissal are also major sources of grievances.

The Union Movement of Tomorrow

Unions are also making inroads with professionals and white-collar workers. Recent reports of IBM sending systems analysts' jobs abroad, Wall Street firms having more security analysis done abroad by foreign nationals, and of hospitals having digitised X-rays read and interpreted by doctors abroad illustrate the concerns many professionals have. In India, UNITES Pro received calls of support from employees of IT/ITES firms that laid off or cut salary.

A recent review of union research and literature provides insights into unions today. Carol Gill (2009) concludes that unions "that have a cooperative relationship with management can play an important role in overcoming barriers to the effective adoption of practices that have been linked to organisational competitiveness." However, she also concludes that employers want to capitalise on that potential need to change the way of thinking, avoiding adversarial industrial relations and emphasising a cooperative partnership with their unions.

Case Study

On March 13, 2013, Renault Chairman and President Carlos Ghosn and representatives of France's CFDT, CFE-CGC and FO unions signed the Renault Agreement, termed as 'Contract for a new dynamic of Renault growth and social development in France'.

The Renault Agreement was submitted the previous day to the Group and Subsidiary Works Councils for consultation.

This agreement, which is the fruit of a particularly rich dialogue with the social partners, is decisive in providing a fresh boost to growth in France.

Within the framework of the Renault Agreement, the different measures negotiated with the unions have enabled the company to make a certain number of key commitments that will ensure continued activity and employment in France in the future.

Renault has committed to producing at least 710,000 vehicles in France by 2016, compared with just over 530,000 vehicles in 2012. This will take the overall utilisation rate of the facilities in France to more than 85 percent and permits long-term visibility for the activity of the company's French sites until 2016, and furthermore up to 2020. This level of activity will also be beneficial to all the French mechanical component plants that produce parts for suspension systems, engines and transmission, as well as to the logistics platforms.

Through the terms of this agreement, Renault has also committed to maintaining activity at all its production sites in France, as well as at its engineering, sales and marketing, and tertiary services departments.

This agreement is the fruit of almost nine months of discussions and negotiations with the unions and has collectively resulted in finding structural and sustainable solutions to face a changing European automotive market. Thanks to this accord, the company will be able to consolidate its French base while at the same time growing on the international front with a view to adapting to today's worldwide automobile industry.

This year, a watchdog committee will be set up to make sure that the terms of the agreement are met. The mission of this committee – which will be made up of three representatives from each of the unions that signed the agreement, along with representatives of the company's senior management – will be to monitor the introduction of the measures specified in the agreement. It will focus notably on four areas: the utilisation rate of manufacturing capacity, the agreement's social measures, research and innovation, and the automotive industry.

The agreement will apply to all Renault S.A.S.'s automobile-based establishments, as well as to its MCA, SOVAB, STA, RST, ACI Villeurbanne, Sofrastock International and Fonderie de Bretagne manufacturing subsidiaries.

Following the official signature, group Chairman and CEO Carlos Ghosn declared, *"I would like to hail the work that has been undertaken over the past several months with a view to producing such an exemplary agreement. I would also like to thank all the unions who fully assumed their role as partners. Thanks to their engagement, as well to our mutual determination to concert and look ahead to the future, we have been able to rise successfully to the challenge of producing an agreement which not only complied with the rules of collective bargaining, but which is also just for the workforce and which provides solid foundations for the company's sustainable growth. This agreement is excellent news for Renault and for those businesses involved in the automotive industry in France. Indeed, it provides proof that an approach based on a spirit of social innovation and responsibility can open up new and promising horizons."*

Questions:
1. What are the major features in the Renault Agreement?
2. Underline the commitments made by the management to the union.

Discussion Questions
1. What is the need for collective bargaining?
2. Highlight the various advantages of collective bargaining.
3. Elaborate on the various types of collective bargaining.
4. Discuss the future of collective bargaining in India.

References

1. Agnihotri V. (1963) Towards Collective Bargaining. Indian Labour Journal, March.
2. Butler Arthur D. (1961) Labour Economics and Institutions, New York: American Publishing Company.
3. Yoder Dale (1959). "Personnel Management: Principles and Policies" New Delhi, Prentice Hall.
4. Human Resource Management. Shashi Gupta, Rosy Joshi, Kalyani Publishers, 2006, Kolkata.
5. K. Kurmanath, "Satyam Freshers attempt Unions" The Hindu Business Line, March 11, 2009.
6. With or without reaching a solution, impasses and union management conflict can leave union members demoralised. Workforce, June 9, 2008, pp 1-18.
7. Carol Gill, "Union Impact on the Effective Adoption of High Performance Work Practices." Human Resource Management Review, 19 (2009) pp 39-50.
8. Human Resource Management, 12th Edition, Gary Dessler and Biju Varkkey, Prentice Hall, 2011.

Chapter 12...

Employee Relations

Contents ...

12.1 Introduction
12.2 Engagement
12.3 Dimensions of Internal Employment Relations
12.4 Termination
• Discussion Questions

Objectives and Summary

This chapter aims to acquaint the reader with concepts related to employee relations and employee engagement. Its objective is to stress upon the importance of employee relations, employee retention and creating an employee-centric organisation. It wishes to bring home the point of how employee retention or talent retention is one of the most important challenges in organisations today. It shares various pieces of legislation related to employees and the reasons for lay-offs and retrenchment.

Employee engagement is one of the biggest challenges of employers today. More and more research verifies how the only distinguishing factor between organisations is the knowledge, skills and attributes of their employees. Employers are going the extra mile to retain employees and conducting exit interviews to analyse their gaps and failings. At the same time understanding the legislation related to retrenchment and lay-offs is also very important as it too becomes an essential part of decisions particularly when the organisations find projects being withdrawn or businesses not remaining commercially viable.

Learning Outcomes:
1. Understanding measures related to employee engagement;
2. Identifying ways to imbibe a work attitude in employees and drive them to bring their best for the organisation;
3. Outlining legislation related to retrenchment and layoffs.

12.1 Introduction

In the factory of the 1960s and 1970s, it would not be uncommon to read a notice board outside the factory gate saying "Hands Required" if a vacancy arose. The 'hand' at that time referred to a recruit and the implication was also that more of manual skills were required at that time. It also meant that the organisation required only a part of the employee skills and not the whole employee himself.

In the modern day, organisations evidently require significantly more than this and that if they wish to be successful, then they need to tap into the ideas and thoughts of their staff. The modern ideology is convinced that "people as well as their work is important " in order to compete effectively in today's world. No more the emphasis on the work alone, individual doing that work also has gained importance.

It also implies that we need to create ways to get a 'buy-in' to their work and engage them more effectively. One of the ways in which this can be achieved in the world of work is through employee engagement and employee involvement. This can be defined as, "A concerted attempt by employers to find participative ways in which to manage their staff by investing in human capital" (Marchington, 2001).

Forms of Employee Involvement

According to the work of Marchington and his colleagues, it is possible to identify a number of initiatives that fall under the 'umbrella' of employee involvement. These are a direct form of employee involvement as they operate directly between the management and the staff. Some of the main forms of Employee Involvement are as follows:

1. **Team working:** Work organised around teams of workers.
2. **Team building (cascading):** Information cascaded from top to bottom via team meetings.
3. **Direct Communication:** Communication as one-to-one meetings.
4. **Suggestion Scheme:** Voluntary schemes for seeking employees' views on change and other initiatives of the organisation.
5. Problem-solving groups.
6. **Quality Circles** or quality improvement groups to enhance a focus of continuous improvement in quality.
7. **TQM:** As a continuous focus on quality improvement.
8. **ESOPS:** Employees' share in ownership schemes.

Thus the focus is more on employee involvement, who is considered to be a valuable stakeholder.

12.2 Engagement

One of the biggest issues facing modern-day organisations is securing loyalty and commitment from employees all the time. Organisations today are grappling with the problem of how to garner this value and competency of generating a willing commitment and passion with loyalty from the employees. This is currently one of the biggest issues facing them. It is a common theme running though the HRM literature available. Today, there is also a realisation that employment relationships are becoming increasingly diverse (diversity of workforce, varied shifts from the traditional 8 hours to the 12-hour work day with more weekends off, flexible working hours, part-time work, and temporary work) are now a common phenomenon even in the traditional sectors, apart from the IT industry, hospitality and aviation. The objective now is to seek an employee engagement rather than a lofty sense of loyalty and commitment. This realisation has been tempered by an acknowledgement that the business driven agenda of much of contemporary HRM, by putting business needs first, served in some cases to undermine moves to secure employee engagement (*Truss et al, 2006*). According to **CIPD (Chartered Institute of Personnel and Development**), "Engagement is an idea whose time has come... It represents an aspiration that employees should understand, identify and commit themselves to the objectives of the organisation that they work for. For employee relations specialists, it means being more strategic and seeing the 'bigger picture' but ultimately it may mean asserting more strongly the employee interest and agenda. This may not fit with the management culture still based on 'command and control'. It's a genuinely transformational message." (*CIPD, 2005*). In India, many organisations, believing employee engagement to be a strategic issue, have appointed and designated special people, away from the HR division, to monitor and design employee engagement programmes. These may also include services like a concierge, who runs errands for the employees like banking, insurance related, paying of bills and so on, to reduce the irritants at their personal level. On the other part of the engagement spectrum, organisations are conscious of developing the holistic aspects of an employee and so, engage them through special food festivals on Fridays, festival celebrations, music through specially invited DJs, health check- up camps, a state-of-the art gymnasium, and so on.

These reflect today's transformational environments in organisations, all centred on employees and their strategic alignment.

Employee Relations

According to Edwards (*2003*), the nature of the relationship carries with it important implications for employee relations. He begins by pointing out that the relationship is made up of two parts: "Market relations and managerial relations... the former covers the price of labour, which embraces not only the basic wage but also hours of work, holidays and pension rights... Managerial relations are the relationships that define how the process takes place:

market relations set a price for a set number of hours of work; managerial relations determine how much work is performed in that time on what specific task or tasks, who has the right to define the tasks and change a particular mix of tasks and what penalties will be deployed for any failure to meet these obligations" (*2003; 8*). The employee relationship by definition is the one between employer and employee, potentially mediated by employee associations (such as trade unions) and the government and has a number of dimensions such as economic, legal, social, psychological, power and political.

According to CIPD, the other dimensions of the employment relationship are:

1. The parties which include the management, employees as well as the trade unions.
2. The structure, i.e., the relationship is made up of formal rules around pay and employment rules, informal understanding through the organisation practices and culture.
3. The operation or the different levels or ways through the style of management in terms of how it operates.
4. The substance, which is the content of the relationship in terms of agreements and individual elements linked to rewards, the job and careers.

There have been changes in employment relationships. Cappell (*1999, 2008*) has suggested that the employment relationship has recently undergone change in more fundamental ways. He has talked of a new employment relationship based on the challenges of the new world of work. In his view the traditional relationship relied on employers accepting significant responsibility and risk for the development and career path of many of their employees - which has now broken down. This burden has now been redistributed to the employees, as a result of the growing competition in the economy.

Employee benefits

These are important components of an employment relationship. The type and extent of perquisites given by Indian organisations are determined by the relevant laws, location-specific practices and tax laws. In addition to the legislated benefits (mentioned in Chapter 10, Law and HRM) many firms provide additional benefits to their employees, like soft loans, housing, transportation, schooling etc. Firms have also extended such benefits to the managers too. For instance, the benefits offered by the MNCs and private companies along with public-sector and government employees at various levels include gym at the office, indoor sports, gaming facilities, flexible timings, work from home facilities, celebrations of festivals and birthdays, group insurance schemes, financial support for education, marriage, buying a house and retirement plans or policies. Some MNCs and public-sector companies provide benefits like residential townships, recreation and entertainment facilities schools and hospital facilities. For example, in Pune, Forbes Marshall has a well-equipped hospital which provides medical facilities for not only the employees of the organisation at Kasarwadi, but also allows poor patients from in and around Kasarwadi area to utilise these medical benefits free of cost.

12.3 Dimensions of Internal Employment Relations

Retirement

Despite organisations initiating wide employee engagement programmes, people still resign. Although research studies state how some percentage of resignations is healthy, as they allow fresh ideas to be reinstated through new recruitments, but there is cause for alarm if the number is high. This is especially so if the talented employees resign in large numbers. Organisations need to seriously adopt a way out to stem the resignations occurring en masse. In order to analyse such trends, the following measures are undertaken:

1. **The Exit Interview: Analysing Voluntary Resignations**

    Even during times of economic recession, or a downturn, when organisations are looking for innovation from their talented employees, it causes a huge business loss to the organisation if they leave. At such times, organisations conduct exit interviews to understand the reasons for employees exit and adopt ways of improvement resulting from the exiting employees' feedback. An exit interview is a means of revealing the real reasons employees leave their jobs, providing the organisation with information on how to correct the causes of discontent and reducing employee turnover. Although money or better salary is considered one of the prime reasons for leaving for better job prospects, there is a multitude of other causes mentioned in the exit interviews of organisations.

    The typical exit interview follows the following format:

    Establishing rapport, stating the purpose of the interview, exploring the employees attitudes regarding the old job, exploring the workers' reasons for leaving, comparing old and new jobs, recording the changes recommended by the employee who resigns and conclusion of the interview. The information provided by the resigning employee at any level may be very valuable in getting insights for the organisation to discover gaps, improve its weaknesses and reinforce its strengths. Many a time, the managers conduct the post-exit interview much after the employee has resigned in order to provide a better context for the employee to reflect on the challenges and the problems of the organisation which he or she has left. Such inputs can be valuable for the exiting employee.

2. **Attitude Surveys and Employee Satisfaction Surveys**

    These surveys seek input from employees to determine their feelings about various topics such as the work they perform, behaviour and competence of their supervisor, their work environment, flexibility in the work place, opportunities for advancement, training and development and compensation systems etc.

    If the exit interview is the reactive response, the Employee Satisfaction Survey or the Attitude Survey is considered to be a proactive effort to gather feedback from the current employees on various policies, management practices, procedures, and work elements and culture related to the organisation. Most of the time, companies prefer to conduct such interviews through questionnaires in an anonymous manner to ensure authentic responses from the employees without fear of reprisal or intimidation. Many private organisations and MNCs conduct such surveys as a norm to monitor their practices and culture and align them with the requirements of the employees. Such inputs regarding the work environment, practices and compensation are very valuable for the management to incorporate changes.

3. **Advance Notice of Resignation**

Most firms insist an advance notice period from a resigning employee. This may range from two weeks to three months depending upon the related policy, shared with the employees through their handbook or manual or some form of communication. There are exceptions, where the organisation asks the employee to leave immediately and pays him or her for the notice period. But these are only in exceptional cases.

12.4 Termination

This measure is the most severe penalty that an organisation imposes on an employee. This is considered to be a form of a disciplinary action. Such a decision is considered to be difficult for both - the employer or the manager and the employee who has been asked to go. Research studies on the feelings of employees who have been asked to go, speak about the trauma, fear, a sense of loss of self worth and depression. Recently an FMCG company terminated one of its employees, a manager, after 17 years of working. The ground of termination as mentioned by the company spokesperson was gross negligence of duty and forging of expense documents. It appears that he had acquired some vices during his tenure with the organisation and needed to maintain these vices, which had by now made him addicted - hence he had to resort to forgery and cheating. Still, the organisation undertook an in-depth investigation of the matter and only then passed this termination order even though the manager was very anxious due to the impact it would have on his family members. The adoption of technology and multimedia has facilitated the verification of forgery, misconduct and frauds, and hence providing proof of such misconduct is considered easy today.

Research has suggested that Friday afternoon is probably the best time to fire an employee, because it gives him or her the weekend to cool off; and ideally it should be done on pay day and the employee can collect the last pay-cheque. Further, firing the employee at the end of the day leaves little chance for discussion among the remaining staff that may interrupt the work place.

In case of individuals who are neither managers nor professionally trained individuals such as accountants and engineers, and if the firm is unionised, the termination procedure is usually well defined in the labour-management agreement. For example, drinking on the job may cause immediate termination whereas regular absences may lead to repeated warnings before a termination notice is served to the employee. Regardless of the size of the organisation and whether it is unionised or not, the management should inform employees of the actions that warrant termination.

In case of termination of the top management except the CEO, who can be terminated only by the Board of Directors, there is no formal procedure for the executives before termination. The reasons for the termination too may be different:

1. **Economic Downturn:** At times, business conditions may force some executives to be terminated. In Pune, during the 2008 downturn, the media was replete with reports of executives from various IT companies like IBM and Wipro which had issued termination orders to executives at various levels.
2. **Downsizing:** In order to improve efficiency or as a result of merging with another company, a firm may reorganise or downsize some of its executives.
3. **Philosophical or ideological differences:** These too lead to termination of employees voluntarily as a sudden resignation or volunteered by the top management in the organisation.
4. **Decline in productivity:** The executive may have been capable of performing satisfactorily in the past but is no longer capable of performing with the same efficiency or productivity due to negligence or health or attitude related problems due to which the organisation may terminate him.

Demotion as an alternative to termination

Demotion is used as an alternative to discharge, especially if the employee has served a long term in the organisation. Sometimes firms downsize and the layers in the organisation structure get eliminated due to a restructuring exercise, with even highly qualified employees being terminated. At such times, rather than lose a valuable employee, the firm decides to demote him or her to a lower level position, sometimes even with the same salary. There are times when the demoted person may suffer a loss of esteem and face. The demotion may make him or her angry and frustrated. It is necessary that an employee is given a positive image of his or her value to the company.

Lay-offs in Today's Environment

The business news today is seldom without a report of lay-offs. In their zeal to control costs and make the organisation lean and trim or reduce the flab and concentrate on core competencies while outsourcing jobs to others, more and more companies are laying off staff in the name of restructuring. MNCs like Sony and Mitsubishi, and even Indian companies along with some PSUs are now in the process of laying off even young professionals or white-collar employees. The model is surely shifting towards a just in time workers or contingent workers. In case the lay-offs are due to low performance, it is necessary that the laid-off worker is given the lower rating as compared to one who is being retained as a higher-performing worker. The impact of a lay-off on a person who has been in the company for many years, and who is 40 years old or older, is deep and very traumatic. Recently companies like Mahindras and Force Motors laid off a line of staff from various levels in the name of cost cutting. Many of these employees, as claimed, were high-performance workers. The flip side of such a decision is that those who are more outspoken and challenging are unfortunately the first ones to face the job axe.

Lay-off/Recall procedures

Even in the rapidly changing environment, recalls are necessary at times. Whether the firm is union free or is unionised, carefully constructed lay-off procedures should be developed. Typically the worker and labour agreements mention the lay-off procedure where typically the senior most are the first to be laid off and the first to be reinstated or recalled. Union-free firms should establish lay-off procedures where the employee's productivity – or lack of it - should be the basis. It is essential to define the lay-off procedures in terms of performance and productivity before hand to avoid any discrepancies that may be likely to occur.

Outplacement

Many organisations, especially during the recession of 2008, which laid off workers systematically designed a plan to help such employees with contacts and securing suitable jobs outside the company. This is called outplacement and it is extended to all levels of employees.

Some of the services provided by the outplacement groups are as follows:

1. Social security options, pensions and reimbursement for attending interviews elsewhere.
2. Career guidance including personality profile test and related assessments.
3. Instructions and understanding of one's competency mapping techniques important for remaining active in the outside recruitment circles.
4. Training and coaching for promotional avenues.
5. Help with enhancing techniques and skills for successful interviews.
6. Development of a personal action plan and continued support.

Case Study on Outplacement

ZCS Consulting Ltd., Hyderabad, has been doing Executive search assignments with large infrastructure clients for almost 15 years. The case study is detailed in their own words:

"Every time this particular client with a turnover exceeding $1billion and a presence in power, renewable energy, construction and real estate, calls, it is generally for hiring senior-level executives across their operations spread globally.

"In July 2012 when there was a call from their CEO, we thought it was one more senior search assignment; but the CEO was little serious said he had a serious problem to be resolved immediately. He continued telling us that the utmost confidentiality was required as this involved moving out one of their senior vice presidents in the construction division who had become redundant in the system because of restructuring of one division. He wanted this assignment to be completed in 6 months.

"The CEO just wanted to know whether ZCS could handle this assignment, and the process to follow to ensure confidentiality and ensure at the same time that the candidate was placed in an assignment where he would be comfortable.

"We gave him the confidence that ZCS had been handling similar assignments on a selective basis for various other clients and we would be able to come out with possible assignments in 3-4 months' time.

"While handling this kind of assignments, we follow a very time-tested process of direct interaction with the candidates and take inputs from the company before we start working on the profile. Generally, in our placement we help in structuring his profile, give interview guidance and in some cases help the candidate to understand their present market value so that they can negotiate on compensation with future employers accordingly.

"The profile of the candidate to be outplaced is shared selectively with a few clients where there is high probability of candidate making it and the job content meets the candidate's requirements.

"We also do personalised counselling regarding opportunities and competencies being sought by the potential employer so that candidate accepts the assignment by choice.

"For this particular Senior Vice President we could zero down on two more large infra companies which were planning to diversify into similar domains of this candidate's strengths, had personal meetings with senior executives of these companies and explained to them the value-add this candidate could bring with his vast experience.

"Subsequently, personal meetings were organised between the senior-level team of these companies and the candidate.

"Today sometimes when I meet this candidate, it gives immense pleasure that he has been promoted and all three involved – the old company, the candidate and the new employer - thank us for all the support we have given. "

Questions:
1. What is outplacement and how is it different from regular placement?
2. What are the issues to be addressed from the candidate's perspective in an outplacement assignment?
3. What is the process flow for an outplacement assignment?

Here's a sample of an Exit Feedback Form for a company let us call as Momentum:

Annexure I
EXIT FEEDBACK FORM
PART A
(To be completed by the separating team member)

Name _____ Emp. No. _____
Present Designation _____ Function _____
Present Supervisor _____ Date of Resignation _____
Last Working Day _____ Feedback Interview Dr. _____

You have been with us for a while. Now that you have taken the firm decision to part association with the **Momentum** family, we would like you to share with us the reason(s) for your decision. The feedback that you will provide would be very valuable for us to look at ourselves and to also make momentum a still better place to work in.

Please complete Sections I and II of Part A and return to HRD before the feedback interview date.

Section I

Reason(s) for leaving. (Please tick as many as applicable).

- Higher salary.
- Going abroad.
- Could not cope with the job.
- Transfer of spouse.
- Higher studies (India/Abroad), Name of course _____
- Non-performance.
- No job satisfaction.
- Not satisfied with company policies (Which ones?)
- Not happy with work environment. Did not get along with the boss.
- Not satisfied with performance evaluation.
- Location constraint.
- Not adequate growth opportunities.
- Health problems.
- Own business.
- Retirement.
- Any other (Please specify) _____

PART B
(HR Team)

Part B is the typical basis of the Feedback Interview Interview/HR Team and is not to be handed over to the exiting team Interviewer to keep the following in mind:

- Listen well and be open-minded it serves no purpose for interviewer to get into an argument with the separating team member.
- Please do not justify actions. However where the member has factually incorrect information, you may provide the correct factual information.
- Throughout the interview stay focused on the team member.
- Leave more space at the end of the interview for general comments.
- Take notes of the high points. It is not essential to get exact quotes always. It is more important to listen than write the essence.
- Immediately after the interview determine if you would rehire the team member. Assume they will reapply.

Type of questions to ask:

1. How did you feel you were managed during your association with us?
2. What do you feel are the best things about Momentum worth remembering?
3. Is Momentum a good place to work (If Yes/No–Why?)
4. Do you think the compensation package of the organisation is competitive with the industry (if Yes/No–Why?)
5. What did you like most (least) about your position?
6. Are the employee promotion decisions handled fairly (If Yes/No–Why)?
7. Under what conditions would you have stayed in Momentum?
8. If you had had a magic wand, what two things would you have changed in momentum?
   (i)
   (ii)
9. What are your outstanding achievements during your work tenure in Momentum.
10. (a) When did you first think of leaving Momentum.
    (b) What things/situations that prompted you to take such a extreme step?
11. Suggestions to improve working conditions or morale.
12. Name one thing that the organisation could have done (hypothetical), to retain you.

Feedback interview conducted by:

Date: Place:

PART C
(Immediate Superior)

This part is to be filled by the immediate superior of the exiting team member.

Kindly answer following questions with respect to your experience while working with Mr./Ms./Dr. _____

1. How will you define your work experience with him/her?
2. What have been his/her outstanding contributions during his work tenure with you?
3. What are his/her strengths and weaknesses identified by you?
4. In your view how would you rate his/her relationship with:
   - Superiors
   - Colleagues
5. If he/she were to reapply to Momentum, considering that you have now worked with him/her what would be your recommendation and why?

   Yes Hire/No, do not hire.

   Please give at least two reasons for your above answer.
6. According to you what could be the reasons for his/her change in job.
7. What could have we as an organisation done to retain him/her?

Name and Signature: Date:

Case Study: Young Talent Hiring and Retention

Rahul is a young engineer from a reputed institute with good academic track record who joined as a Graduate Engineer Trainee (GET) in a big Manufacturing company. There were other trainees who were from different institutes who joined along with him. Initially he was provided classroom induction for over a week and then sent to a few other plants to learn the products and processes.

Then he was finally posted in one of the plants where he was asked to take care of the shift operations for 2 years as per the plan. The purpose of the GET programme is to induct talented and energetic Engineers to make them Production/ Maintenance Managers (heading a complete Department) in 5-6 years. Rahul started working but he thought there was no proper guided process operations and maintenance. There were always high expectations on him and he was unable to cope with those expectations as he thought he had not been properly hand-held and he expected more support and guidance from his superiors, which practically is not possible as he was provided with technical training for a month after his joining.

He continued his work though he was not doing it with utmost passion and dedication. He was not emotionally connected to the job. He never took interest to explore and learn new things and this made Rahul remain as a normal employee and not an outstanding employee after completion of one year.

Questions:
1. What do you think is the problem in the above case?
2. What would you do if you were in place of Rahul?
3. Do you think learning and development happens only via classroom training and by an external source? Justify your answer.
4. Do you think that Rahul as a young aspirant was impatient? If yes, what three actions do you recommend?
5. What are the three actionable recommendations to retain Rahul and ensure he does wonders in the existing job?

Case Study: Zensar: Building an Engaged Workforce

In July 2011, Yogesh Patgaonkar - the Global HR Head - and Ruchi Mathur - the newly inducted OD Head - of Zensar Technologies had a problem. They were reviewing the results of the Employee Engagement Survey conducted across 6000 associates (employees) of the company and were concerned that for the second consecutive year the engagement score had dipped by five percent. With the organisation doing well and poised for 50 percent growth in the financial year 2011-12, how could they tell the CEO and the rest of the management team that this was a problem that needed immediate attention?

Zensar had just set a $1-billion revenue target for itself, to be achieved by March 2017. Achieving this target called for a far higher rate of growth than at present, and would need a strong, engaged workforce operating at hi-performance levels. In the process of scaling up, how would Zensar remain 'large enough to deliver, but small enough to care'?

While HR processes and systems were fully in order, the 6000-strong organisation appeared in need of better human connect. It was essential to achieve this, as engagement is a significant key to employee retention, especially in the IT industry where career options are fairly similar across IT companies and lateral moves are relatively easy. Moreover, Dr. Ganesh Natarajan, Vice Chairman and CEO of Zensar, strongly believed that happy employees make for a more productive workplace. He believed passionately in the '5F' culture instituted at Zensar – Fast, Focused, Flexible and very importantly....Friendly and Fun.

When Ruchi and Yogesh explained their concerns, Ganesh exhorted the newly set up Talent Management Committee comprising all Business Heads as well as Line HR Heads, to cut across party lines and look for solutions. Ganesh's brief: to come up with a plan which would reverse the score decline and enable Employee Engagement to climb at least four percentage points up the chart in the coming year.

People Management in the IT Industry: Whilst deciding on the Engagement strategy for the year, the Talent Management Committee kept the following characteristics of the IT industry in mind:

- Being predominantly in the service industry, the ability to create nonlinear impact depends on the engagement of the associates. To keep the engagement high during the scaling up of operations, front line managers' management plays a key role. Any impact on engagement would not be possible unless the frontline managers are on board.
- The Project-based nature of the industry implies that the composition of teams keep changing. Thus, for a junior level associate to experience engagement throughout the organisation, it is imperative to enable consistent People Management practices by Team leaders.
- These priorities were ratified and fine-tuned by the outcomes of the annual Voice of Associates survey and over 250 Associates that we reached out to through Focus Group Discussions, which reflected the need for better People Management Practices in the areas of Connectedness, Feedback and team Development.

Questions:
1. You are an Organisation Development consultant to Zensar. What would your recommendation be to the Talent Management Committee? What strategy should be adopted in order to build both Engagement and growth?
2. How would you ensure that the initiatives decided upon, are implemented such that they are sustained and woven into the fabric of the organisation?
3. How would you measure the success of the initiatives?

Teaching Notes:

Zensar has a strong culture of 'Growth by participative Management' as evident through its extremely successful Vision Community initiative – through which employees across all levels in Zensar contribute and channel their ideas. This success encouraged Zensar to think about participation on a larger scale through the launch of iZen – I Make Change Happen.

Whilst the iZen Engagement Workshops ensured the involvement of frontline managers, the iZen Action Teams reached out to individual Zensarians.

The term 'iZen' marries the concepts of freedom and accountability – the two being sides of the same coin. It provides a platform for each and every Zensarian to contribute in their special way to Zensar's growth. It says - I am Zensar, and am accountable just like anyone else, for people, processes and systems at Zensar. At the same time, it implies a freedom to make change happen.

Two prongs of iZen were launched in 2011-12:
- iZen Action Teams were formed within each Zensar BU/ location – 6 in total - comprising Associates from across levels in that BU. Each team included the BU and HR head and drove engagement initiatives for their BU. Outcomes of the Focus Group Discussions held earlier in the year were shared with the iZen Action Teams who worked specifically on systems related to:
  o Fun at Work
  o Rewards and Recognition
  o Communication
  o Work Environment
- iZen Engagement Workshops: Building Exceptional Teams were held across Zensar Managers - from the leadership level right upto the Project Manager level. Thus all Managers at Zensar were urged to 'make change happen' within their teams by driving consistent people management practices. This was connected to the overall business goal of $1Bn by 2017, because as Zensar scales up, the Engagement agenda needs to be taken up at the level of each Project Manager in order to continue being a highly engaged organisation. There were 3 key areas covered by the workshops:
  o Building Connected Teams
  o Providing ongoing feedback
  o Creating clear development plans for team members

Branding and Marketing: In order to build excitement around iZen and secure nominations from associates for being part of the iZen Action Teams, the Marketing and HR team swung into action with a teaser campaign, posters, cascades, our global eZenscapes* newsletter doing a special feature on iZen, contests around the theme of 'I Make Change Happen', launch events in both Pune and Hyderabad and finally a sustained call for nominations. This received a whopping response resulting in 150 members in the final iZen Action Teams.

Execution of iZen Engagement Workshops – involvement of Leadership Group.

The iZen Engagement workshops reached out to 500+ people Managers in Zensar through over 25 workshops, across Pune, Hyderabad, South Africa, UK and the US. Moreover, it was the top leadership group including the CEO, business and HR Heads who held the workshops for the Programme Managers and Project Managers at Zensar. This kind of involvement and accountability on the part of leadership drove a sense of urgency and brought in huge credibility to the message of the workshops.

Clear Action Plans: There was a clear Action Plan created for participants at the end of the workshops, with participants writing down the practices and timelines for actions related to building Connected Teams, providing formal and informal feedback and Development of team members.

Follow-ups to Workshops: The success of the workshops lay as much in the post-workshop follow up as in the workshops themselves. There were regular follow-ups to the workshops with participants having an open forum with the CEO and HR Head and voicing their experience of being an Engaged Manager through Connectedness, Feedback and Team Development.

There were no less than three formal, structured follow-up sessions and the last one consisted of presentations being made to the CEO, by individual Managers, in terms of their progress with reference to their Action Plan.

Ultimately by urging consistent and repeated action on the part of Managers, a common language was instilled across the organisation and these practices institutionalized, thus bringing about a fundamental change in culture.

Results: There was immense excitement around iZen with iZen Action Team members proudly sporting their iZen 'badges' at work, and driving initiatives whether related to Fun@Work, Rewards and Recognition, etc.

In parallel, the iZen Engagement Workshops led to concerted action on the part of Managers to drive Connectedness, Feedback and Development; which led to both self-motivation as well as team motivation.

Some of the quantifiable outcomes were:

- Increased Retention vis-à-vis 2010-11.
- Significant increase in the Engagement Score, tracked year on year through a Voice of Associates Survey.
- The iZen workshops were targeted specifically at the mid-management level and the Engagement score for that level went up by 10 percentage points.
- Over 700 Development Action Plans made for team members.

Last Word

iZen is a formal articulation of a philosophy that Zensar has believed in for years – that the best ideas, solutions and inputs come from Zensar's associates. Whether it be through Vision Communities, Every Body Meets, the Voice of Associates survey or more personalized platforms such as Pizza and Coke's; there have always been platforms for expressing oneself.

The iZen initiative carries forward and strengthens this philosophy, at the same time grounding it in Excellence, thus leading to the business goal of $1Bn.

Recommended Reading and References:
1. Human Resource Management by Robert Noe, 9th Edn, and Pearson Education: 2006, UK: South Asia.
2. Human Resource Management, Gary Dessler and Bijju Varkkey, 12th edition, Pearson Education, 2011, New Delhi.
3. Human Resource Management by Adrian Murton, Margaret Inman, Nuala O Sullivan, Hodder Education, 2011, South Asia.
4. Human Resource Management, Michael Muller, Richard Croucher and Susan Leigh, Jaico Publishing House, 2008, New Delhi

HIL HR initiatives and Programmes

Employee Engagement:

Employee engagement initiatives include Rewards and recognition, Employee engagement surveys are also conducted once in 18 months by the World Class Consulting firms like McKinsey and Mercer.

We also have some fun for our employees and their family through Annual Get together, Sports events, Internal competitions etc.

We ensured to have Quarterly Employee Communication programme named "HIL Connect" in which MD addresses across the Organisation on the performance and the vision/goal of the organisation. Employees also get a chance to interact & ask questions to the MD & Senior Leadership Team

A Grievance Redressal Process is also introduced for employees to raise their grievances and concerns without fear.

We have launched an Idea Forum, ICUBE for Employees to share their ideas and creative thoughts openly.

Training and Development

The development and training need assessment is done once a year through Training Need Identification exercise. We emphasize on level based training.

We do provide specialized training for the improvement areas and then based on the strengths, the skill mapping for the role is done.

What's new that we are doing in this industry or new/different compared to what we were doing earlier.

Transformation Journey

We have hired Mc Kinsey to help us with our transformation journey, "Udaan". We have identified Change Leaders and Change Agents, who will work on specific projects under the guidance of Mckinsey team for a certain period and will go back to their original base location to replicate the similar initiatives at each location. By this, we are ensuring that the learning is applied and the changes are constant and the initiative is sustained. This process also helps in making the teams self sufficient to lead the change management and is not expected to be driven from Top.

Hi Pot and Hi Value programme

In our transformational journey, Udaan, we are targeting to create a World Class organisation with maximum value to our shareholders, attain the Customer delight and be the leader in the focused segment of our business. We can achieve this ambitious but achievable target only by having inspirational leaders and a pool of in-house talent on board.

To Development in-house Leaders across all levels, we have launched Hi pot Programme. Colleagues meeting the eligibility criteria undergo Assessment Centers conducted by the external agency. The colleagues successfully clearing the assessment are declared as Hi-POTs. The whole framework of Hi-Pot programme includes,

- All Hi pots having freezed IDP in discussion with their Managers.
- Hi pots selecting their own mentor.
- In-house coaching being provided to mentees.
- Exposure of working in Cross functional teams.
- Exposure to challenging assignments, job rotation, role change with higher responsibilities.
- Organisation investing in one year comprehensive Management development Programme focusing on competencies which includes classroom training, coaching and on the job training.
- Hi pots are identified as successors for the higher roles.

What's the new idea/motivation? How are we measuring the results?

We want to sustain our leadership in the Building material Industry, and as a first stepping stone aiming for the best in the Group Companies. With the help of McKinsey we have identified 3 key initiatives to improve our Organisational Health Index. All our efforts and actions are aligned to ensure that we improve our Organisational Health Index. We have taken targets to build the right organisation for our aspirational journey, increase our Employee Engagement (from 33% to 75%), PMS (from 61% to 90%), Rewards and Recognition (from 36% to 70%).

Attracting young talent and retaining them. How successfully we have done this.

We have been hiring GETs and MT from the premier institutes like IIT and IIMs under our YUVA (Young Unique Vibrant Achievers) program.

We hire them after a stringent talent acquisition process which involves, Group Discussion, psychometric tests and personal rounds of Interviews. Designing specific roles for MT/GETs and laterals from Premier Institutes like ISB,IIMs,IITs,NITs. We provide Individual coach and ensure that they get the visibility and interact with Leadership team and group Chairman on periodic basis.

Succession plan/career growth prospects within the organisation – cross-functional or within the group

- Identified successors have been given leadership, Business acumen training.
- Critical Assignments and coaching.
- Successors for few Key positions to be hired externally. Introduced Assessment Centre as selection process for senior and critical positions.
- Introduced Job portal, IJP, Employee Referral.

Cross functional on the job training to get a 360-degree feel.

In our transformation journey, we expect our teams to work in collaboration.

Hence the project which is identified for hi pots, probable Hi pots, change leaders, change agents involves working with cross functional team. As a growth prospects, employee have an option of moving to a different function through internal job posting. It has reaped good results as employees are familiar with the challenges faced by various teams and are working cohesively to achieve a common goal.

Way forward - what are the new plans being explored. Critical drivers of retention, reasons for attrition etc.

- Fast track growth for Hi pots.
- Job rotation of Hi pots on regular interval of 18/24 months.
- Looking for the differential pay package for hi pots.
- Similar career growth opportunities for Probable high-pots and hi performers.
- Would revamp the Performance Management system to make it more robust and transparent.
- More thrust on Employee engagement programs which would bring the culture of innovation, performance excellence.
- Revamped Rewards and Recognition for timely and appropriate recognition.
- How the personal issues/family relocation are etc. are being addressed.
- We are fortunate to have Pan-India presence. Hence if an employee wants to relocate to some other location due to personal reasons, depending on the individual capabilities and the business requirements we map employee to new location.

- Employee benefits, security to the family in the event of death/disability etc.
- All employees are covered under group personal accident Policy. The family can claim around 40 times of Basic salary in case of death and in proportionate way for disability.
- We are also checking the feasibility of Life term Policy for a cross section of employees.

Discussion Questions

1. What is employee engagement? Why is it important?
2. What are the reasons for retrenchment? How are employees identified for lay-offs?
3. What is the importance of an exit interview?
4. What are the phases in retiring an employee?

Chapter 13...

Employee Health and Safety

Contents ...
13.1 Introduction
13.2 Safety
13.3 Safety Programmes
13.4 Provisions of Factories Act
13.5 Safety Committees in India
• Discussion Questions
• References and Recommended Readings

Objectives and Summary

This chapter is aimed at understanding the importance of following safety norms in organisations, and the consequences of not doing so. It also reflects the importance of wellness among employees at all levels, as there is research to prove that employees' health is reflected in their productivity and performance. It aims to expose the readers to the relevant legislation related to safety and the need for a safety audit to monitor the measures undertaken by organisations.

Safety can be defined as absence of accidents or mishaps at the workplace. Several workers and employees along with people from the surrounding areas have lost their lives or have been maimed forever due to the absence of safety measures. Losses have mounted and productivity has been affected when valuable employees have fallen sick or not reported to work due to alcoholism, depression or such lifestyle-related diseases. It is considered imperative for organisations to extend importance to the areas of safety and health, in order to generate better results from employees and the public at large. Legislation too has incorporated these clauses.

Learning Outcomes:
1. Underline the impact of lack of safety measures in organisations;
2. Highlight the importance of safety and the need for a regular safety audit;

3. Elaborate on the impact of wellness and employee wellbeing;
4. Promote wellbeing through counselling and training employees to counter the effects of smoking, depression, alcoholism, stress and burnout.

13.1 Introduction

"Every twenty seconds of every working minute of every hour throughout the world, someone dies as a result of an industrial accident." This was how the seriousness of industrial accidents was described by the Director General of the British Council, in his message of good wishes at the Seventh National Conference on Industrial Safety and Health organised by the National Safety Council of India this year, in 2013.

Major Industrial Accidents in India in the Year (2011)

PUNE: Twenty people were hospitalised today following a chlorine gas leak from an effluent treatment plant in Pimpri-Chinchwad area in Pune district.

The leakage in the plant triggered a scare in the area with people living in nearby localities shifting temporarily as a precautionary measure.

The patients, who complained of cough and eye irritation after the gas leak, are in a stable condition, hospital sources said. January 18, 2011

Bhagiradha Chemicals & Industries Ltd has informed BSE that at 3.30 A.M., on August 10, 2011, a major fire accident occurred at Production Block III at the factory site of Bhagiradha Chemicals Industries located at Ongole, Andhra Pradesh resulting in loss of two lives and damage to property. The extent of damage and impact on the operations is being ascertained. November 26, 2011

Five people died on Friday in Tamil Nadu's Vaniyambadi district, after inhaling poisonous gas at a local tannery. The victims were cleaning a tank used for chemical treatment of leather, when they were exposed to the gas. April 30, 2010

The risks associated with industrial working have made the life of workforce very cheap.

13.2 Safety

Safety in simple terms means freedom from the risks of injury, loss of limbs, or any form of disability or loss. Industrial safety or employee safety refers to the protection of the workers from the danger of industrial accidents.

An accident can be defined as an unplanned and an uncontrolled event in which an action or reaction of an object, a substance, a person or a radiation results in personal injury.

Accidents are of various types. They can be classified as major or minor ones, fatal or non-fatal depending upon the severity of the injury. A major accident is the one which results in the death or a major disability of the injured. These disabilities may be partial, total, temporary or permanent.

Need for Safety

An accident-free plant provides a safe environment for employees to work. The need for safety also extends to the organisations, which may be prone to accidents due to short-circuits, earthquakes, faulty furniture, lifts in its building etc. International Labour Organisation (ILO) observes April 28 every year as the World Day for Safety and Health at Work. Dow Chemicals, an MNC, in its quest for an accident-free and safe environment, has allocated a specific time, every Monday, for safety meetings. Speakers and experts in the area of safety and accident prevention make presentations and share expertise on areas related to safety.

The following are the advantages of safety and an accident-free organisational environment:

1. **Cost saving:** There are direct costs as well as indirect costs incurred by the organisation in case of an accident. Direct costs include medical expenses reimbursement, compensation payable to the family dependents if the accident is fatal. The indirect costs involve the decline of morale among the employees, who believe that the organisation is negligent as far as safety is concerned. Also, it affects the operational efficiency, damages the equipment and results in a decline of the efficiency of the worker or the employee who has been a victim of the accident.

2. **Increased productivity:** Employees in safe environments are able to enhance their productivity as they do not have to worry about safety and accident issues and can concentrate on efficiency and innovation.

3. **Morale:** The Workmen's Compensation Act 1923 underlines the need to reimburse the dependent family for the loss caused to the employee on account of negligence, accidents and lack of safety. In order to avoid not only the monetary costs involved due to lack of precautions or training given to the employees for a safe working, organisations will benefit from the high morale of the employees who believe that that they are safe in the environment and are adequately trained to meet emergencies if necessary.

4. **Legal:** The law ensures an environment which is accident-free and safe. The Supreme Court has held that:

An enterprise which is engaged in a hazardous or inherently dangerous industry which poses a potential threat to the health and safety to the persons working in the factory and industry in the surrounding areas, owes an absolute and a non-delegable duty to the community to ensure that no harm results to anyone on account of the hazardous or inherently dangerous activities. This implies unlimited liability.

The civil law establishes the extent of damages or compensation. In criminal law, sentences are prescribed; sentences are also prescribed under the pollution control laws.

There is no legal ceiling on the extent of liability. Financial losses can be minimised if the plant and the organisation is accident-free.

13.3 Safety Programmes

These should be governed by the following principles:

1. Most accidents are caused due to a number of factors, namely the systemic problems resulting in human failure and mistakes – the cost of which may be very high. It is necessary that the top management take a more serious view of safety and consider this focus, as its topmost agenda. Apart from the mandatory Safety Week (4th March till 16th March), the management needs to conduct regular training programmes to share and educate the personnel about safety practices in all spheres.

2. Another important function of the management is to identify potential safety hazards, expose the personnel to monitor safety standards in processes and machinery, design systems to identify action in the event of any hazard, and to maintain records of earlier accidents and their causes. These will caution personnel. Also surprise safety checks by the quality and safety managers or outside inspection agencies will leverage the importance of safety. The management must take total precaution to communicate the importance of safety at all times and also incorporate safety standards as an element in the performance appraisal process. To ensure this, proper systems for maintaining the upkeep of equipment and education of the personnel is paramount.

3. The top management as well as managers at all levels should control and monitor safety standards in all areas of work.

4. A typical programme of safety contains the elements of strategic choices, designing safety policies, and organisation of safety, evaluation, implementation and analysis of causes of accidents.

Causes of Accidents and Remedies

1. Inadequate attention paid to inspection aggravates the problems of industrial accidents. For instance, there are the following acts which are in force: The Factories Act, The Boilers Act, The Industry Explosives Act, The Indian Electricity Act, The Pesticides Act, The Environment Protection Act, and The Water (Prevention and Control of Pollution) Act. All these are legal provisions to ensure employee and public safety and prevention of accidents. However, human errors and negligence on the part of inspection bodies result in otherwise avoidable accidents. Hence, accidents like the ones at Sivakasi, at the glass-making units at Faridabad, and Mandya Sugar Mill at Mandya (Karnataka) to mention only a few. Many industrial units where appropriate care about safety is not taken are like potential death traps.

2. Many a time in organisations, safety is traded for the completion of targets and jobs. The importance to be given to safety is undermined by the increased focus on results. If there is an accident, then the managements are blamed.

3. Sivakasi, a major location for cracker units, has as mentioned above become a death trap for many women - and children too - who work there. The 1982 fire which claimed more than 35 lives has not been forgotten. Lack of importance given to safety, haphazard production, employing untrained child labour (more than 45, 000 children have been employed there) and gross indifference by the government on these illegal issues has been a major cause of such accidents. Other examples reported, where there has been gross negligence, include the cotton ginning factory at Andhra Pradesh and Fabine textiles at Bhiwandi, Maharashtra where fire claimed many lives. The lack of fire-fighting equipment had aggravated the disaster. Other industries where the safety norms are grossly disregarded are the diamond cutting industry and coal mines, where and the residue ash or dust can cause untold harm to the people, environment, flora and fauna. Besides, workers being locked up in diamond cutting and polishing units, due to the owners' fear of pilferage, has caused deaths when fires have occurred. Since many of these accidents are in the unorganised sector, the safety precautions have been grossly neglected.

4. Two recent garment factory disasters in Bangladesh highlight the crying need for proper enforcement of existing safety legislation. An eight-storey factory building that collapsed in April 2013 has claimed more than 1,000 lives, making it the worst such disaster in history. Just a fortnight later, a fire in a sweater making unit killed the owner and at least seven workers. The country has a garment industry worth about $20 billion, with customer lists that include the world's top names in the retail trade. While the Rana Plaza building reportedly collapsed because of poor construction and blatant violations of safety regulations – to which the big-name buyers turned a blind eye - the toll in the 11-storey Tung Hai Sweater factory fire was so low because it happened at night, after it had closed for the day. The factory, with its sister unit, has some 7,000 employees who produce about 70 million sweaters and other articles of clothing every year for customers in Europe and the US. Earlier, in November 2012, a fire in the Tazreen garment factory had killed 112 workers. There are about four million Bangladeshis working in garment factories, for hourly wages of 10-30 taka (a taka is worth about one US cent). This obviously keeps costs down for the Western buyer – be it the retail chain or the final customer who wears the clothes.

5. Factory negligence due to lack of training and education to workers and personnel, non-demarcation of areas for hazardous materials and non hazardous materials, and non-implementation of factory regulations and safety standards, have given India a name for some of the highest number of industrial accidents totalling 100,000

workers. This is a huge number compared with those in the developed countries which have single-digit numbers, or almost negligible as in Japan.

Training in Safety

Training should be accorded top priority by the organisations and industry if safety is to be ensured. The content, design, module and methodology changes depend upon the system of training adopted by the enterprise. Today, safety is considered to be a top priority in many industries and hence this function has been leveraged to the top management accountability. The objective of all training programmes is to equip personnel with the skills of education and knowledge of the working of the factory and industry, expose them to the potential accidents and their consequence if safety is not pursued systematically, and empower them to minimize the accident impact and damage in the event of casualty.

Sometimes, organisations recruit specialists to conduct training on the various areas related to the chemicals, emergency showers use for water deluge, use of fire-fighting equipment and their operation and so on.

Organisations like National Organic Chemical Industries (NOCIL) have designed unique training programmes on safety and risk management.

Role of the Top Management and Unions

The top management should believe in the priority of safety measures and safety implementation. They could form special safety committees and appoint a safety officer who will continuously monitor the implementation of safety standards and their administration. They need to also get a buy-in from the trade union that could monitor these activities.

Employee Participation

From the employees' perspective, this should be communicated as an urgent issue and their effective participation should be established. A detailed check-list must be provided to ensure their regular involvement and participation. This should include the following: treat the issue of safety as a very important point, cooperate with inspection and safety officers, suggest ways to improve safety, share the importance of safety, adhere to company safety rules, report on any accidents and damages on account of unsafe conditions, design systems to immediately report on events, keep the work area neat and uncluttered, avoid unsafe acts, report on unsafe procedures and correct them. All this would go a long way improving the safety of organisations.

Safety includes health and wellness of employees too. Many IT and service organisations have woken up to this urgent need. Hence, today there are a plethora of facilities like medical and wellness centre in work places, a well-equipped gymnasium, blood donation camps, yoga classes, meditation and pranayama, psychological counselling for the employees, sharing ambulance numbers in case of emergencies and a tie up with them. These are also included in the domain of safety. Still there have been mishaps and deaths.

There was a recent case in a Technology Solutions organisation where an employee suffered a heart attack. Since the ambulance did not come on time, he died. Ditto is the case of an IBM employee, who reported to work on time. Apparently she received a phone call, and the next thing was to climb up the stairs of the building and jump from the terrace. Reports suggested that counselling on time could have staved off the suicide.

Provisions of the Factories Act, 1948

The provisions are:

S.21 Dangerous part of every piece of machinery must be securely fenced. S.22 stipulates that the machinery in motion must be examined by a trained adult male worker. The section further provides that any young person or a woman should not handle a machine which is in motion. S.23 states that young persons should not be allowed to work on dangerous machines. S.24 says that every factory must provide suitable striking gear. There should also be a locking device to prevent accidental starting of transmission machinery.

According to S.25, no traversing part to be allowed to run within a distance of 45 centimetres from any fixed structure.

S.26 Requires that casting should be done in such a way as to prevent danger.

S.27 Stipulates that women and children should be prohibited from going near cotton openers.

According to S.28, hoists and lifts should be in good condition and should be examined once in every six months. Similarly, lifting machines, chains, ropes and lifting tackles must be in good construction and should be examined once in every 12 months (S.29).

S.30 Requires that notice of maximum safe working speed of grindstone or abrasive wheel, etc. to be kept near the machine.

S.31 Stipulates that safe working pressure should not be exceeded.

S.32 Requires that in every factory all floors, steps, stairs, passages and gangways shall be of sound construction and be properly maintained. Similarly, pits, sumps and openings in floors must be covered or fenced (S.33).

According to S.34, no person shall be employed in any factory to lift or carry weight so as to cause his/her eyesight.

S.35 Mandates provision of goggles or screen to protect persons working on machines which might cause damage to his/her eyesight.

S.36 Prohibits entry of any worker into any chamber, tank, pit or pipe where any gas or fume is present.

S.37 Mandates that measures be taken to prevent explosion on ignition at gas or fume. Similarly, measures must be taken to prevent outbreak of fire and its spread (S.38).

If it appears to the factory inspector that any building, part of a building or machinery is dangerous to human life he/she may ask for details about them or insist on suitable tests to determine their safety.

S.39   Where unsafe condition is reported, the inspector may serve a notice on the occupier to initiate suitable measures to restore safety (S.40).

Where a factory employs 1000 or more workers, there must be a qualified safety officer(s) appointed to ensure compliance of all the safety provisions (S.41).

13.5 Safety Committees in India

Many Indian firms, especially in the manufacturing sector, have established Safety Committees, with adequate representation from employers and employees. Large multidivisional firms like ECIL have multi-tier safety committees. For instance, in ECIL, the corporate-level safety committee looks into broader safety policy and development of a safety culture, while the other level handles the operational aspects of safety. Among the MNCs, ABB's approach to safety is a participatory one, taking into consideration the local requirements of different operations. The participatory forums include health and safety committees and employee forums. In the case of Coal India Ltd, the participatory organisation for safety is rather elaborate. At the apex level is the Standing Committee on Safety in Coal Mines, chaired by the Minister of Coal and Mines. The Coal India Safety Board, headed by the chairman of CIL, has workers and management representatives. A tripartite safety committee of workers, management and government is constituted for each subsidiary company. Area committees and mine committees are also set up with representatives of workers and the management. Designated and trained worker representatives monitor the safety status of mines on a monthly basis. Controlling safety and health costs of all types becomes a more pressing issue in challenging times.

Safety Audit

Audit is a detailed analysis of the facilities, management and employee attitude towards safety, safety planning as well as alignment with safety regulations. The role of the safety auditor is not only to determine the adherence to safety standards but also to measure the overall performance in controlling the operation's safety. Audit is comparable to an inspection. But the main point of difference is that the level of intensity and detail with which the audit is undertaken is much more than an inspection.

In Challenging Times and Downturn

During a downturn and in times of economic uncertainties, the biggest challenge facing the HR is how to cut costs related to safety. The answer to this is a big NO. There should be no compromise on safety. It may result in a short-term saving, but it may prove to be very expensive in the long run, due to accidents and lack of safety awareness. The training programmes may be reduced to a webinar, or online training instead of the expensive conference room and hotel location. But that's all. At any time, the training on safety should not be compromised upon.

Emphasis should also be given to reduce unsafe conditions and acts. These may include the following: identify and eliminate unsafe conditions, use administrative means such as job rotation and also use personal protective equipment. Unsafe acts may be reduced through an emphasis on the top management commitment on safety, establishing a safety policy, reducing unsafe acts through selection, providing continuous safety training, using posters and other propaganda, using positive reinforcement, using behaviour-based safety programmes, encouraging worker participation, and conducting safety and health inspection regularly.

Health

This can be defined as maintenance of the wellbeing of an employee and keeping him/her free from any diseases or accidents. As mentioned in the safety module above, employees at all levels need to be healthy and happy to perform well and enhance their productivity and efficiency. This not only helps the organisation to grow but also facilitates the motto of its contribution towards corporate social responsibility, a key parameter in judging its performance. The Confederation of Indian Industry (CII) institutes awards to organisations on the basis of their endeavour in maintaining the wellness of their employees. Some of the recipients of such awards are; HDFC Bank, L&T, Tata Steel, Birla Cement and ITC.

Some of the health maintenance services rendered by the organisation maybe included as follows:

1. Pre-hiring medical check-up for all individuals at all levels before joining the organisation.
2. Regular medical check-up of all individuals to detect early signs of diabetes, blood pressure, erratic pulse rate, anaemia, tension, ulcers and the like.
3. A fully-equipped first aid centre with all facilities, and training given to employees to handle accidents arising at the workplace.
4. Rehabilitation and proper placement of workers who have been impaired by some disability due to an accident at the workplace or while travelling to or from the workplace.
5. Control of occupational health hazards.
6. Regular examination of eyes, teeth and ears.
7. Treatment available for common colds, coughs, stomach aches and the like.
8. Maternity and child-related welfare for women.
9. Special care of the workers in danger divisions like foundry, welding and painting.
10. Provision of sanitary facilities like supply of drinking water, provision of healthy and nutritious food, good housekeeping, elimination of insects like rodents and cockroaches.

The physical health of the employees can be severely affected by the following diseases or ailments or addictions.

Infectious Diseases: With the rise in mergers, joint ventures and acquisitions, personnel travelling abroad to far-off destinations and coming back, has become common. With this, the advent of many infectious diseases is also on the rise. Employers need to take adequate steps to prevent the entry of infectious diseases.

These steps include the following:

1. Closely monitor the Centre for Disease Control and Prevention's travel alerts. These inform travellers about health concerns and suggest precautions.
2. Provide medical screenings for employees returning from infectious areas.

3. Tell employees to stay at home if they have respiratory problems.
4. Clean the areas of work and surfaces regularly.
5. Stagger break times to reduce the event of overcrowding.
6. Emphasise the use of regular hand washing and make sanitiser use a regular affair.

Alcohol Abuse: Alcoholism is a major cause of industrial health problems and sometimes even accidents. Drinking liquor on the job or off the job, where the employee comes to work with red eyes and a breath stinking of alcohol, can be quite unnerving to fellow employees. Such an addiction and habit affects the productivity of the work and leads to increased absenteeism. Employers deal with such issues by arranging counselling by the HR or even warning the alcohol victim by suspending him or her from work. In extreme cases, outside agencies are roped in or a membership is obtained in Alcoholic Anonymous where a therapeutic approach is taken to counselling and helping the alcoholic to get freed from the habit through training and a change in attitude.

In a recent case in an FMCG Company, the Sales Manager, after several warnings and attempts at counselling, was forced to be terminated. On any day, he typically had red eyes when he came to work. He would speak in a sozzled manner, which made his subordinates quite nervous. Many a time, they did not understand his language and communication. He was known to be a good performer, and hence several attempts were made to coach him and educate him of the mal-effects of drinking. However when his distributors, on whom the organisation's business was dependent, started to complain about his late coming and not getting out of the car while visiting them, the matters came to a head and he was asked to leave.

Stress, Burnout and Depression

Stress is an essential part of work life. According to Fred Luthans, "Stress can be defined as an adaptive response to an external situation that results in physical, psychological and behavioural deviations for organisational participants." The physical or psychological demands from the environment are called stressors. They are known to create stress or the potential for stress when the individual perceives them as representing a demand that may exceed the person's ability to respond. Simply, stress can be defined as an individual's response to a disturbing factor in the environment and the consequence of such a reaction. Stress thus involves the interaction of the environment and the individual.

Stress can be manifested in a positive and a negative manner. Positive stress is called Eustress, a term coined by endocrinologist Hans Selye to describe a pleasant or curative stress; it provides an opportunity for one to gain something from the outcome and or where the situation offers a challenge for the individual. It is negative stress when the situation is associated with marital breakdown, heart disease, child abuse, alcoholism, absenteeism, and a couple of other social, physical, emotional and psychological problems.

Stress is known to be associated with demands and constraints. These often lead to potential stress. They are often related to the uncertainty of outcome especially when the outcome is significant. Not all individuals experience the same level of stress. Some individuals are calm and composed because of their sense of endurance and social support.

However, there are others who are likely to crumble under the stress which they perceive to be intense and so get highly stressed. According to Don Hellreigel, how an individual experiences stress depends upon the following: the person's perception of the situation; the person's past experience; the presence or absence of social support; individual differences with regard to stress reactions.

These can be explained as follows:

1. Perception: This refers to the psychological process where the person selects and organises stimuli into a concept of reality. Employees' perception of a situation can influence whether or not they experience stress. For instance, a challenging assignment with a deadline may cause stress to one employee and may be source of positive challenge to another employee.

2. Past Experience: The relationship between experience and stress can be a positive reinforcement. Positive experience or a positive reinforcement can affect an individual and create eustress or no stress. Alternatively, a negative experience under some event like criticizing the boss and getting into trouble for the same, may act as a negative stressor.

3. Social Support: This is the availability of family and friend network available for the employee to share and counsel him/her about his problems. This network is considered to be very important to stabilise and support an employee undergoing trauma, stress or depression due to work pressures, problems and conflicts with boss and colleagues and such areas. Organisations have woken up to this reality and hire specialists to counsel and support an employee who feels disoriented due to stress and burnout. Also, retrenchment or job lay-offs are known to cause immense pain and loss of self-esteem for the employee concerned.

4. Individual Differences: Differences in values and beliefs have been identified as the main reasons for individual differences. These cause different perceptions, attitudes and behaviours among personnel. Thus even feelings or experiences of stress differ among employees at all levels.

Burnout

This is a phenomenon closely associated with job stress. Experts define burnout as the total depletion of physical and mental resources caused by excessive striving to reach an unrealistic work related goal. Burnout builds gradually, manifesting itself in symptoms such as irritability, discouragement, exhaustion, cynicism, entrapment and resentment.

Employers can head off burnout, for instance, by monitoring employees in potentially high pressure jobs. What can a burn out candidate do? In his book, *Burn Out: How to Beat the High Cost of Success*, Dr Herbert Freudenberger suggests:

1. Break your patterns. First, are you doing a variety of things or the same one repeatedly? The more well-rounded your life is, the better protected you are against burnout.
2. Get away from it all periodically. Plan rounds of introspection among nature, so that you compulsorily get away from it all periodically.
3. Reassess your goals in terms of their intrinsic worth. Are the goals you have set attainable? Are they really worth the effort and the sacrifice?
4. Think about your work. Could you do as good a job without being so intense?

Research mentions how mini-vacations during the work day, such as time off for physical exercise, meditation, power naps and reflective thinking, help to reduce stress and burnout.

Employee Depression

Depression is considered a disease. Typical warning signs of depression include persistent sad, anxious or empty moods; sleeping too little; reduced appetite; loss of interest in activities once enjoyed; restlessness or irritability; and difficulty in concentrating. For example, in Pune, there are organisations like "Connecting" which help to train people at work or in schools or colleges to identify those with depression. These people are then systematically counselled. Even helpline numbers are available to connect on the phone. It has been stated that a number of suicides have been averted due to the availability of such help lines and agencies to connect with those who are depressed due to various reasons. This is also a serious problem at work. It thus results in declines in efficiency and productivity; hence it should be handled carefully and systematically with trained people.

Computer-related ergonomic problems:

With advances in computers and screen technology, there are risks associated with monitor related health problems at work. Problems include short-term eye burning, itching, eyestrain and soreness. Backaches and neck aches are also widespread. There are a number of general recommendations regarding computer screens. Most relate to ergonomics or design of the worker-equipment interface. These include:

1. Employees should take a 3- 5 minute break from working at the computer every 20- 40 minutes, and use the time for other tasks.
2. Design maximum flexibility into the workstation so it can be adapted to the individual operators. For example, use adjustable chairs with mid-back supports. Don't stay in one position for long periods.
3. Reduce glare with devices such as shades over windows and recessed or indirect lighting.
4. Give workers a complete pre-placement vision exam to ensure properly corrected vision for reduced visual strain.
5. Allow the user to position his or her wrists at the same level as the elbow.
6. Put the screen at or just below eye level, at a distance of 45 to 75 cm from the eyes.
7. Let the wrists rest lightly on a pad for support.
8. Put the feet flat on the floor or on a footrest.

Workplace smoking

Smoking is a serious health and cost problem for both employees and employers. For employers, these costs derive from higher health and fire insurance, as well as increased absenteeism and reduced productivity. There are special awareness programmes initiated in organisations to expose the hazards of smoking and appeal to the smokers to quit. Special drives too are created in organisations to curb the same.

Violence at Work

Violence against employers is an enormous problem at work. The recent case in India at the Maruti Manesar plant, involving the killing of the HR manager by the workers and their rampage, by hitting the supervisors with stick and rods, is a case of rampage and violence at work. More and more organisations today are embarking on an improved employee screening to gauge the proneness to employee aggression; heightened security measures are also being adopted by the employers. Reference checking is another measure used by organisations at the time of employment to detect potential character related to frauds, cheating, violent behaviour and psychiatric problems. These also include sexually aggressive behaviour, where the law today is very powerful to deal with such devious behaviour.

Health and Safety at RSB Group:

Workplace safety standards are adhered to at this automotive transmissions manufacturer in its multiple locations including Pune and Jamshedpur, with personal protective equipment being provided to all. Workers provided by contractors also have to adhere to identical safety norms. Supervisors ensure that workers observe safety regulations, drills and procedures laid down. Training on first aid and fire-fighting is organised periodically for employees. Accidents are properly analysed and necessary steps are taken to avoid recurrence. RSB often undertakes the complete responsibility of any worker meeting with an accident, both on and off the RSB premises. Individuals have been, in the past, moved to the best available medical facility available for treatment. Establishments of the RSB Group have been audited and certified for Occupational Health and Safety Management in terms of BS OHSAS 18001 – 2007. OHSAS 18001 is a British Standard for occupational health and safety management systems, recognised and adopted all over the world. The Occupational Health and Safety Advisory Services (OHSAS) Project Group was formed in 1999 to clear the confusion caused by the large number of national standards and proprietary certification schemes and create a single unified approach. This Group had representatives from various national standards bodies, academic institutions, and accreditation and certification agencies. It used the best of existing standards and schemes to create the OHSAS 18000 Series. The OHSAS 18001 specification was updated in July 2007, making it more closely aligned with the ISO 9000 and ISO 14000 structures to let organisations could adopt it more easily alongside their existing management systems. Later, the BSI Group decided to adopt it as a British standard, hence 'BS OHSAS 18001'. An occupational health and safety management system (OHSMS) promotes a safe and healthy working environment by providing a framework that helps organisations to consistently identify and control health and safety risks; reduce the potential for accidents; aid legislative compliance; and improve overall performance.

Medical Treatment: Regular medical check-up of all personnel is undertaken. Awareness training of all personnel to include response to emergencies is also pursued. Turbo ventilators in the plants provide for cleaner environment. Suspended dust particles in the sheds are relatively low and the maintenance of green lawns outside the sheds reduces the dust factor. Administrative buildings housing offices are immaculately maintained. All RSB premises undertake tree plantation in accordance with laid down targets.

At Jamshedpur, besides ESIC and Mediclaim, the company has established a dispensary with both Allopathic and Homeopathy doctors and two pharmacists to provide treatment for minor ailments.

Health and Safety at Forbes Marshall Pvt. Ltd.

Forbes Marshall Group has 7 joint ventures under its umbrella and is one of India's leading players in the steam engineering and control instrumentation space offering energy conservation solutions to businesses. The company is in operation for over 65 years and is also a family-run business being run by the third generation (at RSB, the second generation is just moving into management positions). Values and culture are core philosophies in everyday life and everyone who joins the organisation is called a 'member' and not an employee. Many of them are also the second- or third-generation members of the larger Forbes Marshall family.

This company has been acknowledged on many occasions as safe place to work. The care is not limited only at work but also extended after office hours. There have been instances where members who had situations at home were picked up and dropped at the company guest house in the middle of the night on just a call. In addition, the company also has a functional value council where issues pertaining to sexual harassment can be referred to. The council, consisting of a rotational, cross-functional team of members, has full authority in determining the consequences for issues brought before it.

Safety for the company is not restricted to the shop floor alone. There are safety policies. Despite all the efforts towards adhering to precautions, whenever accidents occur, (most of them are minor) the hospital attached to the premises provides first aid and care accordingly. In severe cases, which are quite rare, like the one when an employee lost his eye, the company took the responsibility of looking after the family. For instance, in the case of this employee, the directors themselves undertook the responsibility of funding the education of all his four children. Also, a lump sum was paid to the wife. All this is funded through a corpus, which is built by all employees working on one Saturday every quarter, and an amount equal to the collected funds is put in by the directors. This corpus is then used judiciously to financially help any employee who becomes a victim of any form of accident.

Recently, one employee, while travelling to another city on company work, suffered a severe heart attack. The company funded his hospitalisation as well as took the responsibility of educating his children. Another employee was killed recently at another location, when a severe storm hit a tin shed of the client's location, which fell on him and killed him. His children were educated through the company's funds and his wife was given employment by the company.

Issues related to safety are not confined to the Safety Week alone, but are regularly promoted. For the young employees, for instance, training was given on how to drive safely. Another training session on safety related to the use of a fire extinguisher, in case of an emergency.

Wellness for the employees is also a core value of Forbes Marshall. At any given time, a register containing all the employees' names and their blood groups and health parameters is kept ready. In case of emergencies, this is used to get a ready reference for the blood group required. Also, there are doctors attached to the hospital in its premises and check-ups are undertaken regularly for all employees. Special programmes on anti-tobacco chewing and fighting alcoholism are also undertaken at periodic levels.

Case Study
SAERTEX INDIA – THE UNIQUE MODEL IN EMPLOYEE SAFETY

SAERTEX INDIA, the wholly owned subsidiary of SAERTEX Group, Germany has established operations in India in year 2006 through the manufacturing plant in Hinjewadi, Pune. The first year of operation the company has reported a minor accident of a technician although they have been following the safety norms strictly. The first and only step adopted by the Company was to ensure that such mistakes does not repeat in future whereby introducing the most innovative way of adopting and implementing 'safety first' programme.

What is safety first program?

Interestingly this unique program is being invented and introduced successfully by the work force through common interest and through group discussion. The team analysed the areas where safety is mandatory which was interestingly started with the canteen where the food quality is the first safety factor. This means hygiene food, consistent quality and vegetarian with high nutrition factors without oil etc. The workforce realised that 'health comes first in safety'. In order to establish a healthy workforce it is important to have healthy food. Proudly to say that 'SAERTEX INDIA never ever had a single incident on anyone reporting stomach upset or any other smallest decease on food poison etc.". Once this is being established strongly rest of the areas became much more easier to identify. Thanks to our 'Super Achievers and Achievers Team'.

SAERTEX INDIA started identifying all other areas like no two wheeler travelling to office on frequent basis, even if one travels 100% ensure that safety measures are being taken care first like helmets, condition of vehicle being informed to HR and starting time and reaching time to be informed to HR so that they can analyse at what speed the vehicle is being driven etc.

This continues to the next level on office staff, and factory technicians by identifying every areas of work and life which has helped the company to celebrate the safety week. When there is a pick up and drop no one is allowed to tell the drivers to drive fast because they are late. Here we train and develop the need and necessity of 'time management' whereby avoiding traffic rush in order to reach office on time. Safety week celebration is a grand affair in SAERTEX INDIA, where we award and reward the 'best safety team and best individual safety commitment and command'.

Very proudly we say since last 6 years we have no accident reported in the Company. We say loudly 'WE TAKE CARE OF OUR PEOPLE'S SAFETY AND THEY TAKE CARE OF OUR COMPANY'S BUSINESS.'

Discussion Questions

1. Elaborate on the need for safety and well being of the employees.
2. Cite examples to show the damages caused due to lack of safety measures and lack of employee care by the organisations.
3. Explain the duties of a Safety Auditor.
4. Highlight the main features of the legislation related to health and safety.
5. Explain the various wellness programmes that organisations could initiate.

References and Recommended Readings

1. Fred Luthans, Organisation Behavior, McGraw Hill, 1998, p330.
2. Don Hellreigel, et al, p 211.
3. Human Resource Management, 6th edition, K. Aswathappa, McGraw Hill, 2010.
4. Christina Maslach and Michael Leiter, "Early Predictors of Job Burnout and Engagement" Journal of Applied Psychology, 93, no (3), 2008, pp 498-512.
5. Mina Westman and Dov Eden" Effects of a Respite from Work on Burnout: Vacation Relief and Fade Out "Journal of Applied Psychology, 82, no 4, (1997) pp 516-527.
6. ibid p 516.
7. Human Resource Management 12th edition. Gary Dessler and Biju Varkkey; Pearson: 2011; Manipal.

Chapter 14...

Ethics

Contents ...

14.1 Introduction
14.2 Human Resource Ethics
14.3 Ethics and Human Resource Manager
• Discussion Questions
• Recommended Readings and References

Objectives and Summary

This chapter aims to underline the need for, and importance of, ethics. The objective is to share the importance of ethics in terms of right or wrong, which is sometimes a piece of confusion in an organisation. It aims to highlight the need for designing an ethical code in an organisation. It explains the deontological concept of using words like always or never. It highlights the advantages of adopting ethics at work.

Ethics is understood as the morally underlined acts of right or wrong or good or bad doings in an organisation. Human Resource needs to be concerned about ethics, including the concepts related to these doings by employees. Every employee needs to be aware of the ethical code and conduct of behaviour expected from him or her in terms of forging relationships with one another, vendors, customers and the public at large. The culture or 'the way we do things here' in an organisation depicts the ethics underlined by the organisation. Hence organisations need to highlight the benefits of following ethics and punish such acts or behaviour which are a gross contravention of ethical norms.

Learning Outcomes:

1. Identify the code of ethics for organisations;
2. Explain Human Resource and ethics;
3. Elaborate on the design of culture in alignment with the ethical practices and expected behaviour;
4. Discuss the benefits of ethics and the advantages of following ethical behaviour norms.

14.1 Introduction

Ethics is the discipline dealing with what is good or bad, or right and wrong or moral duty and obligation. Ethics is a philosophical discipline that describes and directs moral conduct. Laws also offer guides to ethical behaviour, prohibiting such acts that can be harmful to others. For example, if certain behaviour was illegal, most would consider it to be itself unethical. The vision, values and mission statements of an organisation are considered to be sources of ethical guidance, apart from the mentioned ethical standards and behaviour expected from organisations. These are considered sources of ethical guidance and should lead to any employees' belief or convictions about what is right or what is wrong.

Ethics can be defined as "the principles of conduct governing an individual and a group, specifically the standards one uses to decide what one's conduct should be". Making ethical decisions always involves two things - normative judgement in terms of whether something is good or bad or right or wrong, and questions on morality. Morality is considered society's highest expected standard of behaviour. Moral standards are known to guide behaviour of the most serious consequence to society's well being such as murder, lying and slander.

Deontology

An approach to ethics that emphasises duties, rights and principles is known as deontological (from the Greek word for duty). In deontological ethics, good or bad is evident in the act itself, irrespective of the consequences of the act. What is bad about lying is lying itself, without consideration of the effects of the lie. The same would be true of other unethical acts like stealing, cheating, or doing personal work in official time. Deontological propositions often take the form of lists of types of action that should be encouraged or refrained from, using words like 'always' or 'never' respectively. As a categorical imperative proposed by Kant (1724-1804), a leading voice in deontology ethics, (meaning acts which should be done anyway without keeping the end in view) they are always and absolutely the right way to do. An important form of categorical imperative proposed by Kant is called universalisation – meaning we should follow only rules that can be universalised. The second form requires that we should not treat other people only as a means to some desired end, but also as an end in themselves.

What are the implications of this requirement for HRM? For example, if an employer uses the threat of violence or other degrading treatment to persuade employees to obey instructions, or introduces other elements into the employment circumstances, that effectively enslave the employee, then the employee's rights are violated and the arrangement is clearly unethical.

14.2 Human Resource Ethics

HR ethics is the application of ethical principles to human resource relationships and activities. Reading the newspaper, connecting with friends on Facebook and other social networking sites is considered illegal or an unethical practice of individuals in organisations. Sometimes, deciding what is ethical is difficult. It is often assumed that those in human resources have a great deal to do with establishing an organisation's conscience. For judging ethical behaviour for the conduct of business, the Companies Act of 1952 and the Security and Exchange Board of India (SEBI) which is a market regulator have laid down corporate governance laws. Independent regulators like the Reserve bank of India (RBI) for Banking and Telecom Regulatory Authority of India (TRAI) for the telecom sector also set operational norms for ethical behaviour and act as watchdogs. Various labour laws set the framework for dealing with employees who are directly or indirectly employed by firms.

Truly, for organisations to grow and prosper, good ethical people must be employed. Today, even from the potential employees' viewpoint, a preferred company is considered one which adheres to ethical standards. Research studies show that "People who score high on ethics tests tend to do better from a long-term professional standpoint." One of the practices being followed by organisations in the area of ethics is related to pay for performance rather than pay for position, which was the case earlier. An issue relating to ethics which has been largely focused upon is the practice regarding the excessive amount of compensation received by the top CEOs and Managing Directors. For example, Jack Welch owns a business school and the General Electric (GE) is known for corporate excess. His former wife revealed a $9-million annual pension plan payout, plus outrageous perks such as lifetime use of GE's $80,000 per month, Manhattan apartment with free food and free maidservant, lifetime use of GE's fleet of corporate jets, a new Mercedes plus a limousine and a driver, and assorted free sports and opera tickets.

A Code of Ethics

Most organisations have underlined a code of ethics. This is then embedded in the corporate culture of the organisation. Today business schools have a subject called Ethics and Human Resource Management. Even the course work of Ph.D. in many universities has a specialised module on Ethics. The ethical code developed by the Society of Human Resource Management (SHRM) includes ethical areas related to professional responsibility, professional development, ethical leadership, fairness and justice, conflicts of interests and use of information. For example, with regard to conflict of interests the code states as follows: "As HR professionals we must maintain a high level of trust with our stakeholders. We must protect the interests of our stakeholders as well as our professional integrity and should not engage in activities that create actual, apparent and potential conflict of interest..." In short, a code of ethics establishes the rules that need to be followed by employees at all levels in an organisation.

In order to promote the importance and following of ethical behaviour, organisations today have a special ethics officer or promote and establish an ethics committee or a vigilance committee. The chief job of this officer or committee is to point out, through investigation, malpractices happening in organisations and punish or take severe action against those who are engaged in these. For instance, in the Tata Group companies like Tata Tayo, at Tatanagar, Jamshedpur, they have established a Vigilance Committee. The job of this committee is to investigate the practice of gifts, cash or any other valuable items being accepted by those in the purchase or any other department especially during the festivals of Diwali and New Year. The rule is that accept a small box of *mithai*, no other article or valuable is allowed to be accepted. Those found breaking this rule or diktat are immediately asked to tender their resignation. The code of conduct normally includes issues like business conduct, competition, and workplace or HR issues. Wal-Mart too has a similar code where gifts which are received from suppliers are either given to charity or destroyed.

Some of the other firms that have also developed their code of ethics include Infosys and Delhi Metro Rail Corporation. All are known for their commitment to business ethics. A lot of attention has been given to the area of ethics. Hence the scandal at Satyam Computer Services Ltd. affected the promoters who were charged and arrested for misappropriation and embezzlement of funds. A few senior employees of the audit firm PWC that certified the accounts landed in trouble too.

Research Findings: What do we know about ethical behaviour at work? Several experts reviewed the research concerning things that influence ethical behaviour in organisations. Here's what they found:

1. Ethical behaviour starts with moral awareness. In other words, a person has to understand whether he realises or recognises that a moral issue exists in an organisation.
2. Managers need to cultivate the right norms, leadership, management, culture and systems.
3. Ethics slide when people undergo moral disengagement. And by doing so, it frees them from the guilt that one would normally associate with violating ethical standards.
4. The most powerful morality comes from within. In effect, when the moral person asks "Why be moral?" the answer is "Because that is what I am." Then failure to act morally creates emotional discomfort.
5. Offering rewards for ethical behaviour can misfire. Doing so may actually undermine the intrinsic value of ethical behaviour.
6. Don't advertently reward someone for devious or bad behaviour.
7. Employers should punish unethical behaviour. Employees who observe unethical behaviour expect you to discipline the perpetrators.

8. The degree to which the employees talk of ethical behaviour is a good predictor of ethical conduct.

9. Many a time, people tend to alter their moral compasses when they join organisations. They tend to equate what's best for the organisation to what is the right thing to do.

14.3 Ethics and the Human Resource Manager

It is increasingly being considered by various organisations that to understand ethics of employment and HRM one needs to examine the special features of the employment relationship and the contract of employment. It is considered that if labour is a commodity much like any other, then it becomes difficult to see what ethical principles prevent employees from being treated in the same way as these other assets - acquired, used and disposed of as the business purpose determines. The important difference between employees and other assets is how employers need to show respect for persons and to recognise an individual's independence of action.

The employment relationship could also be examined from a consequentialist perspective and identify the net benefits that accrue from certain employment practices, for example the notion of the open-ended employment contract. There is likely to be a positive change in net happiness for workers resulting from reduced uncertainty as well as the social benefits that flow from having a predictable and regular income, like access to managers. From the employers' perspective, the benefits include reliable levels of regular supply together with reduced transaction costs like recruitment and training. The mutual trust engendered by a continuing relationship also provides the basis for employers to invest in training and development to improve the skills of the workers and make the organisation more profitable.

From a libertarian point of view, employment may be considered as an important means by which an employer and labour can freely exchange labour for reward. However, we need to consider that such an exchange is subject to significant inequalities in power between the two parties. Most of the time, the employer exercises greater power in the labour market and so, has more opportunity to exercise choice. In a democratic society it is not surprising that people vote for governments that promise to redress some of the inequalities by legislating to protect employees from the arbitrary exercise of such power. Hence we need to execute legislation related to unjust sacking, discrimination, minimum wages and maximum working hours.

A manager's human resource decisions are usually replete with ethical consequences. For example, one survey found that 6 out of 10 of the most serious ethical work issues - workplace safety, employee records security, theft and privacy rights - were considered to be related to HR. The KPMG India Fraud Survey 2010 reported that over 45% of the surveyed

India companies experienced increased fraudulent activities. The reasons attributed to these are diminishing ethical values and a failure to act against fraud. Another survey conducted by temporary staffing agency TeamLease in 2008 found that 68% of Indian respondents are comfortable doing personal work in office hours. Sixty-one per cent were fined for taking personal printouts or photocopies in office. The study also found that there were differences in different Indian cities in terms of reactions to unethical actions. Even the manner of dealing with the ethical issues differed from place to place or city to city.

Ethics, HRM and the Law

If we consider the legislation, much of it is related to human treatment for the employees and to reduce the unequal balance between the employer and the employees. Recent legislation relates to the ethical considerations of social justice and fairness. Equal opportunity or anti discrimination legislation has an ethical purpose that is requiring employers to behave in ways that will help in redressing the issue of social disadvantage. That is reason for the focus on safety of workers, better working conditions and accepting of people with disabilities.

Much of the legislation enacted in India over the years has its basis on reducing the power gap between the employers on one hand and the employees or workers on the other. All these forms of legislation have an ethical connotation implied in them. Recently, even the legislation relating to women's rights and work and the provisions for maternity leave and equal wages as compared to their male counterparts is an extension of the right to equitable distribution of work and prevention of discrimination among the sexes.

Ethics and Culture

It is important to mention that thinking about right and wrong is strongly influenced by the cultural contexts in which these ideas were formed over the centuries. These become important features in organisations. For example, the teachings of Confucius are a strong influence on Chinese culture and thus on relationships and practices in Chinese organisations. **G. Hofstede (1991:164)** proposed 'Confucian Dynamism' as a separate dimension in understanding the differences between national cultures which embodied a long-term rather than a short-term orientation to work, based on values such as perseverance and thrift. These values, together with the familiar Confucian emphasis on hierarchy, will influence the behaviour and attitudes that are accepted and admired at work. In the world of globalisation and all economies influenced by globalisation, understanding the influence of cultural differences becomes important in managing business relationships across national boundaries. Although the basic ideas of good and bad will not differ from each other, the way in which these ideas are deliberated, lived and implemented will vary and will ultimately affect the conduct of business done ethically in outside countries.

HRM Themes and Ethics

An ethical perspective can help us to understand the overall purpose and strategy of the organisation. For example, the approach of the shareholder emphasises that the purpose of the business is to make as much money as possible for the shareholder and adopt actions that are in alignment with ethical considerations. The shareholders' view is that the businesses have obligations to a wide range of stakeholders like the customers as well as employees at all levels. The power distance in a relationship can contribute towards unfairness and injustice at work. This is considered unethical by many. The culture or "the way we do things around here" of an organisation too can have a major influence on the creation of an environment of an organisation, where if bad things are happening they are dealt with in a strong or firm manner and the employers or the top management do not compromise on the values and ethics. However, in an international context, it must be understood that an issue considered unethical or not in line with the local culture may not be perceived in a similar manner in another country. For example, giving preference for selection in jobs to family or friends or relatives, is considered a best practice in countries like Indonesia but not India or other developed economies.

Corporate Culture is closely related to ethics in an organisation. Mutual of Omaha defines corporate culture as "the personality of the organisation", the shared beliefs, that determine how its people behave and solve business problems. Mutual of Omaha executives believe that its corporate culture provides the foundation for its company's work and objectives, and the company has adopted a set of core values called "Values for Success". It is as follows:

Mutual of Omaha's 'Values for Success'

1. **Openness and Trust:** We encourage an open sharing of ideas and information, displaying a fundamental respect for each other as well as our cultural diversity.
2. **Team work (Win/Win):** We work together to find solutions that carry positive results for others as well as ourselves, creating an environment that brings out the best in everyone.
3. **Accountability/Ownership:** We take ownership and accept accountability for achieving end results, and empower team members to do the same.
4. **Sense of urgency:** We set priorities and handle all tasks and assignments in a timely manner.
5. **Honesty and Integrity:** We are honest and ethical with others, maintaining the highest standards of personal and professional conduct.
6. **Customer focus:** We never lose sight of our customers and constantly challenge ourselves to meet their requirements even better.
7. **Innovation and Risk:** We question "the old way of doing things" and take prudent risks that can lead to innovative performance and process improvements.
8. **Caring /Attentive ('be here now'):** We take time to clear our minds to focus on the present moment, listening to our teammates and customers, and caring enough to hear the concerns.

9. **Leadership:** We provide direction, purpose, support, encouragement and recognition to achieve our vision, meet our objectives and keep to our values.
10. **Personal and professional growth:** We challenge ourselves and look to ways to be even more effective as a team and as individuals.

(**Source:**) "Transforming our culture: The Value of Success" Mutual of Omaha, www.careerlink.org/emp/mut/corp.htm)

The 21st Century: A New Focus on Business Ethics

Although business ethics appeared to become more institutionalised in the 1990s, new evidence emerged in the early 2000s that many business executives and managers had not fully embraced the drive in organisations for ethical standards. The cases of Satyam's Ramalinga Raju, Goldman's Sachs' Rajat Gupta, Barclay's Finance Director, Diamond, are all recent instances of a gross violation of ethics among top personnel in companies around the world. Such abuses have increased public and political demands to improve ethical standards in business. The current trend in India too is away from legally-based ethical regulations in organisations to culture- or integrity-based initiatives that make ethics an integral part of the core cultural values. Many companies in their induction and regular training programmes are compulsorily imparting values and their alignment as an integral part of their learning and training. Even global businesses are working together to establish acceptable standards of behaviour in organisations. There are special people appointed to oversee the ethics aspect of culture adherence and behaviour. They are designated as Ethics officer, Vigilance officer, and so on.

The Advantages of Business Ethics

Among the rewards for being more ethical and socially responsible in an organisation are increased productivity in daily operations, greater employee commitment, increased investor willingness to entrust funds, improved customer trust and satisfaction and better financial performance.

1. **Employee Commitment:** This refers to the perception and experience of the employees at various levels in relation to trust, loyalty and transparency of their organisations. Organisations need to make concerted efforts to create in their working climate an element of trustworthiness, honesty and fairness in all their dealings. From the employees' perspective these include keeping with the contractual obligations made to the employees, imparting trust by maintaining a sense of respect with the employees and all stakeholders, and the upkeep of the reputation of the organisation.
2. **Investor Loyalty:** Gaining investor trust and loyalty is vital to the financial stability of the firm. This will depend upon the sense of commitment and loyalty of the employees, which in turn will affect the profitability and productivity of the firm. Shareholders are likely to trust and invest in organisations which are free from fines and lawsuits, and are known in media circles as being transparent and reputed for honouring commitments with all stakeholders. Investors look at the bottom line for profits or the potential for increased stock prices or dividends.

3. **Ethics contributes to Customer Satisfaction:** Organisations need to be aware of incorporating customer interest with the employee interests and other stakeholders' interests. Customer loyalty and maintaining a long-term relationship is crucial for the success of the firm. Public trust is essential for maintaining a long-term relationship between a business and its consumers. By focusing on customer satisfaction, a company continually deepens the customer's dependence on it, and as the customer's confidence grows the firm gains a better understanding of how to serve the customer so that the relationship may endure. Organisations provide an opportunity for customer feedback, which can engage the customer in cooperative problem solving. Customers today are conscious of adhering to ethics with all stakeholders that the company is engaged with. For instance, consumers today are known to avoid the products of companies that are perceived as treating their employees unfairly.

4. **Ethics contributes to Profits:** It is established that the company cannot nurture and develop an ethical climate unless it has achieved adequate financial performance in terms of profits. Organisations with greater resources have the means to practise social responsibility while serving their customers, valuing their employees and establishing trust with the public. Research evidence shows that being ethical pays off with better performance and higher average total return to shareholders. Employees which perceive their organisations that exhibit honesty and integrity have a higher rate of return.

Indian Organisation Examples

The employees of an Indian utility MNC worked for many days to minimise the effect of a crisis caused due to a flash flood that came upon the company way back in 2006. The main aim was to keep the utility supply going so that consumers got uninterrupted supply and were not affected. Even the employees and their families were affected by the flood in terms of damage to property. Due to such an emergency situation, employees involved in purchase and supplies were allowed to procure directly from the suppliers like local shops without proper bills. Later on, when the company tried to verify the claims made by the employees for such expenses, one of them, whose efforts were huge and appreciated, had claimed extra money. On confessing this, he was expelled from the organisation with immediate effect.

Another example takes the form of the board of Indian IT Company Infosys Ltd, whose CEO then had to be fined for not informing the company about the change in stock ownership within the mandatory one day of the completed transaction. He had inherited these shares from his mother. He was also asked to give the fine of Rs 5 lakh as a donation to charity.

Ethical Training: Ethical training is very important to avoid such instances and to build a fair and open and integrity-related culture in an organisation. Much of the training related to ethics in an organisation relates to exposing the employees at all levels to understand the ethical code of conduct of the organisation. Many organisations have an ethical code of conduct displayed on their boards very prominently. The training module includes an explanation of these, with examples and ethical dilemmas confronted by employees and how they can handle them without compromising on the code. Training is also internet-based and it showcases films and dilemmas faced by employees at various levels and in various situations.

Case Study

At the Chennai-based Armstrong International India Pvt. Ltd, it's all more about how this company conducts its business than what it does. The first thing that strikes you as you drive through the gateway is that it has no gates. "The villagers from all around walk in regularly to fetch water," says managing director Mahijeet Mishra. "They even come to eat in our canteen!" The company's 'culture card' - a little booklet, folded to card size - lists the Armstrong vision and mission of providing many 'enjoyable experiences', its late founder-CEO David M. Armstrong's belief in 'communications through storytelling', core values and strategies. At the end is a 'four Es' summary of the brand: environment, energy efficiency, enjoyable experiences and education. Armstrong International is in the business of providing 'intelligent' system solutions for steam. It does all this without any 'dusty' policy manuals, but through storytelling, in the founder's belief that "Through storytelling, our people can understand very clearly what the company believes in and what needs to be done to keep us successful." In the Indian operation, too, every employee is encouraged to write and put up stories on notice boards for others to read and learn from: just as the company doesn't have manuals, it doesn't put out circulars - everything is conveyed through stories.

Everything from the in gate to the out gate is everyone's department, all employees audit one another. There is a unique 'trust' system in place: employees put the money for their tea or coffee in a tin or a jar, which is kept open – and nobody cheats or steals.

Mishra, too has a number of stories to tell.

One of Armstrong's valued customers had laid out a prerequisite criterion for the company to become their trusted supplier: it had to pass the audit to be conducted by their own auditing agency. The scope of work was to review the manufacturing process, labour law compliance and statutory licences. During the audit, one of the questions was 'What are the major labour union issues?' To the reply that there was no union, they asked: "What do you do to prevent formation of a labour union?" Says Mishra: "We said, the first thing we do is to treat everyone as family members. We are not a company who would hire a security guard to frisk its blue-collared employees at end of every shift and then expect the same set of people to come back next morning carrying a loyalty flag and generate cash for the company. In Armstrong, if a Director gets picked up in an air-conditioned cab every morning, so does the shop floor team member. Armstrong's motto is: Do unto others as you would have them do unto you."

"Instead of spending time on 'How to handle labour union issues', we spend more time in 'How to provide an enjoyable experience to every customer partner and employee'," he says. "By the way, we passed the audit with one 'non-conformity' which said, 'The Company doesn't have any mechanism to monitor attendance of its people still neither the management nor the workers have any complaints with each other.'"

Question: Why are labour unions formed? And what would you do as HR/IR to prevent formation of a labour union?

A factory of approximately 100 people which doesn't have any gate, nor any gated warehouse nor any gated cash vault section, it keeps its inventory, money, snacks and food unmanned, in a spirit of total trust. "During earlier days we did face cases of theft, especially loss of cash from the petty cash vault," Mishra admits. "Since there are no CCTV cameras installed, it was difficult to catch the culprit. The theft continued for couple of weeks till we zeroed in on the guy. The easier option was to fire him and save our culture - but we opted to appoint him as our trusted volunteer to ensure that no theft takes place." This trust transformed him into an honest human being.

Question: What do companies achieve by putting CCTV cameras at various corners of the facility? As HR head, will you recommend your management this measure to improve productivity and ethics at the workplace?

One late Friday evening while leaving the factory for home, Mishra saw a group of employees gathered at the dispatch dock. On reaching the spot, he found a bunch of sales team members struggling to operate the pallet truck, with the GM - operations putting his technical brain onto 'How to nail a wooden box' and the cab drivers and canteen boys cutting the foam sheet. As if this was not enough of a surprise, the operators whose shift was over hadn't gone home but were running around within the factory to help the inventory manager pick materials from inventory racks. On probing, the GM – Operations explained that the Logistics Manager had committed to ship a consignment the same day but since the packing boy had had to rush back home for an emergency, they had all assembled together to make the shipment happen instead of going out to play as they usually did every Friday. "Such gesture of acting beyond 'departmental boundary' made us a truly unique team!" he says.

Question: For better productivity output, is it better to remain within department silos or to perform beyond departmental boundaries? What will be your suggestion as HR head?

Source for the online ethical quiz below:

http:/Encarta.msn.com/encnet/deprtments/elearnings page BusEthics Quiz&Quizid- 1888GS

Source: The Economic Times, March 7, 2013

Discussion Questions

1. What is ethics? How does one understand it in an organisation?
2. What is the relation of deontology and ethics?
3. How does culture relate with ethics?
4. What is the significance of human resource with ethics?

Recommended Readings and References

1. Human Resource Management by Sarah Gilmore and Steve Williams, Oxford University Press, 2009, UK.
2. Hofstede G (1991), Culture and Organisations, London, Profile Books.
3. Business Ethics: Ethical Decision Making and Cases, 6th edition, O.C. Ferrell, John Paul Freadrich, Linda Ferrell, Biztantra US, 2006.
4. Human Resource Management, 9th edn, R.Wayne Mondy, Robert Noe, Pearson Education, London, 2006
5. Dubinsky "Business Ethics".
6. Steve Bates, "Corporate Ethics important in today's job seekers" HR magazine, 47, Nov 2002, '12.
7. Byrne Lovelle,"How To Fix corporate Governance", 71
8. Kenneth Lewis, The responsibility of the CEO providing ethical leadership, Vital speeches of the day, Oct 15, 2002, 6-9.
9. The list of research is based on Linda Trevino, Gary Weaver and Scot J Reynolds, "Behavioural Ethics in Organisations: A Review" Journal of Management, 32, no 6, (2006) pp 951-990.
10. S.K. Chakraborty, "Business Ethics in India" Journal of Business Ethics, October, 1997, pp 1529- 1538
11. Human Resource Management by Gary Dessler and Biju Varkkey. 12th Edition, Pearson, 2011, India.

✽✽✽

Chapter 15...

International Human Resource Management (IHRM)

Contents ...

15.1 Introduction
15.2 Issues in International Human Resource Management
15.3 Expanding the Role of International HRM
15.4 International Human Resource Management
- Discussion Questions
- References
- Recommended Readings

Objectives and Summary

This chapter helps the reader understand and know about the concerns involving international human resource management, a need in today's times when organisations are changing their working models to include collaboration, amalgamation, joint ventures and the setting up of subsidiary companies by the parent company in different countries. The aim of this chapter is to acquaint the reader with concerns relating to the changing cultures, policies, training, performance parameters, tax equalisation, risks, relating to working across countries and geographical boundaries.

International Human Resource Management is being increasingly adopted by companies as they become more and more globalised. It has spawned a new group of people called expatriates, inpatriates and transnationals. The concerns of each of these are different and they need to be met and adapted in order to secure better performance across nations. Culture is a major issue here, and theories of Hofstede and Hall become very relevant to comprehend the needs of the different nationalities, their values and beliefs and their different working habits. All these are likely to influence their motivation, morale and performance. Practitioners are increasingly realising the need to sensitise the employees on various aspects of culture and even the parent companies need to understand the local culture and local needs when they set up subsidiaries in these countries.

Learning Outcomes:
1. Highlighting the differences between domestic HRM and international HRM;
2. Identifying the culture differences among nations through the studies of Hofstede and Hall;
3. Understanding the different training needs, ethnic issues, performance parameters when working across boundaries.

15.1 Introduction

The field of IHRM has been characterised by approaches related to cross-cultural management, which examines human behaviour from an international perspective. It also includes understanding the various HRM systems in different countries and understanding HRM from an MNC's perspective. After globalisation in India, the field of HRM has undergone a transformation. This is particularly related to acquisitions, mergers, joint ventures, international subsidiaries; sales subsidiaries. A study of International Human Resource becomes necessary to examine the traditional HR issues from an international perspective.

This includes the following:
1. Human Resource Planning as a pre-condition to the international operations. This includes decisions related to deputing personnel on international assignments .The objective is to determine the availability of appropriate personnel who are adequately trained with competence and capabilities to fit the requirements of the post.
2. Staffing includes the recruitment and selection of the personnel.
3. Performance management to create systems and designs, and determine parameters to measure metrics for performance.
4. Training and development designed in alignment with the competencies and capabilities required by the various categories of personnel.
5. Compensation and benefits determine the design and the components of compensation to include Basic, HRA, DA, Incentives, LTA and medical components.
6. Industrial relations to understand the laws and legislation which governs the relationship and working of personnel falling in the ambit of industrial relations.

The above activities change when one includes international human relations in one's approach. International HR includes independencies and interconnectedness among personnel from various countries which fall under the ambit of an MNC - whether as an expatriate, an inpatriate or third-party personnel supplying materials and services as a vendor. In order to understand these implications, it is necessary to understand the following terms:
1. The home country or a parent country where the firm is headquartered.

2. The host country where the subsidiary may be located.
3. Other countries that may be the source of labour, finance and other inputs.

So, the three categories of employees in an international firm include:
1. Host country nationals
2. Parent company nationals
3. Third country nationals

For understanding international HRM, some commonly-used terms need to be understood:

1. **Expatriates:** Personnel who are deputed to work in the host country from the parent or the company headquarters.
2. **Inpatriates:** Personnel who are deputed from the host country where the subsidiary is located, to the parent company for work or training.
3. **Repatriates:** Personnel who are relocated to their headquarters after working for some time in the host country from the parent country. They bring with them the sensibilities in culture garnered from the host country to understand a broader framework of issues.

Differences between Domestic HRM and International HRM

1. **More Comprehensive HR activities:** For an international HRM purview, unlike in a domestic purview, care should be taken about myriad issues with which a domestic HR manager is not really concerned. For instance, tax equalisation policies need to be understood.
2. **More expertise and knowledge:** The HR personnel need to learn and acquire expertise about the various employment laws of different countries, global models of strategy and structures, quality systems, differential compensation systems along with allowances and adjustments, as well as currency fluctuations; training needs identification due to differences in cultures and performance parameters whose focus may differ from country to country.
3. **More involvement with the employee and his spouse and family:** This issue becomes more detailed as the visa formalities for the inpatriate include declaration about family details, medical history, AIDS test, political and social developments abroad and relevant corporate news.
4. **Diversity and complexity:** This is especially important to understand for an MNC with a mix of expatriates and inpatriates. The issue of diversity of thinking and perceptions, complexity in comprehension and adjustment need to be learned for a smooth transition for both the parties.
5. **Change in focus and training:** These include dimensions relating to pre-departure and post-arrival training, orientation with the new country, climate and culture, living style, cost of living issues, relocation help, political orientation and understanding as well as gender differences.

6. **Risk management:** With the increase in kidnapping and terrorist attacks, the sensitivity of the host country as well as the foreign country needs to be sharpened. This becomes more accentuated especially if the laws of the foreign country are contrary to the host laws as in Middle East countries in comparison to countries like the US and the UK.

7. **Public relations work:** This holds a very important place in order to enhance the image of the MNC with different interest groups as well as NGOs and human rights agencies operating in different countries. The job of the HR personnel is to promote the image and values of the organisation in the foreign countries and represent the company on important occasions as well as coordinate the research and development work related to differences in culture, language and ethics.

15.2 Issues in International Human Resource Management

With the increasing trend towards globalisation and as more and more countries become interdependent, combined with the constant movement of people between countries, most organisations including the Small and Medium Enterprises (SMEs) are vying to collaborate with other organisations through various business models - from the franchisee, acquisitions, joint ventures, mergers or even a subsidiary. Examples in India include the McDonald's, Pizza Hut, Tata Costa Coffee, Tata Air Asia, Mahindra Navistar, and so on.

The following are the challenges confronted by them:

1. **Management of International Assignments:** The expatriate is constantly faced with the challenge of acquiring a global mindset with a local culture. Consequently, many MNC's prefer to hire local talent even at the top level nowadays. For instance LG, a Korean company, till some time ago in India, had all Koreans heading their Strategic Business Units (SBUs) in India. Recently, however, in their restructuring exercise, they have replaced all the Korean heads with Indian personnel. Nevertheless, the challenge is to adopt and adapt global best practices for some of their policies and systems.

2. **Employee and family adjustment:** This also poses a deep challenge. Indians working in Korea on deputation have been troubled by the Koreans' lack of sensitivity to vegetarian food. They are not aware of the elements of vegetarian food and serve chicken or fish, calling it vegetarian. Vegetarian ingredients for cooking are not easily available, either. In India, the expats are appalled at the traffic problems in the cities or the work culture. For example, when a German expatriate came to Pune as a head of its automobile major, he couldn't understand why the Indians "never do it right the first time". Or the English man who came as Managing Director of an air-conditioner manufacturing company, couldn't fathom why nobody wanted to play with him in the cricket match that he organised for all his employees on a national holiday. As he narrated, "perhaps there is too much emphasis on hierarchy here."

3. **Selecting the right person for a foreign assignment:** Care should be taken to select expatriates according to their knack for adjustment and passion for change and

adaptation, along with their families' orientation towards these. Although there are vendors available to train expatriates on adjustment or relocation, it can be quite traumatic for the spouse and family, especially if the spouse has been working in the parent country. Schools and education become a huge area of adjustment for the children too. All these factors should be considered before selecting the expatriate for the new assignment. Research has shown that typically, the performance initially dips, as reflected by the measure and speed of adjustment with the new environment, language and culture.

4. **Language and Communication:** These are important considerations in an international assignment. It is necessary for the expatriate to learn the local language, especially some common terms, or employ an interpreter.

5. **Legal aspects:** Due to the multi-country employment by MNCs, IHRM has become more complex. Companies should carefully analyse the status of employees and subsidiaries to determine whether they are covered under home country or host country Acts.

6. **Variations in country environment:** The biggest challenges as mentioned above are the worldwide variations in the social, cultural, economic, political and technological environment. These also affect the HR practices in terms of learning styles, compensation and allowance expectations, policies related to employee welfare and benefits, work or employment security, organisational working culture and also sharing employee records across countries. These are not always allowed across geographical boundaries and thus may affect the overall global labour market.

7. **Balance:** Every MNC needs to strike the right balance between globally acknowledged best practices and the local custom practices. MNCs should learn to foster a sense of balance to achieve a smooth integration in the local environment. For example, in countries like India, believing intensely in hospitality, it is not uncommon to personally receive guests from the parent country at the airport and make them comfortable in the hotel booked for them. This gesture may be relatively alien to some from other countries. Or for instance, in countries like Mexico, the working locals believe in a leisurely lunch and not a time-bound one as in India and elsewhere. Companies collaborating with Mexican ones need to adjust this custom to suit the Mexicans who work in India.

15.3 Expanding the Role of International HRM

The United Nations Conference on Trade and Development (UNCTAD) in its annual survey of foreign direct investment calculates what it refers to as an index of 'transnationality' which is an average of the ratios of foreign assets to total assets, foreign sales to total sales and foreign employment to total employment (The Economist, 1997). Based on this index of transnationality the most foreign-oriented multinational is Nestle, with 87% of assets, 98% of sales, and 87% of employees located outside Switzerland. The top ten multinationals are as follows:

1. Nestle (Switzerland)
2. Thomson (Canada)

3. Hoderbank Finaciere (Switzerland)
4. Seagram (Canada)
5. Solvay (Belgium)
6. Asea Brown Boveri (Sweden)
7. Electrolux (Sweden)
8. Unilever (Britain, Netherlands)
9. Philips (Britain, Netherlands)
10. Roche (Switzerland)

The reason cited for the US not being mentioned is the huge size of the domestic market, which is not the case with the above small advanced economies.

The approach and attitude of the top management towards internationalisation and a global mindset

In order to foster an international orientation, it is necessary for the top management to inculcate an orientation towards the best global practices and a global mindset. The world's boundaries are now considered history, and with the growth of technology and social networking, internationalisation is here to stay. Organisations are even undertaking intensive research to design and cater to the new economies or markets. On their side, even the new economies are customising products according to the culture and ethnicity of the countries. The shape of cars and the design of seats in India are very different from those in other countries. Brands like Apple are another example to restructure their approach to treating India as an established market for their i-phones. The higher-ups there have learnt not to underestimate emerging markets and so, the Apple strategy to launch and customise its products for the India market is well under way.

15.4 International Human Resource Management Approaches

The HRM uses four different attitudes and approaches to managing and staffing their subsidiaries. Perlmutter (1969) has formulated and identified the three attitudes as ethnocentric, polycentric and geocentric; the fourth one has been derived with Heanan (1979) as regiocentric. These approaches are known to influence designing a multinational enterprise based on top-management assumptions upon which the key product, functional and geographic decisions are made.

These can be described as under:

1. Ethnocentric: This attitude reflects a sense of superiority over others and assumes that its practices and strategies are better than those of its subsidiaries. To put it simply, the parent country or the headquarters decides and designs all the strategies for the host country to execute and follow. It is regarded by the parent country that its practices meet with the globally established benchmarks and hence these need to be enforced rather than taking inputs or giving discretion to the subsidiary.

2. **Polycentric:** Here the MNC treats each subsidiary as a locally distinct identity and allows it the power to strategise and be led or headed by only local nationals. These leaders may not be promoted in the headquarters country, but in the subsidiary location they are considered and are given complete power to manage and control its local operations.

3. **Geocentric:** The approach and attitude in this case are that of meritocracy and capability rather than a headquarters or local approach. The belief in this approach is that each function and member of the top management requires distinct competencies, knowledge and skills. These may be sourced from the world at large, rather than being restricted to the local country or the headquarter one. MNCs are becoming more open to such an approach as they increasingly realise that the colour of the passport does not matter, but competency and skill matter more.

4. **Regiocentric:** The approach here is to confine the selection to the geographic structure and strategy. It attempts to combine the benefits of capability with the geographic position, assuming a similarity of culture and values due to a geographic proximity. For example, FMCG companies like Unilever and Proctor and Gamble have a head for the Asia Pacific region.

Although these are a reflection of the management attitudes and approaches, many a time due to the laws and local customs of the subsidiary companies, MNCs are forced to adopt the approaches as practised in the subsidiary companies.

Strategies for International Organisations

One of the key aspects considered of the strategic management of modern organisations is the balance between differentiation and integration (*Lawrence, Lorch, 1967*). This design not only refers to operation and international activities but also to developing and deploying people in the organisation.

A popular model used in India is the Bartlett and Ghoshal model. They distinguish organisations as: multinational, global, international and transnational:

1. **Multinational:** This type of organisation responds to the needs of national diversity and national culture. In terms of communication and culture, there is hardly any semblance with the parent company. There is exchange of technology, culture and communication, but it is limited. An example is Cadbury Kraft, which to a large extent has retained its national culture and diversity.

2. **Global:** Here the organisation takes advantage of the centralised global base, its global strategies and its expertise, knowledge and global scale operations. It is sensitive to the global trends in food, fashion, technology and consumer demand. An example is Burberry, which has globalised its perfumes and fashion worldwide.

3. **International:** This type of organisation is considered ideal. Examples are companies like Proctor and Gamble, Unilever and so on. The ideal mix is to exploit and take advantage of the parent company's competency, skills and knowledge and

adapt them to the local conditions, customs and culture. Knowledge is developed at the centre and then transferred to the overseas subsidiaries.

4. **Transnational:** The purpose is to integrate the separate forces operating in the international marketplace. These include the global integration of global tastes like Coca Cola, local differentiation like development of local tastes like lipstick colours to suit the local fashion, and worldwide cost-effective innovation as in consumer durables like Samsung TV or LG washing machines.

Human Resource management is crucial to organisational competiveness and productivity. Due to the growing diversity of the world's workforce, the need to manage this diversity has become a major challenge of international organisations. The woman as a growing workforce is also increasing the complexity of the workforce.

Selection

As far as the human resource selection for international operations is considered, it differs widely from one country to another. Asians for example are known for their extensive screening and testing techniques. Testing in the US has been restricted and also in Canada with human rights and the legislation being very restrictive.

Compensation and Benefits

Compensation decisions are strategic ones and play a key role in achieving performance and sustainable competitive advantage for international firms. The area of international compensation is complex primarily because the MNCs must cater to the three categories of employees like Parent Country Nationals (PCNs), Third Country Nationals (TCNs) and the Host Country Nationals (HCNs). The common components include the base salary, foreign service inducement, or hardship premium, allowances and benefits. The approaches to compensation could be a going-rate approach where the base salary for international transfer is linked to the salary structure of the host country, or a balance-sheet approach where it links the base salary of the PCN or the TCN to the salary structure of the relevant home country.

Training and Development

Expatriates are given pre-departure training apart from the ongoing training during their work in the host country. The common components of this training include cultural awareness programmes, cultural assimilation, language training, sensitivity training, preliminary visits, corporate language, practical assistance, job-related factors and cross-cultural training.

Performance Management

One of the most challenging aspects for a firm operating internationally is managing the performance of its various international facilities. The evaluation of the performance of the expatriates is very much linked with the performance of the subsidiaries, which they are sent to manage. Some of the parameters included in the performance appraisal include the tasks -

both transactional and relational - adjustment with the host environment, and, most importantly, cultural adjustment.

Repatriation

The process of bringing the expatriate back to the home country is called repatriation. This also needs careful managing. Re entry into the home country presents new challenges as the repatriate copes with what has been called the re-entry shock or reverse culture shock. While people generally expect life in a new country to be different, they may be less prepared for homecoming to present problems of adjustment. And so, it may be traumatic for some. From the multinational perspective, repatriation is generally considered the final stage of the expatriation process. The typical four phases of repatriation include preparation for the new position, physical relocation, transition and readjustment. As far as the job is concerned, there may be feelings of anxiety about career, employment and coping with new role demands.

Multicultural model

The interesting aspect of working internationally is to work with people with different cultural heritages. There are differences in cultural values and ideas on life. IBM is an appropriate example of an organisation where people from different cultures assimilate and adjust.

Hofstede (1980a) was one of the first to attempt to develop a universal framework for understanding cultural differences in managers' and employees' values based on a worldwide survey, although not the only one. Hofstede's work focuses on 'value systems' of national cultures, which are represented by four dimensions:

- **Power Distance:** This is the extent to which inequalities among people are seen as normal. This dimension stretches from equal relations being seen as normal to wide inequalities being viewed as normal.
- **Uncertainty avoidance:** This refers to a preference for structured situations versus unstructured situations. This dimension runs from being comfortable with flexibility and ambiguity to a need for extreme rigidity and situations with a high degree of certainty.
- **Individualism:** This looks at whether individuals are used to acting as individuals or as part of cohesive groups, which may be based on the family or the corporation. This dimension ranges from collectivism to individualism (*Hui, 1990*).
- **Masculinity:** Hofstede *(1980a)* distinguishes 'hard values' such as assertiveness and competition, and the 'soft' or 'feminine' values of personal relations, quality of life and caring about others, whereas in a masculine society gender role differentiation is emphasised.

Adapting the Organisational Culture

Gannon and Associates (1994) outline three main facets of Swedish culture:

- **Love of nature:** Sweden was late to develop as an industrial nation but this industrialization was rapid. This industrialisation with an emphasis on engineering has given international prominence to such companies as Volvo, Saab, Scania, Ericsson, ASEA, SKF and Electrolux.
- **Individualism through self development:** Individualism is connected to a person's own self-development and tied to him or her, rather than the competitive thrust of corporate life. Five weeks' holidays are the norm, and absenteeism and excessive sick leave are an issue, with an average of 27 sick days per year - which is more than five times the US average. Quality of life is more important.
- **Equality:** This is quite often expressed through complex systems of welfare and other state mechanisms designed to provide the same service to everybody: health service, child benefits, maternity/paternity leave, pensions, and so on. Taxation is high in order to support these systems, and also serves as a leveller of social inequalities.

Indians too verbose

This cultural trait of Indians is narrated by Shilpa Hulikawi, the HR manager of Schindler, an Indo-Swiss venture manufacturing elevators. Headquartered in Switzerland, the company has a subsidiary at Kasarwadi, Pune. One of the common traits of the Indian employees of Schindler, noticed at the headquarters in Switzerland, is their detailed talking and verbosity. To a question asked by the parent company employee, the answer by an Indian engineer goes into the history of the matter, his experience at dealing with the issue, his suggestions and wordy conclusions. A sharp contrast to this is the German engineer in the company headquarters, who answers exactly to the point. This trait which can divert the attention and interest focus of the German, who is sometimes made to feel less superior, as the Indian engineer explains in meticulous detail. This is one dominant point of the adaptation which the parent company employees have to make while interacting with their Indian counterparts.

Indian employees in the parent company also need to make drastic adaptation, trying to understand the German language so commonly spoken there. Not to mention the food habits. With globalisation, the expatriates from the parent company have very smoothly adapted to the Indian food, culture of greeting by shaking hands and the non-hierarchical style of working, with nobody occupying any corner offices. Even the fancy titles and the designations have now been done away with the transformational working of today.

HR Managers have often faced the music because they were not aware of the local laws. Some countries, for example, include same-gender partners in the definition of 'spouse', whereas same-gender marriages are not legalised in many countries. There can be many such cultural diversities - the law of sexual harassment in the U.S., for instance, is extremely stringent, and what is an acceptable conversational or behavioural norm in India may be unacceptable there.

Case Study: Research Report

International Human Resource Management demands global leadership attributes for successful international working models. The following is a research paper written and investigated by a global leadership expert and mentions the dimensions to be acquired by all personnel in today's globalised working.

A Formal Evaluation of a Novel Leadership Programme

Principal Investigator: Gerald Huesch, President and CEO, Global Leadership School, Berlin, Germany.

ABSTRACT

Introduction: There are numerous leadership courses available that claim to provide excellent results improving employee efficiency and imparting maintained leadership improvements. However there is currently a lack of quality evaluation of these leadership and managerial programmes in the literature supporting claims. The purpose of this study is to assess nine dimensions of leadership of a novel programmes implemented by the Global Leadership School.

Methods: A leadership regimen was developed by the Global Leadership School and implemented at a paper mill for a period of one year. This course consisted of monthly meetings, training provided by an experienced leadership professional, a number of leadership instruments and a mandate from the company promoting and focusing on leadership over a one-year period. A survey was completed following this one-year period which measured 9 dimensions of leadership for both pre-training and post-training time periods.

Results: Five-hundred and sixty-seven (77.99%) of the eligible invitees responded to the survey. Results from the survey demonstrated a significant improvement in eight of the nine leadership dimensions in both the perceived leadership imparted upon employees (reported by superior) and the leadership received by employees (reported by employees). Divisional analysis indicated that all of the divisions had an improvement in the leadership dimensions. The open question administered during the survey identified a number of areas employees identified for company improvement as well as highlighting areas of success.

Conclusion: The implementation of this leadership programme provided significant improvements in eight of nine dimensions of leadership measured. This finding clearly demonstrates the effectiveness of this programme over the one-year period.

INTRODUCTION

Leadership is a key component to the motivation and productivity of employees and thus the success of any company. Though quality leadership is an integral part of corporate success it remains a complex concept to implement successfully. There are many proponents for different leadership methods and styles throughout the literature and corporate world, and there is currently a lack of a gold standard for successful implementation. These methods vary greatly, from a self-leadership approach, a process by which an individual monitors and controls their own behaviour, to the more traditional leadership approach, where a leader exerts social influence over employees to accomplish common goals and tasks (1).

The most common form of leadership is this traditional method, and while it appears to be an easy concept, many managers thrust in to this leader's role fail to provide adequate leadership to their reporting employees. The inability of managerial teams to effectively motivate and achieve high levels of productivity from employees while maintaining company morale has led to the development of a number leadership training programmes. These programmes provide a proposed improvement in leadership skills, leading to increased productivity and company morale. However there is currently a lack of quality evaluations examining the claims of such programmes and courses (2).

The Global Leadership School is a leading provider of such leadership programmes and focuses on a brand of leadership training that emphasises transformational leadership. Transformational leadership is an approach that enhances motivation through the emphasis of positivity and ownership to optimized performance (3).

The purpose of the current study is to implement and evaluate a leadership regimen designed by the Global Leadership School and monitor its effects on 9 dimensions of leadership management performance over a one-year period.

METHODS

The Leadership Programme

A leadership regimen was instituted by Gerald Huesch of the Global Leadership School at the mill for one year. It included two major components, as follows: 1) The CEO of the company raised awareness and set a strong focus on the importance of good leadership for a one-year time period and 2) During the same time period, Gerald Huesch conducted leadership training for the management team. All managers, including middle- and top-level managers, received the same leadership training.

The leadership programme included a special meeting place, which created a safe environment for monthly meetings. The monthly meetings (half day) were followed by leadership training with different leadership instruments, which were connected to real time challenges. Every top manager could also have individual coaching and team development training. All managers, regardless of level, used the same leadership instruments throughout the training programme. In addition to these instruments, board members visibly demonstrated support for one other (i.e. one talks, the other writes the notes on the flipchart) throughout the training process. Every meeting closed with a question and answer session allowing for equal participation and an opportunity to provide feedback. Finally, a buddy system was implemented in which managers were pair to provide support during training exercise such as choosing the correct instruments for the right challenges.

Table 15.1 summarises the leadership instruments that were utilised by the Global Leadership School during this training programme.

Table 15.1: Leadership Instruments

- Leadership climate
- Nine chambers of decision making
- Shark and dolphin
- Percentage of successes
- Three point technique
- Pilot technique
- Laser meeting
- Eight chairs from 'No' – to 'Yes'
- Braveheart speech
- Apocalyptical communicator
- 5 + 1 baskets of delegation
- Retrospective
- Happy box
- One – Two – Three
- Situational leadership model
- Red call principle
- H_2O technique

Evaluation of the Leadership Programme

Subsequent to the year of leadership training and raising awareness, a Leadership Survey was administered. The respondents answered the questions twice, based on "today" (the day they completed the survey) as well as the situation one year ago (prior to the leadership training). The questions were asked from the view of the superior as well as the view of the employee.

The Leadership Survey was developed having questions in nine different dimensions of leadership: (1) clarity and transparency, (2), unnecessary rules, procedures and administration, (3) real involvement and responsibility, (4) performance, goals, and learning, (5) feedback, support and acknowledgment, (6) team spirit and togetherness, (7) values and ethics, (8) my superior superior's and (9) management. Each question on the survey was rated on a scale from 1 to 10 with 10 representing the "best" answer. Employees were also given an opportunity to respond to an open question to ascertain an employee "wish list" for the company's future.

Following survey completion respondents were categorized into four divisions based on their role within the company. Employees were grouped into commercial, finance, management and technical divisions to allow for analysis of these subgroups.

RESULTS

Response Rate

The survey was conducted from December 2010 to March 2011. Seven-hundred and twenty-seven eligible employees were invited to participate in the survey. Five-hundred and sixty-seven of the eligible invitees responded, representing a 77.99% response rate.

Employee Characteristics

The average age of respondents was 40.38 years; sixty percent of these respondents were male. Eighty percent had completed a college degree as their highest level of education and responders had been employed for an average of 15 years. Responders supervised 47 people on average.

Table 15.2: Employee Demographics

	Total (n=567)
Women (%)	39.50
Men (%)	60.50
Age (mean±SD)	40.38±9.22
Highest Level of Education (%)	
College degree	80.39
Other	9.94
Masters degree	8.56
PhD	0.55
Not displayed	0.55
Years with company (mean±SD)	15.24±9.49
Employees supervised	47

Evaluation of the Leadership Programme

Results from the survey demonstrated a significant improvement in eight of the nine leadership dimensions in both the perceived leadership imparted upon employees (reported by superior) and the leadership received by employees (reported by employees). The unnecessary rules, procedures and administration dimension of survey did not reach significance following the leadership promotion and training, but did demonstrate a trend of improvement.

Fig. 15.1. Superior (A) and employee (B) rated dimensions of leadership.

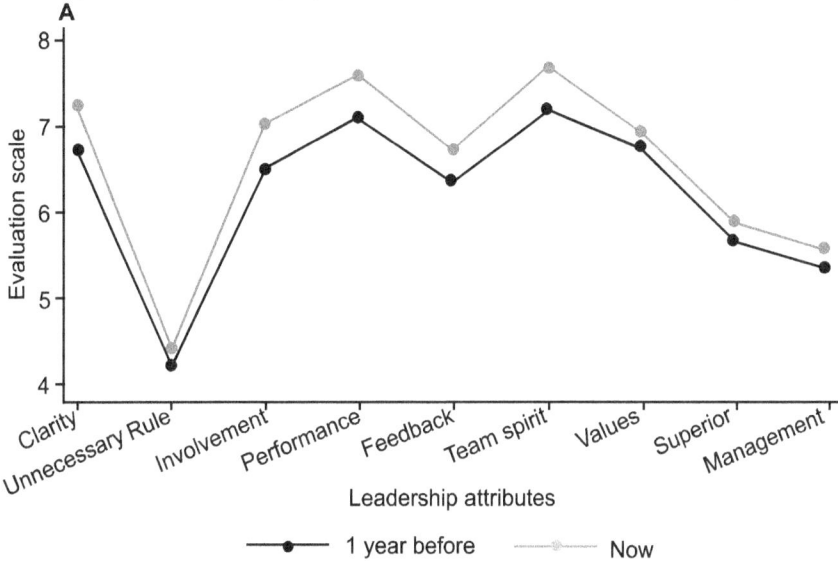

Fig. 15.1 (a): Leadership one gives to his employees (Now and 1 year ago)

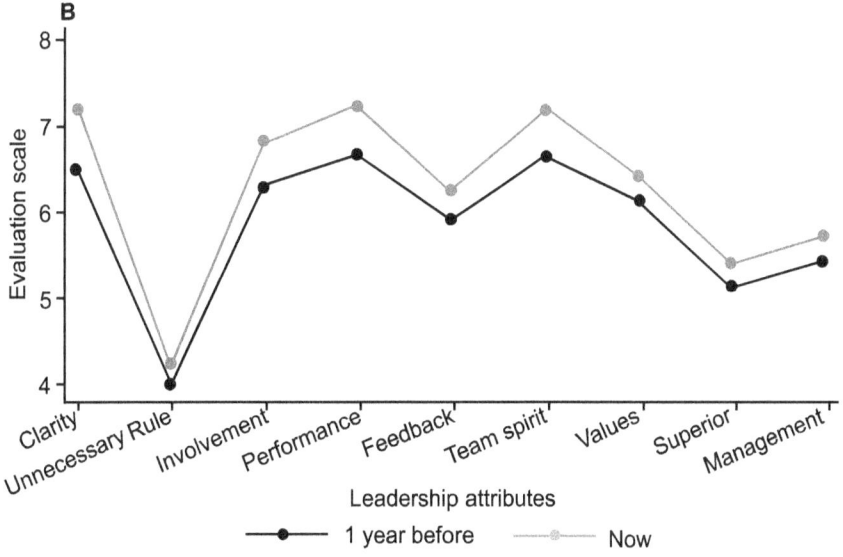

Fig. 15.1 (b): Leadership one receives from his employees (Now and 1 year ago)

All superiors who responded to the survey reported imparting more leadership than was actually perceived by the employees.

Grouping of the responders resulted 45 (8%) of employees in the commercial division, 68 (12%) in the finance division, 147 (26%) in the management division and 305 (54%) in the technical division. All of the divisions demonstrated on average an improvement in the leadership dimensions. The greatest improvement appeared in the "team spirit" dimension for all subgroups. The commercial group demonstrated the greatest variance in responses and was the weakest of the 4 divisions while the finance group was the strongest.

Fig. 15.2. Superior-rated dimensions of leadership across divisions (A) now (B) one year ago.

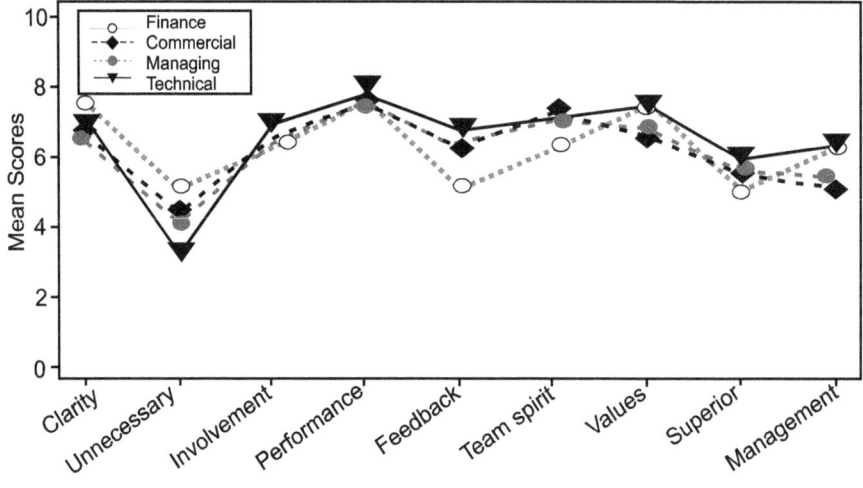

Fig. 15.2 (a): Comparison of leadership one gives to his employees between four divisions (A year ago)

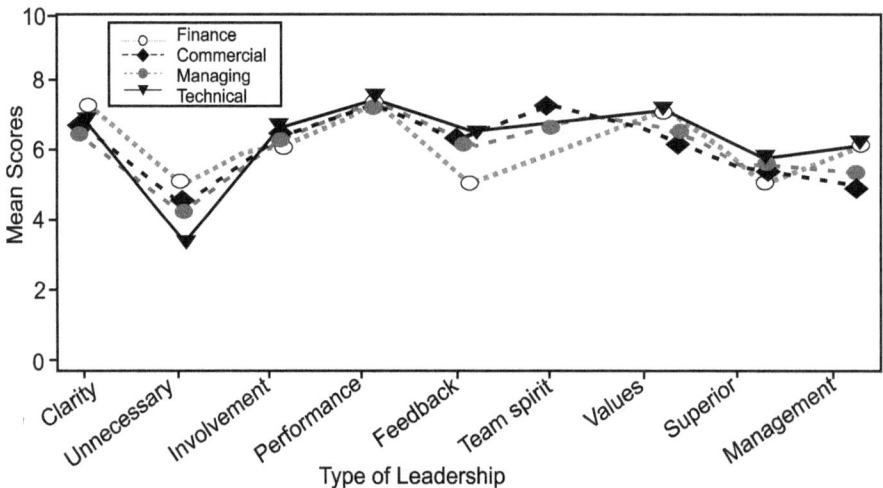

Fig. 15.2 (b): Comparison of leadership one gives to his employees between four divisions (A year ago)

Fig. 15.3. Employee-rated dimensions of leadership across divisions (A) now (B) one year ago.

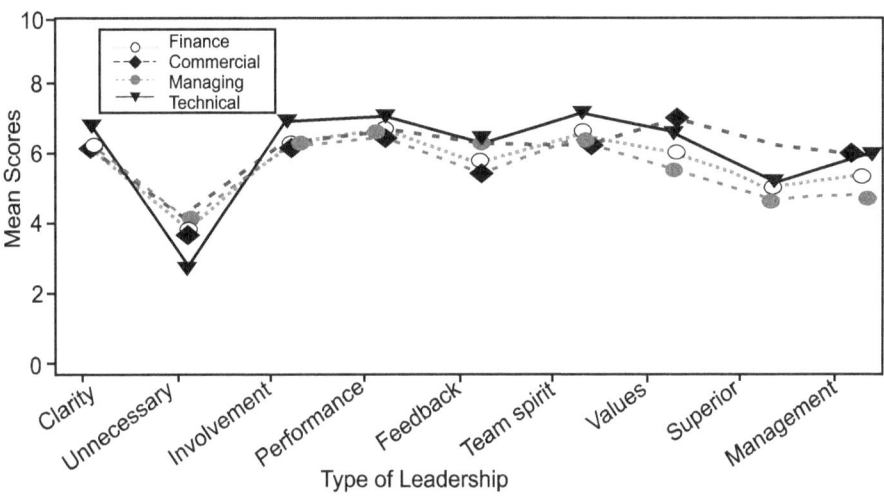

Fig. 15.3 (a): Comparison of leadership one receives from his employees between four divisions (Now)

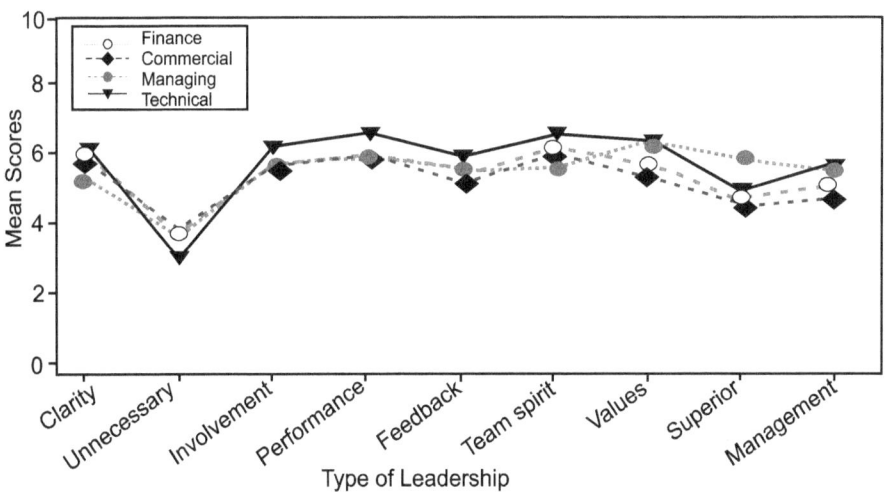

Fig. 15.3 (b): Comparison of leadership one receives from his employees between four divisions (A year ago)

Superior responses categorised by division are detailed in Figs. 15.2 (a) and (b) and employee responses are detailed in Fig. 15.3 (a) and (b).

Evaluation of the open question identified seven common employee responses, which were ordered according to frequency. These common responses form an employee "wish list" for future consideration by the company (Table 15.3). The most commonly reported theme was an expression of gratitude for being an employee of this company. Employees also requested more regular meetings across specialities, discussions for mutual events, and team discussions/analysis. Employees commonly indicated that they would like an improved system for bonuses, incentives and acknowledgement of performance. This should be accompanied by consequences for the inability to accomplish targets. The open question also indicated a desire for increased opportunities to become involved with decision making and the opportunity to utilise the creative potential within the company. Scouting of young creative talent also frequently appeared in the responses. Finally, the employees would like to improve their time management skills and create timelines for achievements, reducing the number of postponed meetings.

Table 15.3: Employee Wishlist

- Expression of gratitude for being a Mondi employee
- Request for more regular meetings across specialities for discussion, mutual events, team discussion and analysis
- An improved system for bonuses, incentives and acknowledgement of performance
- Consequences for inability to accomplish targets
- Increased opportunities to become involved with decision making
- Utilise the creative potential within the company, and increase the involvement of young specialists through talent scouting
- Improve time management
- Create timelines for achievements
- Reduce postponement of meetings
- Ensure the health and safety of employees in the work place

DISCUSSION

The implementation of the leadership programme resulted in substantial improvement in 8 of the 9 dimensions of leadership measured. These improvements were apparent for both superior perceived "leadership imparted" and employee perceived "leadership received", indicating that training methods were retained and applied over the one year period. The improvement demonstrated in these dimensions are supported by Lady Shewsky et al, who demonstrated that the administration of a leadership development programme in a highly educated population, similar to the one used in the current study, resulted in participants retaining and an utilising leadership behaviours (5).

There was a discrepancy noted between the level of imparted leadership and received leadership, with superiors reporting imparting greater leadership than the employees report receiving. This is a common occurrence in management assessments, with higher self-evaluations when compared to perceived reality which was shown by Kets de Vries et al (6).

The one dimension that did not demonstrate a significant improvement over the one year leadership training period was the unnecessary rules, procedures and administration dimension. This dimension demonstrated a very small improvement which was expected due to an increase in reporting required by the head office over the one-year period.

The "team spirit" dimension demonstrated the greatest improvement of the nine dimensions and is a strong indicator of the success of this programme. Team spirit is heavily influenced by all aspects of the training programme. This dimensions demonstrating the greatest improvement signifies that the leadership training and education did have a significant effect on the leadership within the company. This is supported by the findings of Gundersen et al who found that mangers with transformational training, similar to the training employed at the company, tend to have better adjusted and higher performing teams (4).

When respondents were categorised into the commercial, financial, managerial and technical sub groups, it was found that all groups demonstrated an average improvement over the one year training period. Respondents in the commercial group had the weakest leadership dimension scores. The responses from this division demonstrated the greatest variance which can be attributed to greater group diversity, and is a possible explanation for the lower scores.

Analysis of the open question provided insight into the employee's perception of the company and possible improvements that could influence leadership and employee satisfaction in the suture. In general employees were thankful for the employment opportunity they receive from the company, and suggested increase meetings across specialities within the company while also utilizing the full creative potential of the company. Employees also indicated that an improvement in time management and communication is necessary. The employee's expressed a desire for an improved incentive and acknowledgement system for high quality work. These suggestions are an excellent starting point for continued improvement in leadership within the company.

This study provided and excellent formal evaluation of the leadership programme provided by the Global Leadership School. The strengths of this study were its large population size, extending the survey to 727 managers, and its excellent response rate. 567 of the 727 managers (77.98%) offered the survey responded. Limitations of this study include the method with which the survey was conducted. The survey depended on participant recall of leadership situations from a pre-training time period, almost one year ago. A better method may be to implement two surveys, one conducted with the commencement of training and the other conducted upon completion of the one-year time frame.

CONCLUSION

The implementation of this leadership programme provided significant improvements in eight of nine dimensions of leadership measured, with the ninth dimension demonstrating a trend towards improvement. The results from this survey clearly demonstrate the effectiveness of this programme in a large company, where leadership is an integral part of success. The open question aspect of the survey also allowed for employees to make constructive suggestions on how to improve leadership within the company, these suggestions could be used as a basis for the continuing improvement of leadership within the company.

References

1. Andressen, P. The Relation Between Self-Leadership and Transformational Leadership: **Competing Models and the Moderating Role of Virtuality. Journal of Leadership & Organisational Studies February 2012 19: 68-82.**
2. Black A. M, Earnest G. W. Measuring the Outcomes of Leadership Development Programmes. **Journal of Leadership & Organisational Studies** November **2009:16(2):184-196.**

3. Zhu W, Riggio R, Avolio B, Sosik. J. The Effect of Leadership on Follower Moral Identity: Does Transformational/Transactional Style Make a Difference? Journal of Leadership & Organisational Studies May 2011 18: 150-163.

3. **Gundersen G, Hellesøy B, Raeder S.** Leading International Project Teams: The Effectiveness of Transformational Leadership in Dynamic Work Environments. Journal of Leadership & Organisational Studies February 2012 vol. 19 no. 146-57

4. **Ladyshewsky**http://ema.sagepub.com.libaccess.lib.mcmaster.ca/content/40/1/127 - corresp-1 **R, Flavell H.**Transfer of Training in an Academic Leadership Development Programme for Programme Coordinators. Educational Management Administration Leadership January 2012 vol. 40 no. 1 127-147.

5. **Kets de Vries M, Hellwig T, GuillénRamo L, Florent-Treacy E, Korotov K.** Long-term Effectiveness of a Transitional Leadership Development Programme: An Exploratory Study. Printed at INSEAD, Fontainebleau, France 2008.

Discussion Questions

1. Why has International Human resource management become important today?
2. Explain the differences between domestic HRM and International HRM.
3. Explain the cultural philosophies of different countries using the Model of Hofstede and Hall.
4. What is the future of IHRM and why will it stay?

References

1. Bartlett C A and Ghoshal S (1989) Organizing for World effectiveness. The transnational solution. California Management Review. Full.
2. Lawrence P.R and Lorsche W J (1967) Organisation and Environment. Cambridge MA. Harvard University Press.
3. Hofstede G (1980) Culture's Consequences: International differences in Work Related Values. Beverly Hills, CA. Sage.

4. Gannon M.J. and Associates (1994) Understanding Global Cultures. Metaphorical Journey through 17 Countries. Thousand Oaks, CA.

5. Perlmutter. H. V, 1969 The Tortuous Evolution of the Multinational Corporation, Columbia Journal of World Business, vol. 4, no.1, p9.

Recommended Readings

1. International Human Resource Management by P. L. Rao, Excel Books, 2008, New Delhi.

✱✱✱

Chapter **16**...

Human Resource Information Management (HRIM)

Contents ...

16.1 Introduction
16.2 Processes relating to Human Resource Information Systems
16.3 Organisation and Individual issues in HRIS Implementation
16.4 Practical Approaches to Implementation
16.5 Future Trends in the Field of IT/IS and HRIS
- Discussion Questions
- Recommended Readings and References

Objectives and Summary

This chapter is aimed at helping students understand the use and integration of technology with the Human Resource function. It aims to move away from the purely administrative function of Human Resource to using a technology-enabled service which perceives HR function beyond a database to a more analytical and decision-making role for their performance appraisal, forecasting needs and career planning to secure the right job fit for the case of promoting talent management. The future of HR lies in HRIS and other technology-related services.

Today with the increasing workforce in organisations, the strength sometimes crosses 60,000 across geographical boundaries. With companies working through such a model, the need for organising, planning and controlling the human resource function becomes very important. HRIS plays an important role in analysing, forecasting and monitoring the HR workforce. It is used for their career development, performance appraisals, analysis of the causes for attrition and utilising the information to make the right decisions. There are various HRIS-enabled tools in the market like PeopleSoft. However, more and more companies are developing their own web-based services rather than being dependent on the standard software tools available from vendors. With the increasing levels of workforce in organisations and the need to create innovation and optimise their talent, the need for HRIS has become acute today.

Learning Outcomes:
1. Identify the dire need for HRIS versus the purely documentation and administrative role of HR;
2. Underline the various advantages accrued for adopting HRIS and its contribution in stemming attrition in companies;
3. Specify the technology-enabled role of HRIS in organisations for analysis and computing decisions related to the workforce for this;
4. Elaborate on the future of HRIS.

16.1 Introduction

Planning, Organising and Control of Human resources require a sound information base. The human resource workforce has to take various decisions regarding the various levels of employees' related to their varied needs. The quality and depth of the decisions will depend upon the type and intensity of information provided to the human resource management. This information is supplied by the system for the effective management of the human resources in an organisation.

"Human Resource Information System (HRIS) can be defined as a computer-based system of gathering, classifying, processing, recording and disseminating the information required for the efficient and effective management of the human resources in the organisation." Bhattacharya, 2006.Thus, in simple words, HRIS is a system designed to supply appropriate information to the human resources department and the leadership team to help them manage the employees at all levels in an organisation.

The Need for HRIS
1. Today there are large organisations having a workforce of sometimes even 60,000 or more personnel. Hence the need to manage this large pool of personnel becomes inevitable.
2. The need is more intense for organisations which are dispersed geographically in several regions. For such organisations, timely and apt information is necessary to manage the dispersed employees effectively. Examples are Accenture, Hindustan Unilever, and Proctor and Gamble.
3. Compensation packages and elements are becoming more and more customised today. Hence, HRIS is needed to calculate and determine correctly the

compensations of the employees, sometimes deployed elsewhere, due to expatriation or repatriation.

4. As a statutory requirement, an employer and the Human Resource personnel have to maintain records of the large workforce. So HRIS is needed to secure compliance with the labour laws.

5. HRIS is not required for just record-keeping. This is a supplementary need. The primary need is to analyse, forecast and manage information for appropriate decision-making.

Important Uses of HRIS can be summarised as follows:

1. HR Planning and Analysis - manpower inventory, manpower requirements, skills requirements, turnover analysis, absenteeism analysis, placements, job matching, job descriptions, workforce utilisation.

2. HR Development - employee profiles, training requirements, succession planning, career interests and planning.

3. Staffing - sources of recruitment, application tracking and job offer refusal analysis.

4. Compensation - pay structure, compensation administration, incentive plans analysis, legal regulations implementation, Tax calculations etc.

5. Performance Appraisal - Employee competency records, comparing actual performance with standards.

6. Health, Safety and Security - safety training, accident records, health records, compliance with Acts.

7. Labour Relations - union negotiation records, attitude survey results, exit interview analysis, employee job history etc.

16.2 Processes relating to Human Resource Information Systems

1. Data Collection: The first step in the process of designing an HRIS system is collecting data related to the human resource function in detail. After collection of the data, the next step is to tabulate and classify the mounds of data depending upon the purpose for which the data is to be collected. Also the context of data analysis should be shared to measure the effectiveness and determine the nature of data collection methods to be adopted. The following types of information are required for the data collection:

(a) **Talent Acquisition Function:** Inventory of the present and future needs of manpower, reliable and scientific performance standards, location and fitting of required skills, valid measures for testing and selection and ultimately costs of recruitment and replacement.

(b) **Development and Progression Function:** Parameters of employee performance coast and benefit calculation of training and development, linkages between organisation and individual needs, career and succession planning.

(c) **Remuneration Function:** Relationship between productivity and wages, impact on incentives and bonus on employee motivation and morale building, cost of employee turnover, impact on inflation on salaries and incentives, value and nature of collective bargaining and trade unions on the welfare of the organisation.

(d) **Maintenance Function:** Organisational health indicators like absenteeism, turnover, accidents and grievances, physical and mental working conditions of employees, causes and costs of employee separation, incentives for voluntary retirement from service.

(e) **Integration Function:** Communication, management and leadership climate in the organisation, adaptation to the environmental climate, causes of deterioration in the productivity levels, and impact of technology and market changes.

16.3 Organisation and Individual issues in HRIS Implementation

Cultural Issues: One of the major challenges in getting people to adapt to the updated HRIS is making them adopt the new technology. It also involves a change in the organisation's culture for affecting the change effort and transformation.

Researchers define organisation culture as a complex set of shared beliefs, guiding values, behavioural norms and basic assumptions acquired over time that shape our thinking and behaviour. They are a part of the social fabric of the organisation. Not understanding a firm's culture before implementing an HRIS project can be fatal.

Data Management System

A good and effective data management system consists of processing the data through classification, analysis and summarisation of data and editing them.

Storage of data: This takes the form of indexing, coding and filing.

Retrieval of data: Whenever required, judging and assessment of the value and relevance of the data, and finally dissemination in terms of extending information whenever required. An efficient system accesses data whenever required at the right time and in the right form.

The design of the data management systems should not be rigid. An efficient system should be able to quickly respond to changes in the environment.

Designing of an HRIS

Levels of Information Systems: Companies tend to install information systems from the bottom up, level by organisation level. Transaction Processing Systems often come first; they provide the company's managers and accountants with detailed information about short term daily activities, such as account payables, tax liabilities and order status.

Management information systems are a level up; they help managers make better decisions by producing standardised, summarised reports on a regular basis. For example, an MIS can take raw data related to human resource and integrate it into the HRIS. As organisations grow, they often tend to integrate human resource information systems to collect, process, store and disseminate information to support decision-making, coordination, control, analysis and visualisation of an organisation's human resource management activities. There are several reasons for installing an HRIS as mentioned above.

HRIS should be implemented with other systems within HR and the rest of the organisation when appropriate to obtain maximum benefits and efficiencies. Systems should certainly be integrated with payroll and automated time systems. Benefits enrolment systems and other similar vendor software can also be integrated to avoid duplicate entries and prevent errors. Ideally, other corporate functions such as financial systems should be integrated for efficient flow of information.

16.4 Practical Approaches to Implementation

Implementation can be completed all at once or in phases. An implementation undertaken in a phased manner allows for testing of the system with smaller groups so that unforeseen problems can be fixed and success can be communicated and celebrated.

Case Study

In 1998, Proctor and Gamble (P &G) had more than 98,000 employees in 80 countries. Identifying common measures, improving service and reducing HR administrative costs were strategic imperatives for this global consumer products company.

The human resource managers at P &G considered a variety of solutions. Should they maintain a decentralised global operation in HRM and use technology such as internet service portals to improve efficiency, join the trend towards shared service centres (SSC) to centralise their operations, or investigate outsourcing for select human resource functions? With so many countries and governmental regulations, how could P& G achieve sufficient standardisation through HRIS to gain increased savings and still meet its varied responsibilities to those multiple entities? Would its internal customers view the move from decentralized to centralized shared services to meeting their needs? How would such changes be measured from an internal customer satisfaction perspective? Which measures for the various administrative approaches would best align the HR function with the P & G balanced scorecard strategic goals and objectives? These are some of the problems of HRM which are solved by an HRIS.

HR Administration and HRIS Environment

As mentioned earlier, HRM administration deals with the efficient performance of transactional activities like record-keeping, updating policy and informational materials for a self-service portal, generating and disseminating internal reports, complying with governmentally mandated external reporting and also administering external contracts. These are all examples of HRM administration associated with an organisation's workforce.

HRIS is a vital tool for managing increasing complex transactional requirements. Employee data base is carefully constructed so that the information is accurate and timely. HRIS is known to assist managers charged with improving the efficiency of HR administration by reducing costs, enhancing the reliability of reporting and improving service to internal customers.

Historically HR managers operated as adjunct staff to organisations, overseeing the daily transactions associated with hiring, paying and training employees and reporting on employee issues as required by managers.

How to implement a global HRIS System

With employers increasingly relying on local rather than expatriate employees, transferring ones selection, training, appraisal, pay, and other human resource management practices abroad is a top priority. There is less focus on employees today on expatriate issues and more on how to manage your local employees abroad. Considering cross-cultural differences in human resource management practices, most employers refer to local managers on specific human resource management policy issues. As in most successful multinationals, the objective is to successfully implement global HR systems by applying several best practices. This enables them to install uniform global human resource policies and practices around the world. The basic idea is to develop systems that are acceptable to employees in units around the world and ones that the employees can implement more effectively.

HRIS Applications in MNEs

Most of the HRIS Applications designed for a domestic user or company can also be used by MNCs or MNEs. Of course, some modifications are necessary to demystify the complex database in an MNC. For example, in areas relating to Performance Management Systems or Compensation Management it is necessary to collate a database of all countries and adapt to their labour market, culture and legislation relating to the administration of the issues related to compensation elements of countries, or performance appraisal. A number of modifications to an HRIS in MNEs would be driven by the different labour laws and regulations of the country. There is software available for IHRM but the use of this software demands that the database be timely and accurate. Being able to create and access reports based on employee data, and to do it quickly requires that the data be accurate and up to date.

Tends in HRIS

These trends are reflected in the paradigm shifts in HRM. According to a survey and report created by the Society of Human Resource Management (SHRM) which is concerned with research and best practices related to HRM, identifying 12 future trends important for HR, the following are underlined:

1. The need to integrate Corporate Social Responsibility (CSR) as an important activity in an organisation's HR activity has been underlined. It has been emphasised that CSR should not be treated as a one shot affair but a continuous process where time, funds and sharing of expertise are engaged by the corporates. Recently, it has been announced by the controller of company affair, that at least 2 per cent of the profits of an organisation should be veered towards any area of CSR. Social responsibility also includes in its ambit measures to reduce the gap between the haves and the have-nots. It also includes tackling the issues of differences of priorities among generations, which is, aging workers versus new entrants.

2. The second trend of importance is the new focus and concern relating to the employees health, safety and security. Labour legislation related to this matter is being enforced in many countries including India. There is also an increased monitoring of possible fraud by employees using legislation for enforcing workmen's compensation and other related areas. Recent additions include issues related to email frauds and monitoring. Also there are generational differences in terms of topics values, retention, and drug testing and environment concerns.

3. Employee retention and talent management are becoming increasingly important in today's time which is fraught with scarcity of valuable talent in terms of skills, knowledge and expertise. Organisations are initiating programmes relating to measures for implementing talent management systems to retain top performers. For such areas, most organisations have integrated these in their strategies and have catapulted HR into the top slots on par with the top management. Talent has now become a crucial concern for all organisations and has not been entrusted to the HR alone. These trends should be incorporated in the strategic framework of organisations. Companies also need to address the problems and challenges of managing a multigenerational workforce related to its recruitment, selection and talent management. The increasing trend of mergers, acquisitions and joint ventures has reinforced the need for attaching the strategy related to HR with the overall vision, mission and the organisation strategy.

4. The management of ethics in an organisation - MNE or other - is an important concern today. Organisations need to clarify and underline their ethical standards which may act as a basis for determining employee behaviour and action. It must be stressed that ethics is not universal, as is probably assumed. Hence the need to state in writing the ethical norms expected from the workforce. These become more

complex as organisations are becoming more diverse in terms of the generational gaps of the employees at all levels.

5. With an increasing trend of MNEs, it has become important to understand multicultural differences existing among employees from various countries. The need to sensitivise employees about differences in understanding of the various cultures in terms of individualism vs collectivism, power distance, uncertainty of avoidance, communication and non-verbal gestures, use of language, understanding of policies relating to recruitment and selection and so on. In countries like India, which is considered to be a melting pot, these issues related to perception and interpretation also become significant as the merger of rural and urban culture, generational differences make obvious differences in perceptions and understanding of issues at the workplace.

6. The growing importance of the role of HR professional s as consultants has changed the focus of HR. They are expected to manage vendors and outsource specialised activities after consultation with the top management. A new concept of HR capital and HR accounting has designed metrics to quantify the values and services of HR in order to measure their effectiveness.

7. Labour relations and collective bargaining are becoming increasingly important to negotiate and manage and reconcile differences with the union representatives. The objective is to generate a win and win situation. The case of the strike in the Maruti plant at Manesar in Haryana, which lasted 45 days, killed an HR manager and injured many personnel and incurred a total loss of Rs 450 crore, is an example of a deadlock of negotiations.

8. There is an increased awareness of organisational development and learning among the workforce in organisations. These related to team building, understanding differences among demographic differences in the work force, orienting the new workforce with the adoption and use of new technology, new methods and new perceptions required for improved working and better productivity.

9. Human resource planning and staffing management is becoming increasingly important today. More and more organisations are increasingly developing metrics to forecast staffing requirements, and planning learning and designing learning modules to enhance the fit between the employee and the requirements of the job. These are constantly being revised and reviewed to suit the changing trends in the environment.

10. MySpace, blogs and other social networking sites including Twitter are being increasingly used by Human Resource to engage with customers – both internal and external - on a regular basis. If HCL Technologies boasts a low attrition rate of 8 per

cent for last year, the Chairman, Vineet Nayyar, attributes this to his constant communication and sharing of insights and pearls of wisdom through the sites like Face book, Twitter, MySpace and so on. He is convinced of the dire need and use of these networking sites to constantly communicate with his personnel. Zig Ziegler, the motivation speaker, speaks of such communication as bathing. It is constantly required and should not be a one-off affair.

11. The design of compensation and rewards systems has become very creative and innovative. More and more organisations are pulling out all stops to design customised compensations and reward systems with a view to attract and retain personnel. There is an increasing body of research to substantiate the correlation between retention and compensation and reward systems.

12. There is a significant focus today on improving diversity among the workforce and incorporate diversity policies with overall strategy. More and more organisations are earmarking percentages to recruit women and differently-abled people for their various positions. For instance, when one of the HR managers of an organisation was not able to draw women to fill the top positions available, he even went to the extent of saying that he would have to force somebody for a sex change so that a woman could fill a position at the top level! More and more companies from the campus recruitment phase to the social networking recruitment are increasingly adopting a diversity policy to fill various positions. There is an adequate body of research to prove that diversity inclusion in organisations helps to create innovation and creativity, so important to secure a competitive edge.

16.5 Future Trends in the Field of IT/IS and HRIS

When examining future trends in HRIS, it is impossible to separate the future trends in IT/IS without relating them to the field of HRM. The knowledge economy is being profoundly influenced not only by the intensity but also by the speed of technological evolution. Information technologies have been steadily evolving and improving from mainframes to client services and now to Internet /web interfaces (Roberts, 2006). Some of the technological trends include broadband and wireless-related networked communication technologies, convergence technologies, collaborative tools, service oriented architecture, business-oriented systems are some of the notable developments affecting HRIS and its related technologies. Apart from achieving better coordination and integration of different systems within an enterprise, these technologies are empowering both employers and employees to deploy, share and use their knowledge for the common benefit of their company.

Future Trends in Workforce Technologies

In terms of future workforce technologies, Henson (2005) predicted that:
1. The technology of the future will be both collaborative and connected;

2. There will be increased and more widespread use of intelligent self-service via employee portals;
3. There will be increased use of HR scorecards coupled with workforce analytics and decision trees;
4. There will be an increase in process automation and the use of online analytical processing (OLAP) for processing raw data;
5. Faster and cheaper access to accurate real time HR information will be possible due to advancement in communication tools;
6. The worker of the future will be able to work anywhere, any time and on any device which would not only help work life balance but also turn the workplace into a 24/7 cycle.

According to Cedar Crestone (2006), survey on human capital management, the following are the findings on the survey of future trends:

1. Organisations using more HRIS software applications experienced more operating income growth than organisations with fewer applications. Some of the applications include: career planning, workforce measurement, talent acquisition, performance management.
2. One of the key objectives of HRIS software applications is to help the organisation in meeting its strategic objectives like providing and gathering HR metrics for budgeting and forecasting.
3. In terms of HR technologies what was important was analytics, reporting and decision tools, employee development and recruitment services.
4. The use of self-service portals allows reduced transaction and compliance costs.
5. The market for Strategic, HCM and measure/plan software applications is growing at an early stage.
6. Organisations today are moving away from solutions from third-party vendors towards web self-service.
7. Use of in-house HRIS solutions increases employee productivity and integrate new services as their key drivers for growth.
8. Talent management as a software application is receiving maximum attention due to its multitude of benefits.

One must remember at all times that technology cannot be a substitute for managerial competence and employees' discretionary behaviour. It can only be a messenger not a message. It is also impractical to expect information systems to supplant the soft functions of HR like online character, or replacing a good executive coach. In short, technology is extremely important in the field of HRIS, but people are simply the most important.

HRIS at Honeywell

Honeywell, a multinational company with global presence in several countries, has adopted Human Resource Information Systems (HRIS) for all the administrative work of its 13,000 employees in India. These are spread across all major cities in India. This MNC with the parent company in the US is engaged in designing energy efficient solutions, producing various types of safety products and has also started manufacturing of turbochargers, a component used in the automobiles, for enhancing mileage of vehicles.

Vimo James, Head of HRIS Engagement Leader in India, shares the functions of the HRIS team. "Our purpose is to free the HR personnel across all locations from administrative work. We take care of all the administrative requirements of the employees from their induction to their exit. These include the online induction training, onboarding, joining formalities like the collection of documents, bank statements, photographs, medical certificates, issue of identity cards and so on. During the course of working, the employee needs letters of experience for taking home loans, or taking a house on rent or even working certificates for pursuing higher education or certificate courses. All these are provided by our HRIS team. We even have digital signatures of all our team heads and managers, so that they are not disturbed at all. Apart from these routine administrative activities, we also collect data related to employees for determining their bonuses and rewards in kind, under our reward and recognition policy. These are collated and employees are disbursed the same through their team heads in the team meetings or any public functions organised to felicitate them. During the time of the employee's exit or retirement, we work closely with the payroll team to calculate the dues due to him and complete all the exit formalities like the exit interview and so on."

The benefits accruing to the organisation by adopting HRIS are substantial. The Human Resource personnel are able to focus on their core areas of analytics related to recruitment and filling vacancies, working closely with the business heads or functional heads for designing initiatives for optimising the performance of the employees, improving their productivity, managing talent, coaching and counselling the employees as well as the managers. It has been measured that the savings in terms of HR to employee ratio has increased a lot, and also the HR personnel are able to fully concentrate on strategic issues.

The only flip side of intensively adopting HRIS is the lack of human touch experienced by the personnel. Sometimes they never interact with the HR and their only contact with the HR function is through the mail box and technology. For Indians, this is a big barrier, as they are prone to more of a human interaction than technology alone.

The future definitely focuses on the increasing use of technology to facilitate HR and administrative functions.

Discussion Questions

1. Why is HRIS is important in today's working times?
2. Underline the main benefits of using HRIS.
3. Forecast with examples the future of HRIS in organisations.

Recommended Readings and References

1. Human Resource Management by Shashi Gupta, Rosy Joshi. Kalyani Publishers, 2006, Kolkata
2. Human Resource Information Systems (Basics, Applications and Future Directions) by Michael Kavanagh and Mohan Thite, Sage Publications, New Delhi, 2009.
3. Cedar Crestone (2006) Workforce technologies and Service delivery approaches, Alfaretta, GA: Author.
4. Henson R. (2005) The next decade of HR: Trends, Technologies and recommendations. In H. G. Gueutal and D. Stone (Eds) The brave new world of HR. pp 255-292 San Francisco: Jossey Bass.
5. Roberts B. (2006) New HR systems in the Horizon HR magazine 51 (5) pp 103-107.
6. Dipak Kumar Bhattacharya (2006). Human Resource Planning (2nd edition), New Delhi.

www.ingramcontent.com/pod-product-compliance
Lightning Source LLC
Chambersburg PA
CBHW082053230426
43670CB00016B/2874